CALIFORNIA RDA COMBINED

General Written & Law Examination

PREPARATION BOOK

Colleen Kirby-Banas, CDA, RDAEF, BS, MS

Published By:

DENTAL ARTS

The California RDA General Written and Law Examination Prep Book and Study Card Set
Blended Edition 2018

ISBN: 978-0-578-63343-5

Published by:
KB Dental Arts
1959 Playa Street
San Mateo, CA 94403
www.kb-dental-arts.com

Design and print services provided by Art of Marketing – Rancho Cordova, California.

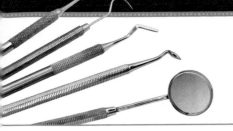

Table of Contents

SECTIONS

PREFACE

Included in the Preface is:

- Disclosure Page
- Examination Outline
- RDA Examination Plan for General & Law/Ethics
  Combined as written by the Dental Board of California

1

UNIT ONE - Patient Treatment and Care

15   Chapter One: Dental Fundamentals
29   Chapter Two: A Review of Basic Chairside Skills
37   Chapter Three: Patient Screening and Education
55   Chapter Four: Medical Emergency Preparedness
69   Chapter Five: Legal Requirements and Ethical Principles

2

UNIT TWO - Dental Procedures

75   Chapter One: Direct and Indirect Restorations
99   Chapter Two: Preventive Dental Procedures

3

UNIT THREE - Dental Specialty Procedures

113   Chapter One: Endodontic & Periodontal Procedures
123   Chapter Two: Orthodontic Procedures
133   Chapter Three: Implants, Oral Surgery & Extractions
137   Chapter Four: Prosthetic Appliances

4

UNIT FOUR - Safety

141   Chapter One: Infection Control
167   Chapter Two: Radiation Safety Procedures
171   Chapter Three: Occupational Safety

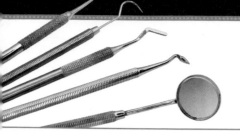

Table of Contents

S E C T I O N S

BONUS CHAPTERS
185 Chapter I: Dental Instrument Review
191 Chapter II: Legal Duties, Settings and Licensure

201 **GLOSSARY OF KEY TERMS**

213 **CHARTING ADDENDUM**

217 **ANSWER KEY TO CRITICAL THINKING QUESTIONS (CTQ'S)**

235 **TEST BANK**

269 **TEST BANK ANSWER KEY**

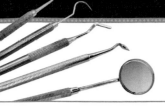

RDA Written and Law Combined Examination Outline
Dental Board of California

History: In December 2016, the Dental Board of California (Board) and the Dental Assisting Council (DAC) agreed to combine both the Registered Dental Assistant (RDA) Written and the RDA Law and Ethics examinations into one examination based solely upon the conclusions of the 2016 RDA Occupational Analysis. Each seven (7) years, the Department of Consumer Affairs' (DCA) Office of Professional Examination Services (OPES) is required to analyze data from surveys issued to current dental health personnel regarding the workplace functions of dental assistants in today's dental offices. The Occupational Analysis provides OPES with the necessary data to recommend, to the Board, changes necessary to maintain a relevant licensure process in our profession. In addition, OPES carries the responsibility to ensure that the licensing examination is legally defensible and meets the requirements of Business and Professions Code Section 139.

In 2017, the Board and the DAC voted to eliminate the RDA practical examination and combine the two existing written examinations into one comprehensive examination, following the recommendations of the OPES.

Today, the Registered Dental Assistant Combined (RDAC) written examination is the sole licensing examination for the California RDA. It includes 150 scored and 25 pretest (unscored) multiple-choice items. It is functional in nature, covering the duties and settings for Registered Dental Assistants as defined in the California Dental Practice Act. Candidates will have three (3) hours to complete the examination.

The following is an outline of the RDAC examination. The numbers in parentheses indicate the approximate percentage of scored questions covering the topic in the examination.

This examination outline is issued by the Board and is the basis for this examination textbook. All chapters relate specifically to the Board's outline and the examination plan that follows this outline.

Questions may require knowledge of rationale (indications, contraindications), instrumentation, technique, and evaluation criteria in the following content areas:

1. Patient Treatment and Care (25%)

2. Dental Procedures (35%)
    a) Direct and Indirect Restorations
    b) Preventative Procedures

3. Dental Specialty Procedures (10%)
    a) Endodontic Procedures
    b) Periodontal Procedures
    c) Orthodontic Procedures
    d) Implants, Oral Surgery and Extractions
    e) Prosthetic Appliances

4. Safety (30%)
    a) Infection Control

RDA Examination Plan (Revised August 2018)
General and Law/Ethics Combined

1. PATIENT TREATMENT AND CARE (25%)

Task Statements	Knowledge Statements
• Review and report to dentist patient medical conditions, medications, and areas of medical/dental treatment history that may affect dental treatment.	• Knowledge of effects of coexisting medical/dental conditions on dental treatment.
• Take patient's blood pressure and vital signs.	• Knowledge of common medical conditions that may affect dental treatment (e.g., asthma, cardiac conditions, diabetes).
• Inspect patient's oral condition with mouth mirror.	• Knowledge of allergic reactions and sensitivities associated with dental treatment and materials (e.g., latex, epinephrine).
• Chart existing oral conditions and diagnostic findings at the direction of the licensed provider.	• Knowledge of purposes and effects of commonly prescribed medications that may affect dental treatment (e.g., Coumadin, psychotropics).
• Perform intraoral diagnostic imaging of patient's mouth and dentition (e.g., radiographs, photographs).	• Knowledge of medical conditions that may require premedication for dental treatment (e.g., joint replacement, infective endocarditis, artificial heart valves).
• Respond to patient questions about existing conditions and treatment following dentist's diagnosis.	• Knowledge of acceptable levels of blood pressure for performing dental procedures.
• Observe for signs and conditions that may indicate abuse or neglect.	• Knowledge of methods and techniques for using medical equipment to take vital signs.
• Perform dental procedures using professional chairside manner.	• Knowledge of techniques and procedures for using imaging equipment to perform intraoral and extraoral diagnostic imaging.
• Educate patient about behaviors that could affect oral health or dental treatment.	• Knowledge of types of plaque, calculus, and stain formations of the oral cavity and their etiology.
• Instruct patient about pre- and postoperative care and maintenance for dental procedures and appliances.	• Knowledge of conditions of the tooth surfaces (e.g., decalcification, caries, stains, and fractures lines) and how to document them.
• Utilize caries detection materials and devices to gather information for dentist.	• Knowledge of effects of substance abuse on patient's physical condition including oral tissues.
• Assist in the administration of nitrous oxide/oxygen when used for analgesia or sedation by dentist.	• Knowledge of effects of nutrition and malnutrition on the oral cavity.
• Assist in the administration of oxygen to patients as instructed by dentist.	• Knowledge of effects of smoking and smokeless tobacco on oral tissue.
• Assist in emergency care of patient.	• Knowledge of the professional and ethical principles related to communicating with, and fair treatment of, the patient.
	• Knowledge of professional and ethical principles regarding patient care.
	• Knowledge of legal requirements and ethical principles regarding patient confidentiality.
	• Knowledge of types of dental conditions of hard and soft tissue and how to identify and document them.

- Knowledge of basic oral and dental anatomy (e.g., nomenclature, morphology, and tooth notation).

- Knowledge of legal requirements and ethical principles regarding mandated reporting (abuse and neglect).

- Knowledge of the RDA/RDAEFs legal and ethical responsibilities to report violations of the state dental practice act, administrative rules or regulations to the proper authorities.

- Knowledge of methods and techniques patients can perform to improve oral health.

- Knowledge of pre- and postoperative care and maintenance for dental procedures and appliances.

- Knowledge of requirements for the supervision of RDAs and RDAEFs related to different dental procedures.

- Knowledge of scope of practice for RDAs and RDAEFs related to initial patient assessment.

- Knowledge of types of automated caries detection devices, materials, and procedures for their use.

- Knowledge of scope of practice for RDAs related to use of caries detection devices and materials.

- Knowledge of procedures for the use and care of equipment used to administer oxygen and nitrous oxide/oxygen.

- Knowledge of signs and symptoms indicating the need to implement first aid and basic life support measures.

- Knowledge of signs and symptoms indicating possible allergic reactions and/or sensitivities to medications or materials used in dentistry.

2. DENTAL PROCEDURES (35%)

2A Dental Procedures: Direct and Indirect Restorations (30%)

Task Statements	Knowledge Statements
<ul><li>Place bases and liners.</li><li>Place matrices and wedges.</li><li>Place temporary filling material.</li><li>Apply etchant to tooth surface (tooth dentin or enamel) for direct and indirect provisional restorations.</li><li>Place bonding agent.</li><li>Fabricate and adjust indirect provisional restorations.</li><li>Place, adjust, and finish direct provisional restorations.</li><li>Perform cementation procedure for indirect provisional restorations.</li><li>Obtain intraoral images using computer generated imaging system (e.g., CADCAM).</li><li>Take impressions for indirect provisional restorations.</li><li>Remove indirect provisional restorations.</li><li>Perform in-office whitening (bleaching) procedures (e.g., Boost, Opalescence).</li></ul>	<ul><li>Knowledge of types of base and liner materials and the techniques and procedures for their application and placement.</li><li>Knowledge of types of wedges and the techniques and procedures for their use.</li><li>Knowledge of techniques and procedures for using matrix bands with or without band retainers.</li><li>Knowledge of types of temporary filling materials and the techniques and procedures to mix, place, and contour them.</li><li>Knowledge of types of bonding agents and the techniques and procedures for their application and placement.</li><li>Knowledge of types of etchants and the techniques and procedures for their application and placement.</li><li>Knowledge of irregularities in margins that affect direct and indirect provisional restorations.</li><li>Knowledge of techniques used to eliminate open margins when placing restorative materials.</li><li>Knowledge of methods for identifying improper occlusal contacts, proximal contacts, or embrasure contours of provisional restorations.</li><li>Knowledge of techniques and procedures for mitigating the effects of improper occlusal contacts, proximal contacts, or embrasure contours of provisional restorations.</li><li>Knowledge of instrumentation and techniques related to the removal of indirect provisional restorations.</li><li>Knowledge of scope of practice for RDAs and RDAEFs related to applying bases, liners, and bonding agents.</li><li>Knowledge of equipment and procedures used to obtain intraoral images for computer-aided, milled restorations.</li><li>Knowledge of types of impression materials and techniques and procedures for their application and placement.</li><li>Knowledge of techniques and procedures used to mix and place provisional materials.</li></ul>

- Knowledge of techniques and procedures for bonding provisional veneers.
- Knowledge of indications and contraindications for the use of whitening (bleaching) agents.
- Knowledge of indications and contraindications for the use of bonding agents.
- Knowledge of indications and contraindications for the use of etching agents.
- Knowledge of types of whitening (bleaching) agents and the techniques and procedures for their application.
- Knowledge of types of cements and the techniques and procedures for their application, placement, and removal.
- Knowledge of scope of practice for RDAs and RDAEFs related to applying and activating whitening (bleaching) agents.
- Knowledge of RDA and RDAEF scopes of practice related to direct restorations.
- Knowledge of RDA and RDAEF scopes of practice related to indirect restorations.
- Knowledge of RDA and RDAEF scopes of practice related to final impressions.

2B Dental Procedures: Preventive Procedures (5%)

Task Statements
- Perform coronal polishing.
- Prepare teeth and apply pit and fissure sealants.

Knowledge Statements
- Knowledge of scope of practice for RDAs related to coronal polishing and the application of pit and fissure sealants.

3. DENTAL SPECIALTY PROCEDURES (10%)

3A Dental Specialty Procedures: Endodontic Procedures (2%)

Task Statements	Knowledge Statements
• Test pulp vitality. • Dry canals with absorbent points.	• Knowledge of techniques and procedures for testing pulp vitality. • Knowledge of techniques and procedures for measuring canal length and size. • Knowledge of scope of practice for RDAs and RDAEFs related to initial pulp vitality testing and other endodontic procedures.

3B Dental Specialty Procedures: Periodontal Procedures (1%)

Task Statements	Knowledge Statements
• Place periodontal dressings at surgical site.	• Knowledge of scope of practice for RDAs and RDAEFs related to the placement of periodontal dressing materials. • Knowledge of types of periodontal dressings and techniques for their application.

3C Dental Specialty Procedures: Orthodontic Procedures (3%)

Task Statements	Knowledge Statements
• Place orthodontic separators. • Place and remove ligature ties and arch wires. • Place elastic ties to secure arch wires. • Remove orthodontic bands. • Take impression for fixed and removable orthodontic appliances.	• Knowledge of scope of practice for RDAs and RDAEFs related to the placement of orthodontic materials. • Knowledge of techniques for placement and removal of orthodontic separators and bands, arch wires, and ties. • Knowledge of techniques for placement and removal of removable orthodontic appliances. • Knowledge of types of materials for taking impressions for removable orthodontic appliances and the techniques for their application.

3D Dental Specialty Procedures: Implants, Oral Surgery and Extractions (3%)

Task Statements	Knowledge Statements
• Remove post-extraction and post-surgery sutures as directed by dentist. • Place and remove dry socket dressing as directed by dentist.	• Knowledge of techniques for removing post-extraction and post-surgery sutures. • Knowledge of methods for treating dry socket.

3E Dental Specialty Procedures: Prosthetic Appliances (1%)

Task Statements	Knowledge Statements
• Adjust prosthetic appliances extraorally.	• Knowledge of methods for identifying pressure points (sore spots) related to ill-fitting prosthetic appliances. • Knowledge of materials, equipment, and techniques used for adjustment of prosthetic appliances. • Knowledge of scope of practice for RDAs and RDAEFs related to the adjustment of extraoral prosthetic appliances.

4. SAFETY (30%)

4A Safety: Infection Control (24%)

Task Statements	Knowledge Statements
• Wear personal protective equipment during patient-based and non-patient-based procedures as specific to the tasks.	• Knowledge of laws and regulations pertaining to infection control procedures related to "Dental Healthcare Personnel" (DHCP) environments.
• Purge dental unit lines with air or water prior to attachment of devices.	• Knowledge of protocols and procedures for purging dental unit waterlines and hand pieces (DUWL).
• Use germicides for surface disinfection (e.g., tables, chairs, counters).	• Knowledge of procedures and protocols for the disposal of biological hazardous waste and Other Potentially Infectious Materials (OPIM).
• Use surface barriers for prevention of cross-contamination.	
• Perform instrument sterilization in compliance with the office's infection control program.	
• Disinfect and sterilize laboratory and operatory equipment in compliance with the office's infection control program.	
• Use hand hygiene procedures.	
• Conduct biological spore testing to ensure functioning of sterilization devices.	
• Dispose of biological hazardous waste and Other Potentially Infectious Materials (OPIM).	
• Dispose of pharmaceuticals and sharps in appropriate container.	

4B Safety: Radiation Safety (3%)

Task Statements	Knowledge Statements
• Implement measures to minimize radiation exposure to patient during radiographic procedures.	• Knowledge of legal and ethical requirements for RDAs and RDAEFs related to radiation safety.
• Implement measures to prevent and monitor scatter radiation exposure (e.g., lead shields, radiation dosimeter) to self and others during radiographic procedures.	• Knowledge of methods for the storage and disposal of radiographic film.
• Implement measures for the storage and disposal of radiographic film.	

4C Safety: Occupational Safety (3%)

Task Statements	Knowledge Statements
• Implement protocols and procedures to protect operator from exposure during hazardous waste management. • Package, prepare, and store hazardous waste for disposal. • Store, label, and log chemicals used in a dental practice.	• Knowledge of what constitutes hazardous waste and the protocols and procedures for its disposal. • Knowledge of requirements for placing hazardous substances in secondary containers, (e.g., labeling, handling, applicable containers).

Notes

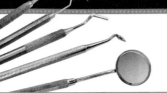

UNIT ONE – PATIENT TREATMENT AND CARE
CHAPTER ONE: DENTAL FUNDAMENTALS

EXAMINATION PLAN DATA:

Topic Area	Patient Treatment and Care
Total Weight of Topic Area on Examination	25%
Subject Area of This Chapter	Dental Fundamentals
Percentage of Examination Questions in Dental Fundamentals	N/A

DENTAL FUNDAMENTALS – TASKS AND KNOWLEDGE STATEMENTS

Tasks Associated with Topic Area	Knowledge Statements Associated with Topic Area
Chart existing oral conditions and diagnostic findings at the direction of the licensed provider	Knowledge of basic oral and dental anatomy (e.g., nomenclature, morphology, and tooth notation)

SCOPE OF PRACTICE – SPECIFIC TO DENTAL FUNDAMENTALS

Unlicensed Dental Assistant	Registered Dental Assistant
Extra-oral duties or procedures specified by the supervising licensed dentist provided that these duties or procedures meet the definition of a basic supportive	All duties that a dental assistant is allowed to perform
Operate dental radiography equipment for the purpose of oral radiography if the dental assistant has complied with certification requirements	Mouth-mirror inspections of the oral cavity, to include charting of obvious lesions, existing restorations, and missing teeth
Perform intraoral and extraoral photography	

Licensed Registered Dental Assistant in Extended Functions (RDAEF):
(a) A registered dental assistant in extended functions licensed on or after January 1, 2010, is authorized to perform all duties and procedures that a registered dental assistant is authorized to perform and those duties that the board may prescribe by regulation.
(b) A registered dental assistant in extended functions licensed on or after January 1, 2010, is authorized to perform the following additional procedures under _direct supervision_ and pursuant to the order, control, and _full professional responsibility of a licensed dentist_:
(1) Conduct preliminary evaluation of the patient's oral health, including, but not limited to, charting, intraoral and extra-oral evaluation of soft tissue, classifying occlusion, and myofunctional evaluation.
(2) Perform oral health assessments in school-based, community health project settings under the direction of a dentist, registered dental hygienist, or registered dental hygienist in alternative practice.

KEY TERMS

Black's Cavity Classifications	System by which carious lesions are classified based on size and surfaces involved
Buccal/Facial	Surface of the tooth closest to the cheeks or face
Contact	An area where the mesial or distal surface of one tooth touches the adjacent tooth
Contour	A curved surface
Cuspids	Considered anterior teeth; referred to as canine teeth; located at the corners of the dental arches
Dental Caries	Tooth disease caused by bacteria (aka: Dental Decay, Cavity, or Carious Lesion)
Dentition	A set of natural teeth in the dental arch
Distal	Surface of the tooth facing away from the midline
Embrasure	A V-shaped space formed by the curved proximal surfaces of adjacent teeth. There are four (4) interproximal embrasures surrounding the proximal contacts.
Incisors	Central and lateral; located in the anterior region of the dental arch
Lingual	Surface of the tooth facing the tongue
Malocclusion	The abnormal or unnatural contact of the maxillary and mandibular teeth when closed together
Mastication	The process of chewing
Mesial	Surface of the tooth facing the midline
Midline	Imaginary vertical line that divides the mouth in half
Molars	Largest teeth in the mouth; located in the posterior region of the dental arch
Occlusal/Incisal	Biting or tearing surface of the tooth

Occlusion	The natural contact of the maxillary and mandibular teeth when closed together
Premolars	Smaller version of a molar; two cusps; located in posterior region of the dental arch
Quadrant	Division of an entire dentition into four equal parts: two quadrants in the upper arch; two quadrants in the lower arch
Third Molars	Referred to as "wisdom" teeth; last teeth to erupt into the mouth

REVIEW OF THE DENTITIONS

A **dentition** is a set of natural teeth in the dental arch. Humans have two sets of dentitions during their lifetime, the primary dentition (baby teeth) and the permanent dentition (adult teeth). Children enter the mixed dentition phase at approximately age 6 to 12 years old. The mixed dentition phase is when both primary and permanent teeth are present in the mouth at the same time. There are 20 teeth in the primary dentition. Children do not have bicuspids, or premolars, in the primary dentition.

Primary Dentition - Eruption Table – Maxillary Arch

Tooth	Eruption	Pt.'s age when lost
Central Incisor	6-10 months	6-7 yrs. old
Lateral Incisor	9-12 months	7-8 yrs. old
1st molar	12-18 months	9-11 yrs. old
Cuspid	16-22 months	10-12 yrs. old
2nd molar	24-32 months	10-12 yrs. old

Primary Dentition – Eruption Table – Mandibular Arch

Tooth	Eruption	Pt.'s age when lost
Central Incisor	6-10 months	6-7 yrs. old
Lateral Incisor	7-10 months	7-8 yrs. old
1st molar	12-18 months	9-11 yrs. old
Cuspid	16-22 months	9-12 yrs. old
2nd molar	20-32 months	10-12 yrs. old

There are 32 teeth in the permanent dentition. The permanent dentition begins when the last primary tooth is lost, typically around age 12.

The California RDA General Written and Law Examination Prep Book © 2017, 2018 • KB Dental Arts – Publisher

Permanent Dentition – Eruption Table – Maxillary Arch

Tooth	Eruption
1st molar	6-7 yrs. old
Central Incisor	7-8 yrs. old
Lateral Incisor	8-9 yrs. old
1st premolar	10-11 yrs. old

Tooth	Eruption
2nd premolar	10-12 yrs. old
Cuspid	11-12 yrs. old
2nd molar	12-13 yrs. old
3rd molar	17-21 yrs. old

Permanent Dentition – Eruption Table – Mandibular Arch

Tooth	Eruption
1st molar	6-7 yrs. old
Central Incisor	6-7 yrs. old
Lateral Incisor	7-8 yrs. old
Cuspid	9-10 yrs. old
1st premolar	10-11 yrs. old
2nd premolar	12-13 yrs. old
2nd molar	11-13 yrs. old
3rd molar	17-21 yrs. old

NAMES AND FUNCTIONS OF THE TEETH

Each tooth has a name to aid in locating it in the mouth. The mouth has two dental arches: the maxillary and the mandibular arches. In the adult mouth, each arch has 16 teeth. In the child's mouth, each arch has ten teeth. The teeth are identified by name and each is located in the same spot in each arch. The names of the teeth are: incisors, cuspids, premolars, and molars. The primary dentition does not have premolars.

Human teeth serve the very distinct purpose of tearing, grinding and cutting of a variety of foods. Therefore, the teeth are shaped and located in certain places to assist in the mastication of food.

Incisors are located in the **anterior**, or front, of the mouth. They have a thin, flat, sharp edge, termed the **incisal edge**, that tears and cuts food by using force. The surface of the incisors closest to the tongue is shovel-like in its shape, which moves the food to the back of the mouth for more effective chewing. There are four central incisors in the mouth; two in the maxillary arch and two in the mandibular arch. There are four lateral incisors in the mouth; two in the maxillary arch and two in the mandibular arch.

Cuspids, also known as canines, are located at the corner of each dental arch. Cuspids are positioned in the anterior area of each arch and have a distinct anatomy. Most cuspids have a pointed appearance and this appearance will vary in severity from patient to patient. Cuspids are also used for the tearing and cutting of food similar to the incisors. There are four cuspids in the mouth; two in the maxillary arch and two in the mandibular arch. Cuspids are single rooted and possess the distinction of being the longest rooted tooth in the mouth.

In each dental arch, there are six anterior teeth: two central incisors, two lateral incisors and two cuspids. There is a total of 12 anterior teeth in the mouth between the two dental arches.

Premolars, or bicuspids, are a cross between cuspids and molars. They are located in the **posterior**, or rear, region of the mouth. Premolars are not as long as cuspids.

Traditionally, premolars have two cusps, but it is not uncommon for a premolar to have three cusps. Premolars are designed to grind food down in preparation for swallowing and, therefore, have a wide surface for chewing food. There are four premolars in each dental arch, for a total of eight in the full adult dentition.

Molars are located in the posterior region of the mouth. Their primary function is for the chewing and grinding up of food. Molars are much larger than premolars or any of the other teeth in the mouth.
There are 12 molars total in the adult dentition, with six molars in each dental arch or three molars in each **quadrant.** Maxillary and mandibular molars are very different from one another. Maxillary molars have three roots (trifurcated) where mandibular molars have two roots (bifurcated). Maxillary first molars have an extra lingual cusp termed the "Cusp of Carabelli." The Carabelli cusp is a distinguishing feature of the maxillary first molar only.

Third molars, commonly referred to as "wisdom teeth", may form or not form. The formation and eruption pattern of third molars will vary from individual to individual; some may fully erupt into the dentition while others may never experience full eruption causing impaction and needing surgical removal. Additionally, the anatomical features of an erupted third molar will vary greatly from patient to patient.

MIDLINE

The **midline** is a parallel imaginary line used to divide the patient's mouth into two (2) sections – left and right. The midline runs between the two central incisors of both the maxillary and mandibular arches.

QUADRANTS

If the midline divides the oral cavity into two sections, left and right, a **quadrant** is established when each dental arch is divided in half horizontally creating a total of four sections. The maxillary arch is split into the upper right (UR) and upper left (UL) quadrants. The mandibular arch is split into the lower left (LL) and the lower right (LR) quadrants. There are eight (8) teeth in each quadrant in the permanent dentition and five (5) teeth in each quadrant in the primary dentition.

SURFACES OF THE TEETH

Each tooth has five (5) surfaces.
- The surface of the tooth closest to or facing toward the midline is called the **mesial**.
- The **distal** surface of the tooth is the surface facing away from the midline.
- Both mesial and distal surfaces are considered to be interproximal surfaces.
- The **lingual** surface is the surface of the tooth closest to the tongue.
- The **occlusal** surface of the tooth is found on the biting area of posterior teeth (premolars and molars) only.
- The **incisal edge** is found on the sharp, thin edge of the anterior teeth (incisors and cuspids) only.

The term **occlusal** is used when describing the biting surface of posterior teeth and the term incisal edge is used when describing the tearing edge of anterior teeth.

The California RDA General Written and Law Examination Prep Book © 2017, 2018 • KB Dental Arts – Publisher
This book and the individual contributions contained within are protected under Copyright by the Publisher

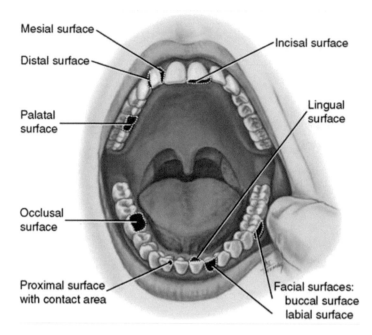

The **buccal** or **facial** surfaces are those surfaces of the teeth closest to the cheeks or face. In the posterior, the surface is called the buccal surface (cheeks). In the anterior, the surface is called the facial (face) or labial (lips) surface.

REVIEW OF BASIC TOOTH ANATOMY

Each tooth in the oral cavity is made up of **contours, embrasures** and **contacts**.

A **contour** is a curved surface. Each tooth will have some curvature to it unless it is damaged by wear. These curvatures help with food passage and natural cleansing of the mouth.

An **embrasure** is the V-shaped space formed by the curved proximal surfaces of adjacent teeth. There are four (4) interproximal embrasures surrounding the proximal contacts:

- The embrasures of anterior teeth: gingival, incisal, labial and lingual embrasures.
- The embrasures of posterior teeth: gingival, occlusal, buccal and lingual embrasures.

A **contact** area is an area where the mesial or distal surface touches the adjacent tooth. Teeth like to touch. If a tooth does not have a contact, over time, the teeth will begin to drift and super-erupt until they are touching. Contact areas provide stabilization of the arches, protection of the interproximal gingiva and prevent food from being trapped in between the teeth.

REVIEW OF BASIC TOOTH MORPHOLOGY

Tooth morphology is the study of the shape of teeth. Teeth are shaped accordingly to their position in the mouth. While certain teeth adhere to some universal basic shapes, it is smart to remember that teeth will have variations.

TOOTH NUMBERING SYSTEMS

Numbering systems are another common method of identifying the teeth for purposes of charting and during treatment. There are two (2) principle numbering systems used in dentistry today – Universal and Palmer.

PERMANANT TEETH

The Universal Numbering System – Permanent Dentition

- Most common system used in the United States.
- Permanent teeth are numbered #1 to #32.
- Tooth #1 begins with the upper right third molar and the numbering works around to the upper left third molar, tooth #16.
- Numbering then drops down to the lower left third molar, tooth #17, working its way around to the lower right third molar, tooth #32.

PRIMARY TEETH

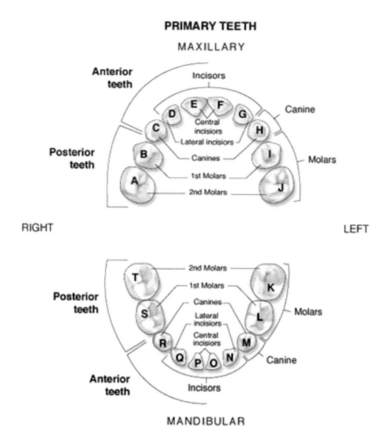

The Universal Numbering System – Primary Dentition

- Primary teeth are identified by capital lettering, using letters A through T.
- Tooth A starts with the upper right second primary molar and works its way around the upper left second primary molar, Tooth J.
- Lettering then drops down to the lower left second primary molar, Tooth K, working its way around to the lower right second primary molar, Tooth T.
- This numbering system is common in general dentistry and pedodontic (Pediatric) practices.

Palmer Notation

Permanent Teeth															
upper right								upper left							
8⌋	7⌋	6⌋	5⌋	4⌋	3⌋	2⌋	1⌋	L1	L2	L3	L4	L5	L6	L7	L8
8⌐	7⌐	6⌐	5⌐	4⌐	3⌐	2⌐	1⌐	Γ1	Γ2	Γ3	Γ4	Γ5	Γ6	Γ7	Γ8
lower right								lower left							

Deciduous Teeth															
upper right								upper left							
		E⌋	D⌋	C⌋	B⌋	A⌋	LA	LB	LC	LD	LE				
		E⌐	D⌐	C⌐	B⌐	A⌐	ΓA	ΓB	ΓC	ΓD	ΓE				
lower right								lower left							

Palmer Notation System

- Palmer is a numbering system used in orthodontic practices.
- The mouth is divided into the four quadrants; in each quadrant, the teeth are numbered #1 to #8 beginning with the central incisor as #1, continuing back through the quadrant with the third molar being #8; therefore, all central incisors are #1, all lateral incisors are #2 and so forth.
- Each quadrant is assigned a bracket noting the upper right (UR), the upper left (UL), the lower left (LL), and the lower right (LR) quadrants.
- The charting is completed by noting the bracket (the quadrant where the tooth is located) and noting the number of the tooth needing treatment.

REVIEW OF BASIC HEAD AND NECK ANATOMY

The head is divided into 11 regions which are: frontal, parietal, temporal, occipital, orbital, infraorbital, zygomatic, nasal, buccal, mental, and oral.

The skull is divided into the cranium and the face. There are eight (8) cranium bones: frontal, sphenoid, ethmoid, occipital, parietal and temporal. There are two parietal and two temporal bones, one located on each side of the head. These bones cover and protect the brain. The face has 14 bones. The two most widely known bones of the face are the maxilla bone and the mandible bone, which comprise the maxillary and mandibular dental arches.

The mandible is the only bone in the body that can move. That is only possible because of the TMJ. The temporomandibular joint (TMJ) is located on each side of the head, which allows the mandible to move for chewing (mastication) and speaking. The mandible bone, via ligaments, meets with the temporal bones of the skull and the muscles of the face thus creating a movable joint.

The muscles of the head and neck are split into seven groups:
1. Muscles of the Neck
2. Muscles of Facial Expression
3. Muscles of Mastication
4. Muscles of the Tongue
5. Muscles of the Floor of the Mouth
6. Muscles of the Pharynx
7. Muscles of the Soft Palate

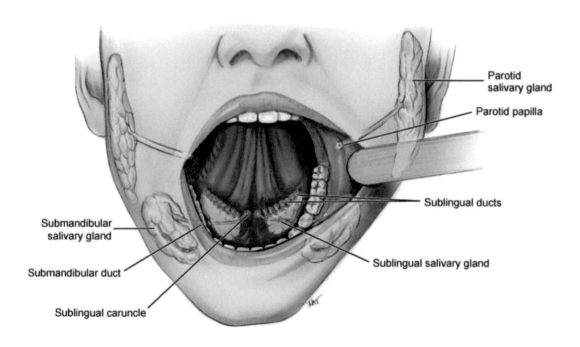

- Parotid salivary gland
- Parotid papilla
- Sublingual ducts
- Sublingual salivary gland
- Submandibular salivary gland
- Submandibular duct
- Sublingual caruncle

The California RDA General Written and Law Examination Prep Book © 2017, 2018 • KB Dental Arts – Publisher
This book and the individual contributions contained within are protected under Copyright by the Publisher

REVIEW OF THE SALIVARY GLANDS

There are three (3) major salivary glands located in the face. Each major salivary gland is a pair.
They are the:

1. Parotid Salivary Glands
    *   Largest of the major salivary glands
    *   Located just below the zygomatic arch, in front of and below the ear
    *   Stensen's Duct (aka, the parotid duct) delivers saliva into the mouth from the gland
    *   Stensen's Duct empties saliva into the mouth opposite the buccal surface of the maxillary first molars
    *   Supplies 25% of all saliva present in the mouth
2. Submandibular Salivary Glands
    *   Second largest of the major salivary glands
    *   Similar in size to a walnut
    *   Located just below the mandible
    *   Saliva is carried from the gland to the mouth via Wharton's Duct (aka, the submandibular duct)
    *   Supplies 60 - 65% of all saliva present in the mouth
3. Sublingual Salivary Glands
    *   Smallest of the three (3) major salivary glands
    *   Located just under and alongside the tongue
    *   Bartholin's Duct (aka, the sublingual duct) delivers saliva into the mouth from the gland.
    *   Supplies 10% of all saliva present in the mouth

REVIEW OF THE ORAL TISSUES

There are two (2) types of oral tissue found in the oral cavity. They are:

*   Mucous membrane tissue -
    *   The entire oral cavity is lined with this soft, thin tissue.
    *   Tissue can easily adapt to the alveolar process.
    *   Tissue is usually darker in color than tissue closer to the teeth; can be described as a dark pink to red in color.
*   Gingiva -
    *   Typically referred to as the "gums" or gum tissue.
    *   Gingival tissue is tougher, stronger and more resistant to the forces of mastication (chewing) than mucous membrane tissue.
    *   Surrounds the tooth at the cervical line covering the roots of teeth and bone (alveolar process) while providing protection.
    *   Gingiva is usually light pink to deep pink in color depending on the individual patient's coloring; fair-skinned patients generally exhibit light-pink gingival tissue while darker-skinned patients exhibit darker pink gingival tissue.
    *   Unattached gingiva: the area of tissue that surrounds the tooth at the cervical edge; floss is inserted here to maintain oral hygiene (aka, "free" gingiva).
    *   Attached gingiva: the part of the tissue that covers the alveolar process; tissue is firmly and tightly secured over the bone for protection.

CLASSIFICATIONS OF OCCLUSION

The term *occlusion* describes the natural contact of the maxillary and mandibular teeth when closed together. The term *malocclusion* describes the abnormal or unnatural contact of the maxillary and mandibular teeth when closed together.

Dr. Edward Angle invented a classification system by which different types of occlusion and malocclusions are described by using the relationship of the maxillary and mandibular first molars as the guide.

The relationship of the permanent first molars determines the classification.

A.   Class I, Neutrocclusion – "Normal Bite"
 o   The first molars are in an aligned relationship.
 o   The mesiobuccal cusp of the maxillary first molar occludes with the mesiobuccal groove of the mandibular first molar.
 o   The cusp of the upper molar meets with the groove of the lower molar determining proper molar alignment.
 o   The anterior teeth may be crowded, crooked or rotated; this makes no impact on the classification of the occlusion.

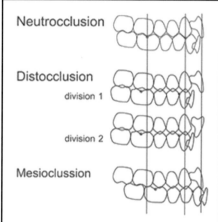

B.   Class II, Distocclusion – "Buck Tooth Appearance"
 o   The mesiobuccal cusp of the maxillary first molar is mesial to the mesiobuccal groove of the mandibular first molar.
 o   This gives the appearance of the maxillary arch protruding over the mandibular arch.
 o   Simply stated, the maxillary first molar is too far forward to be in alignment with the mandibular MB groove effectively shifting the entire arch mesial giving the protrusive appearance.

C.   Class III, Mesioclusion – "Bulldog Appearance"
 o   The mesiobuccal cusp of the maxillary first molar is distal to the mesiobuccal groove of the mandibular first molar.
 o   This gives the appearance of the mandibular arch protruding past the maxillary arch.
 o   Simply stated, the maxillary first molar is too far back to be in alignment with the mandibular MB groove effectively shifting the entire arch distal giving the appearance of a protrusive mandible.

DENTAL CARIES

The term *dental caries* is a technical name for **dental decay** or a cavity. A **carious lesion (cavity)** is a tooth disease caused by the complex interaction of food (starches and sugars) with bacteria that form dental plaque. Bacterial plaque produces acids that cause demineralization of enamel and enzymes that attack the protein component of the tooth. This process, if untreated, ultimately leads to the formation of deep cavities and bacterial infection of the pulp chamber. The development of dental caries in a health-compromised patient is of special concern due to the potential impact oral infections may have on the body.

In addition, teeth that are decayed are painful, prohibit proper chewing, and can lead to dietary changes that may cause nutritional and digestive disorders.

The cause of dental caries is based on three (3) primary factors:
1. A susceptible tooth
2. A diet rich in fermentable carbohydrates
3. The presence of bacteria

There are two (2) types of bacteria that must be present in the mouth for dental caries to develop - mutans streptococci (MS) and lactobacilli (LB). Carious lesions develop through a repeating process of demineralization and remineralization involving adjustments in the valuable minerals that form the enamel. Over time, the changing presence of minerals weakens the tooth structure making the tooth more susceptible to decay (caries).

The following are descriptions of the various stages and sizes of carious lesions:
- Incipient: the start of a cavity; very small at this point
- Overt or Frank: an obvious, visible hole has formed in the tooth structure
- Rampant: decay is present on almost every tooth in the mouth

Oral hygiene, such as tooth brushing and flossing techniques, are useful in reducing the bacteria present in the oral cavity. A patient should establish an oral hygiene routine to prevent caries from occurring.

CAVITY CLASSIFICATIONS

Once a carious lesion is diagnosed by the dentist, it is classified by its size and location by using a system called **Black's Cavity Classifications**. This system is universal to all dentists.

Class I: decay on the occlusal surfaces of premolars and molars; buccal or lingual pits of molars and lingual pits of maxillary incisors
- o Examples: #3 O, #8 L, #14 B

Class II: interproximal decay located on premolars and molars (posterior teeth)
- o Examples: #30 MO, #18 DO, #20 MOD

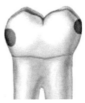

Class III: interproximal decay located on incisors and cuspids (anterior teeth)
- o Examples: #9 M, #25 MD, #22 D

The California RDA General Written and Law Examination Prep Book © 2017, 2018 • KB Dental Arts – Publisher

Class IV: anterior interproximal decay involving the incisal edge
- Examples: #10DI, #23MI, #8 MID

Class V: decay that occurs at the gingival third, or gum line, on the buccal or lingual surface of any tooth; also known as smooth surface decay
- Examples: #2 B, #25 F, #19 L

Class VI: decay on the incisal edges of anterior teeth and/or the cusp tips of posterior teeth caused by wear

ANATOMICAL REVIEW:

- Each tooth has a **crown** and **root** portion.

- The crown is covered with **enamel**.

- The root is covered with **cementum**.

- The crown and root are joined at the **cementoenamel junction (CEJ)**.

- The line that demarcates the CEJ is the **cervical line**.

- The crown portion of the tooth erupts through the **bone** and gum tissue.

- Gum tissue is called **gingiva**.

- After eruption, the crown of the tooth will never again be covered with gum tissue.

- Only the cervical third of the crown in healthy young adults is covered by gingiva.

- The **anatomic crown** is the whole crown of the tooth that is covered by enamel regardless of whether it is erupted.

- The **clinical crown** of the tooth is only that part seen above the gingiva. Any portion of the non-erupted tooth is not part of the clinical crown.

- The tooth may have a **single root** or **multiple roots** with a bifurcation or a trifurcation.

- Each root has one **apex** or **terminal end**.

- The root is held into place by the portion of the jaw called the **alveolar process**.

- The bony socket in which the tooth fits is called the **alveolus**.

- Teeth in the upper jaw (maxilla) are called **maxillary teeth**.

- Teeth in the lower jaw (mandible) are called **mandibular teeth**.

The California RDA General Written and Law Examination Prep Book © 2017, 2018 • KB Dental Arts – Publisher
This book and the individual contributions contained within are protected under Copyright by the Publisher

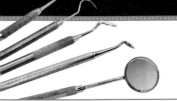

UNIT ONE – PATIENT TREATMENT AND CARE
CHAPTER TWO: A REVIEW OF BASIC CHAIRSIDE SKILLS

EXAMINATION PLAN DATA:

Topic Area	Patient Treatment and Care
Total Weight of Topic Area on Examination	25%
Subject Area of This Chapter	Basic Chairside Skills
Percentage of Examination Questions in Basic Chairside Skills	N/A

BASIC CHAIRSIDE SKILLS – TASK STATEMENT

Task Associated with Topic Area
Perform dental procedures using professional chairside manner

KEY TERMS

Clock Concept	Indicates operating zones for all dental healthcare personnel
Four-Handed Dentistry	One dentist and one assistant practicing at the chair
HVE	High Volume Evacuation
Instrument Grasp	How the instrument is held by the operator
Position of Use	Transferring of the instrument positioned towards the area where it will be used
Six-Handed Dentistry	One dentist and two assistants practicing at the chair
Subsupine	Patient's head is lower than their feet
Supine	Patient is lying flat on their back and the chair is parallel to the floor
Transfer Zone	Area where instruments are exchanged between the dentist and the assistant
Upright	90-degree position of the chair; used when patient enters or exits chair

REVIEW OF THE VARIOUS ROLES OF THE DENTAL ASSISTANT

A dental assistant is a member of the dental health care team and takes on various roles or titles in the dental office. A dental assistant may assist in the front office with scheduling appointments, answering the phone, greeting patients and is often referred to as the business or administrative assistant. A dental assistant may work directly with patients alongside the dentist providing patient care and is often referred to as the chairside or clinical dental assistant. This chapter will focus primarily on the responsibilities and skills of the chairside assistant.

In California, a dental assistant (DA) is defined in law as a person who, without a license, may perform tasks that are considered basic and elementary in nature. A Registered Dental Assistant (RDA) is a person who has completed the education and/or work experience necessary to pass a licensing examination; in addition, the law allows many more skills and functions to be performed by a licensed RDA. It is the responsibility of the dental office employee to know what duties and functions he/she is legally allowed to perform under California law.

REVIEW OF DENTAL EQUIPMENT AND CARE OF DENTAL EQUIPMENT

Basic equipment found in each treatment room includes, but is not limited to:
- **Patient Dental Chair**: designed for patient comfort and support during dental treatment; operated either by hand or foot controls located on or near the chair.
- **Operator's Stool**: designed to support the operator during patient treatment; should have large seat and back rest with the ability to be adjusted to access the patient with ease. *(NOTE: the operator can be the dentist, the hygienist or the dental assistant depending on the type of procedure being performed)*
- **Dental Assistant's Stool**: designed to support the dental assistant during patient treatment with a large, wide seat for extra stability; may include an abdominal bar for upper body support; allows the assistant to turn and access instruments and supplies during treatment without obstruction; contains a foot ring at the chair base for back support and balance.
- **Dental Unit**: provides necessary electricity and hoses with air and water to the dental chair; the dental handpiece(s), air/water syringe and oral evacuation system are located here; arranged in delivery systems chosen by the dentist. Types of delivery systems include:
    - Front delivery: the dental unit is positioned over the patient's chest.
    - Side delivery: the dental unit is positioned at either side of the dental chair.
    - Rear delivery: the dental unit is positioned behind the patient's head.
- **Overhead Light**: used to provide light into the oral cavity during dental treatment; the positioning of the overhead light is the assistant's responsibility during patient treatment.
- **Air/Water Syringe**: provides air, water, and/or a combination of both into the oral cavity during patient dental treatment.
- **Rheostat**: a foot pedal that controls the dental handpieces attached to the dental unit via hoses; placed on the floor near the back of the dental chair towards the operator's side.
- **Waterlines/Hoses**: transports water and air through the hoses to the dental handpiece or the air/water syringe; water is critical during dental treatment to keep the tooth cool.
- **Oral Evacuation System:**
    - Saliva ejector: low-volume suction system to remove fluids, such as water or saliva, from the oral cavity; tip is disposable.
    - High Volume/Velocity Evacuator (HVE): provides removal of large amounts of fluid and debris from the oral cavity; more powerful than the saliva ejector and used with the majority of dental procedures; tip is disposable.

CARE OF DENTAL EQUIPMENT

It is important to always follow the manufacturer's instructions in regard to the cleaning and maintenance of all dental equipment in the office. A dental sales representative or equipment specialist should be consulted if the manuals are outdated or cannot be located in the office. Routine maintenance of equipment is usually one of the many duties delegated to the chairside dental assistant. These duties may include, but are not limited to:

- changing the traps located in each dental unit and in the central vacuum,
- care of the overhead light (ensure the light is cool prior to wiping down),
- flushing of the dental operatory lines/hoses to maintain the evacuation and vacuum systems in the dental office, and
- making sure the operatory is free of dust especially around the base of the dental chair and on stationary objects in the operatory.

PATIENT POSITIONING

When the patient is escorted into the operatory, the assistant will ask the patient to sit in the dental chair. At this point, the dental chair is positioned in the **upright** position. The upright position is used when the patient is entering or exiting the chair, the exposing of dental x-rays and alginate impressions. The back of the dental chair is at a 90-degree angle.

In the **supine** position, the patient is lying flat on their back and the chair is parallel with the floor. The majority of dental work is completed with the patient in this position.

The **subsupine** position places the patient's head lower than their feet. The subsupine position is not recommended for performing dental treatment; instead, it is intended for use during an emergency situation.

ASSISTANT POSITIONING AT THE CHAIR

Prior to the start of dental treatment, both the dentist and the assistant are required to don (place on) personal protective equipment (PPE). The assistant needs to sit in a way that provides visualization of the mouth while achieving correct ergonomics. The chairside dental assistant should position his/her stool as close as possible to the dental chair. The assistant should sit completely on the seat and as far back as possible on the stool with their feet planted side by side either on the floor or on the foot ring provided on every dental assistant stool. Legs are parallel to the dental chair with the knees pointed slightly towards the patient's head.

The assistant's stool should be positioned four (4) to six (6) inches higher than the operator. The above tips for assistant positioning help the assistant gain access and visualization into the patient's mouth. If needed, the dental assistant should adjust the stool to achieve these desired positions.

OPERATOR POSITIONING AT THE CHAIR

It is important to review the operator's position at the chair since dental assistants often sit in the operator's position to perform various tasks during patient treatment. Like the assistant, the operator needs to sit in a way that provides visualization of the mouth while achieving correct ergonomics. The operator should be seated as far back on the chair, so the backrest touches the lower back of the operator.

The operator will feel the front edge of the stool touching the backs of their knees and should have their thighs parallel to the floor. When bent, the operator's forearms should be parallel to the floor with their feet placed flat on the floor. If needed, the operator should adjust the stool to achieve these desired positions.

The California RDA General Written and Law Examination Prep Book © 2017, 2018 • KB Dental Arts – Publisher
This book and the individual contributions contained within are protected under Copyright by the Publisher

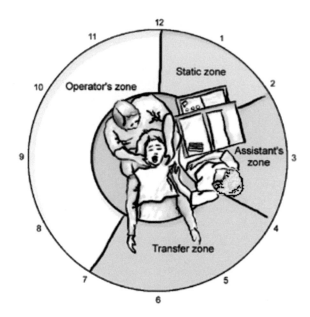

Right Handed Dentist   *Left Handed Dentist*

THE CLOCK CONCEPT

The clock concept, also known as "operating zones", designate working areas for each member of the dental team providing direct patient care, as well as the supplies, and equipment needed to accomplish treatment. These times on the clock change for a right-handed operator versus a left-handed operator.

The time zones are:

- Operator's Zone: 7 to 12 o'clock – right handed; 12 to 5 o'clock - left handed
  - This is where the dental professional performing treatment is seated, usually the dentist
  - The hygienist or the assistant can also be the operator for procedures; if performing or completing a procedure the hygienist or assistant should be seated in the operator's position.

- Transfer Zone: 4 to 7 o'clock – right handed; 5 to 8 o'clock – left handed
  - Area where items, instruments or supplies are exchanged from operator to assistant.
  - Transferring always occurs under the patient's chin, over the chest, between the patient's shoulders and never over the patient's face; items/instruments should not be placed here as a resting place.

- Assistant's Zone: 2 to 4 o'clock – right handed; 8 to 10 o'clock – left handed
  - Area where the assistant is located.
  - The assistant stays in one seated position and pivots the upper body to reach supplies, materials or instruments.

- Static Zone: 12 to 2 o'clock – right handed; 10 to 12 o'clock – left handed
  - Area where a rear delivery system dental unit, a countertop or mobile cabinet, may be located.

The California RDA General Written and Law Examination Prep Book © 2017, 2018 • KB Dental Arts – Publisher

FOUR-HANDED DENTISTRY

Four-handed dentistry is a team approach to delivering dental care. In four-handed dentistry, a dentist and one assistant perform dental care on a patient in ergonomically pleasing, seated positions around the dental chair. Modern dentistry is practiced utilizing the four-handed dentistry concept. Some practices have expanded on the concept by incorporating six-handed and eight-handed dentistry.

- Four-handed dentistry: 1 dentist and 1 dental assistant
  - Both dentist and assistant are seated at the chair.
  - Assistant is responsible for all aspects of the dental procedure including, but not limited to, patient comfort and safety, suctioning, retraction, adjusting of the overhead light, mixing and transferring of dental materials, and instrument transfer.
  - Standard operating procedure in most modern dental practices.

- Six-handed dentistry: 1 dentist and 2 assistants
  - Dentist and one assistant are seated – the chairside clinician.
  - Second assistant is standing behind the chairside clinician – the chairside assistant.
  - Each assistant has a specific set of duties prescribed to them by the dentist; typically, the chairside clinician is responsible for patient comfort and safety, suctioning, retraction, and overall assessment of the patient's well-being; the second assistant is responsible for the mixing and transfer of any dental materials, instrument transfer, and procedural control measures.
  - The tasks performed during six-handed dentistry are commonly involving surgical procedures and varies by dentist preferences.

- Eight-handed dentistry: 1 dentist and 3 assistants
  - Dentist and first assistant are seated.
  - Second and third assistants are standing; one behind the chairside clinician and the one towards the bottom of the dental chair on the operator's side.
  - Duties will be much like those described in six-handed dentistry with the dentist prescribing the duties for each assistant.
  - Most often seen in surgical practices and hospital-based dentistry.

THE CLASSIFICATIONS OF MOTION

Motions are categorized into five categories dependent upon the extent of the motion and nature of the movement.
1. Class I movement is defined as movement of fingers only such as picking up a single item from a flat surface.
2. Class II movement is defined as movement of the fingers and wrist such as instrument transfer using the pen grasp technique.
3. Class III movement is defined as movement involving fingers, wrist and elbow such as using a computer mouse or a dental handpiece to perform an intraoral procedure.
4. Class IV movement is defined as movement involving the entire arm and shoulder such as moving a piece of equipment in the operatory.
5. Class V movement is defined as movement involving the upper torso such as bending over to look into a patient mouth or pulling supplies from a cabinet.

The California RDA General Written and Law Examination Prep Book © 2017, 2018 • KB Dental Arts – Publisher

OVERHEAD LIGHT

The placement, adjustment and care of the overhead patient light is the responsibility of the chairside assistant. The light should be pushed up towards the ceiling and back towards the foot of the chair allowing the patient to enter and exit the chair with ease. Once the chair is back in the operator's desired position, and the operator and assistant are getting into place, the assistant will bring the light forward, turning it on and pointing it straight down at the patient's chest.

Light placement tips for treatment on the maxillary arch:
- Begin with the light on and pointed towards the patient's chest.
- Ask the patient to open, tipping their chin towards the ceiling.
- Grasping the handle of the light, gently tip the light up until the light beam is shining directly onto the maxillary arch.
- Adjust as needed during the procedure for a visible operating field.

Light placement tips for treatment on the mandibular arch:
- Begin with the light on and pointed towards the patient's chest.
- Ask the patient to open, moving their chin toward their chest.
- Grasping the handle of the light, gently pull the light forward until the light beam is directly shining down on the mandibular arch.
- Adjust as needed during the procedure for a visible operating field.

Once treatment is over, turn the light off, and move it out of the way as the operator repositions the chair into the upright position. Take care to handle the light by the handles only as the other surfaces of the light will be extremely hot. The assistant should wait for the light to cool down before trying to wipe it down with any surface disinfectant or placement of new barriers.

INSTRUMENT EXCHANGE

Instrument exchange is the process of the assistant and dentist transferring the desired instruments for the procedure to one another through the transfer zone. In order for this process to be as efficient and smooth as possible, the assistant should be knowledgeable and proficient in the following areas:
- The Procedure: knowledge of the procedure allows for proper preparation of the treatment room, instruments, materials, and supplies; the assistant should arrange the instruments in their order of use during the procedure on the tray or in the cassette.
- Instrument Position: also termed the "position of use" - the working end of the instrument is pointed toward the working surface.
- Passing Technique: passing the instrument appropriately to the dentist using either the single-handed transfer or double-handed transfer technique.
- Transfer Control: firmly placing the correct instrument into the dentist's hand so the dentist does not lose their focal point on the procedure or their fulcrum.

FULCRUM AND OPERATOR INSTRUMENT GRASPS

A **fulcrum** is a stabilizing point for the operator using a finger rest whenever treatment is being performed in a patient's mouth. A fulcrum helps prevent injury to the patient if the operator's hand or the instrument slips while in use during treatment. It is preferred that an intraoral fulcrum be established for the greatest stability; however, a fulcrum may be established on the patient's chin or face (an extraoral fulcrum). A fulcrum should always be established by an operator prior to initiating treatment with an instrument or handpiece during treatment.

The California RDA General Written and Law Examination Prep Book © 2017, 2018 • KB Dental Arts – Publisher

An operator's **instrument grasp** depends on the type of instrument being exchanged, the location in the mouth where the instrument will be used, and how the instrument will be utilized during treatment. An assistant should be aware of these grasps for ease of instrument exchange. The three (3) operator instrument grasps are:

- Pen grasp: the fingers hold the instrument similar to that of a pen.
- Palm grasp: the instrument is held in the palm of the operator's hand.
- Palm-thumb grasp: the instrument is held in the operator's palm as the thumb guides and stabilizes the instrument.

RECORDKEEPING

There is a saying in dentistry, "if it's not in the chart, it did not happen" which denotes exactly how vital accurate and efficient recordkeeping is to a dental practice. The patient's chart, or **patient record**, contains the patient registration form, medical and dental histories, dental x-rays, treatment plans, diagnosis and examination conclusions, consent forms, updates to health history and medications, and a detailed recording of treatment provided to the patient. Everything that happens while the patient is in the dental chair is recorded and documented with constant updating of the treatment plan occurring each time the patient is treated. The patient record can be either a hard copy (paper) version, an electronic version or, in some offices, a combination of both. A patient's financial records are not included with the patient record and are kept separate from the treatment record. The financial records are stored as part of the practice's business office records. NOTE: The dentist is the owner of the patient chart including the radiographs, models and other records pertaining to the patient.

CHAPTER REVIEW COMMENTS:

Four-handed dentistry is a concept that describes the manner in which a dentist and a dental assistant work together to perform dental procedures on patients in a safe and ergonomically appropriate manner.

By working efficiently and effectively, the procedures performed in dental healthcare can be accomplished without causing fatigue, stress and repetitive motion injuries when using the following principles each day:

- Follow the principles of motion economy during the transfer of instruments and materials while working chairside.
- Utilizing ergonomically correct dental equipment.
- Utilizing ergonomically correct positioning of the patient and operators for each type of dental procedure by actively adjusting the patient during treatment procedures.
- Utilize instrument techniques and moisture control devices that assist in retraction of tissues for better visibility.

The California RDA General Written and Law Examination Prep Book © 2017, 2018 • KB Dental Arts – Publisher
This book and the individual contributions contained within are protected under Copyright by the Publisher

END OF CHAPTER - CRITICAL THINKING QUESTIONS:

1. Describe the various roles dental assistants assume in the dental office.

2. Who is responsible for knowing what duties dental assistants are allowed to perform under California Law?

3. What is the rheostat and where is it located in the dental office?

4. Name and describe the patient positions in the dental chair.

5. The assistant's stool should be how many inches higher than the operator's stool?

6. Why should the assistant's stool be adjusted higher than the operator's stool?

7. What information does the clock concept provide?

8. Draw a clock and label each zone for both a right and left-handed operator.

9. What is four-handed dentistry?

10. Why is light positioning important?

11. What does "position of use" mean and when is it important?

12. Which hand is used for instrument exchange?

CRITICAL THINKING QUESTION ANSWERS FOUND IN APPENDIX

The California RDA General Written and Law Examination Prep Book © 2017, 2018 • KB Dental Arts – Publisher

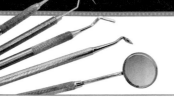

Unit 1 - Chapter 3

UNIT ONE – PATIENT TREATMENT AND CARE
CHAPTER THREE: PATIENT SCREENING AND EDUCATION

EXAMINATION PLAN DATA:

Topic Area	Patient Treatment and Care
Total Weight of Topic Area on Examination	25%
Subject Area	Patient Screening and Education
Percentage of Examination Questions in Patient Screening and Education	N/A

PATIENT SCREENING AND EDUCATION – TASK AND KNOWLEDGE STATEMENTS

Tasks Associated with Topic Area	Knowledge Statements Associated with Topic Area
Take patient's blood pressure and vital signs	Knowledge of common medical conditions that may affect dental treatment (e.g., asthma, cardiac conditions, diabetes)
Review and report to dentist patient medical conditions, medications, and areas of medical/dental treatment history that may affect dental treatment	Knowledge of effects of coexisting medical/dental conditions on dental treatment
Inspect patient's oral condition with mouth mirror	Knowledge of allergic reactions and sensitivities associated with dental treatment and materials (e.g., latex, epinephrine)
Chart existing oral conditions and diagnostic findings at the direction of the licensed provider	Knowledge of purposes and effects of commonly prescribed medications that may affect dental treatment (e.g., Coumadin, psychotropics)
Perform intraoral diagnostic imaging of patient's mouth and dentition (e.g., radiographs, photographs)	Knowledge of medical conditions that may require premedication for dental treatment (e.g., joint replacement, infective endocarditis, artificial heart valves)
Respond to patient questions about existing conditions and treatment following dentist's diagnosis	Knowledge of acceptable levels of blood pressure for performing dental procedures
Observe for signs and conditions that may indicate abuse or neglect	Knowledge of methods and techniques for using medical equipment to take vital signs
Perform dental procedures using professional chairside manner	Knowledge of techniques and procedures for using imaging equipment to perform intraoral and extraoral diagnostic imaging

The California RDA General Written and Law Examination Prep Book © 2017, 2018 • KB Dental Arts – Publisher

PATIENT SCREENING – TASK AND KNOWLEDGE STATEMENTS (CONTINUED)

Tasks Associated with Topic Area	Knowledge Statements Associated with Topic Area
Instruct patient about pre- and postoperative care and maintenance for dental procedures and appliances	Knowledge of methods and techniques patients can perform to improve oral health
Educate patient about behaviors that could affect oral health or dental treatment	Knowledge of types of plaque, calculus, and stain formations of the oral cavity and their etiology
Utilize caries detection materials and devices to gather information for dentist	Knowledge of pre- and postoperative care and maintenance for dental procedures and appliances
	Knowledge of requirements for the supervision of RDAs and RDAEFs related to different dental procedures
	Knowledge of scope of practice for RDAs and RDAEFs related to initial patient assessment
	Knowledge of types of automated caries detection devices, materials, and procedures for their use
	Knowledge of scope of practice for RDAs related to use of caries detection devices and materials
	Knowledge of conditions of the tooth surfaces (e.g., decalcification, caries, stains, and fractures lines) and how to document them

SCOPE OF PRACTICE – SPECIFIC TO PATIENT SCREENING AND CARE

Unlicensed Dental Assistant	Registered Dental Assistant
Extra-oral duties or procedures specified by the supervising licensed dentist provided that these duties or procedures meet the definition of a basic supportive	All duties that a dental assistant is allowed to perform
Operate dental radiography equipment for the purpose of oral radiography if the dental assistant has complied with certification requirements	Mouth-mirror inspections of the oral cavity, to include charting of obvious lesions, existing restorations, and missing teeth
Perform intraoral and extraoral photography	Use of automated caries detection devices and materials to gather information for diagnosis by the dentist

Licensed Registered Dental Assistant in Extended Functions (RDAEF):

(a) A registered dental assistant in extended functions licensed on or after January 1, 2010, is authorized to perform all duties and procedures that a registered dental assistant is authorized to perform and those duties that the board may prescribe by regulation.

(b) A registered dental assistant in extended functions licensed on or after January 1, 2010, is authorized to perform the following additional procedures under _direct supervision_ and pursuant to the order, control, and _full professional responsibility of a licensed dentist_:

   (1) Conduct preliminary evaluation of the patient's oral health, including, but not limited to, charting, intraoral and extra-oral evaluation of soft tissue, classifying occlusion, and myofunctional evaluation.

   (2) Perform oral health assessments in school-based, community health project settings under the direction of a dentist, registered dental hygienist, or registered dental hygienist in alternative practice.

KEY TERMS

Allergic Reaction	A hypersensitivity to a material, product, food or animal that produces an immune response that can be life threatening
Bleach	Tooth whitening agent that produces whiter, brighter teeth
Bitewing	Type of image used for interproximal examination and shows the crowns of both arches on one film
Charting	A documentation process of previous and needed dental work using symbols and colors
Control Panel	Portion of the x-ray unit that contains the master switch, the indicator light, selector and exposure buttons
Digital Image	Electronic signals captured by sensors and displayed on a computer monitor
Drug Addiction	A physical dependency on a drug
Endogenous Stains	Occur within the tooth structure during development and occur due to systemic disturbances
Exogenous Stains	Occur outside the tooth and are caused by environmental factors
Extrinsic Stains	Occur on the external surfaces of the tooth and can be removed by means of coronal polishing
Hemostasis	The process of arresting bleeding using vasoconstrictors to encourage coagulation
Intrinsic Stains	Occur within the tooth surfaces caused by environmental sources and cannot be removed by means of coronal polishing
Panoramic Film/Image	Extraoral image taken either on film or digitally that provides a wide view of both the upper and lower jaws

Periapical	Radiographic view that shows the crown, root tip and surrounding structures
Plaque	Colorless, soft deposit found on teeth that contains bacteria
Positioning Device	Intraoral device used to position and hold the film or sensor
Post-Op Instructions	Directions given to a patient following treatment that will aid in healing or encourage patient comfort
Premedicate	Taking of pre-treatment medication (antibiotics) to prevent disease (premedication or antibiotic prophylaxis)
Pulse Oximetry	Measurement of the level of oxygen in the blood
Radiograph	Image produced on photosensitive film by exposing the film to radiation and processing the image using chemistry
Sensitivity	A heightened response to a substance but not as strong as an allergic reaction
Sensor	A solid image receptor that contains a silicon chip with an electric current
Standard of Care	Level of knowledge and care comparable with that of other dentists who are treating similar patients under similar conditions
Treatment Plan	A map or plan of action created for the patient based upon the findings recorded during the charting portion of new patient appointment or recall visit
Tubehead	Part of the x-ray machine that contains the x-ray tube and the high voltage and low voltage transformers
Vasoconstrictors	A medicament that shrinks the capillaries in tissues thereby decreasing the blood flow temporarily to an area

During clinical care, an effective dental assistant understands the role that proficient patient communications plays in overall patient success. Patients spend a significant amount of time with the chairside assistant during their visits to the dental office and frequently look to the assistant for answers to questions pertaining to their planned dental services. It is, therefore, extremely important the dental assistant develop a strong understanding of all aspects of the dental procedures performed in the office, possess a deep knowledge of the materials, indications and contra-indications regarding the procedures, and demonstrate a thorough knowledge of pre-op and post-op education.

MEDICAL AND DENTAL HISTORIES

The chairside dental assistant is often responsible to review both medical and dental histories with patients prior to the commencement of dental treatment. The assistant must utilize all means necessary to perform an oral interview while using discretion to secure the patient's privacy. If there are any questions the patient missed on the form, this is the perfect opportunity to receive a direct answer from the patient. It is customary to record additional notes based on the patient's communication during the review process.

In the event the patient identifies having an **allergic reaction** or **sensitivity** to drugs, materials or chemicals that may be used during treatment, it is advisable to verbally confirm the nature of the allergy or sensitivity, including the name of the drug, material or product and the resulting symptom. Be sure to verify with the patient what type of reaction they experience when they take or come in contact with the specific drug or material – document the **signs and symptoms** experienced by the patient.

It is helpful to have a list of medications the patient may be taking for the dentist to review to make certain an adverse drug interaction does not occur. In some instances, patients cannot remember specifics about their medications. Ask the patient if they have a list of their medications with them, such as a medical card or a note page in their phone that they carry with them.

If the patient does not have a listing of their medications with them, it is important to tell the patient to please call the office later that day with the medication information or to bring in a detailed list of their medications the next time they come in to the office. It is the dental team's responsibility to explain to the patient that no work can be scheduled or performed until the medication list is complete. This is the safest way to ensure that every patient is receiving the best dental care possible without compromising their overall health and well-being. For example, some medications, such as those taken to treat epileptic seizures, can cause side effects that manifest in the oral cavity. It is important to know this prior to initiating a routine cleaning and examination whereby the cause of swelling, puffiness or redness noted by the dental team may be diagnosed as a medication side effect.

If the patient is currently under a physician's care for a disease or condition, it is advisable that the dentist conducts a phone consultation with the medical provider to determine if dental treatment is allowable and will not produce adverse effects toward the patient's medical condition or treatment.

Other patients will present with no health issues, are not taking medications, and appear to be in stable health; however, it is crucial for the dental team to keep in mind the fact that patients tend to not disclose their full medical history or may not have been diagnosed for a condition. For every patient with a known diagnosed condition there are many that may seek dental care with undiagnosed health conditions.

> *As a side note: It is imperative to maintain all infection control and OSHA recommended protocols regardless of what the medical and dental histories may or may not demonstrate. Patients may be undiagnosed or completely unaware that they harbor infection or disease at the time of their visit to the dental office. The concept is referred to as "Standard Precautions" and is reviewed later in this book.*

There are patients who are required to premedicate prior to dental treatment due to a preexisting health condition. **Premedication**, also known as **antibiotic prophylaxis**, is the taking of pre-treatment medication to prevent disease. A patient is directed to premedicate by their medical doctor, usually due to a heart condition or a joint replacement surgery. If known, the patient will have noted this on the health history form. If, when reviewing a patient's medical history, there is any question as to whether the patient should premedicate and the patient has not been instructed to do so by their medical doctor, the dentist should call the treating medical doctor to confirm.

The California RDA General Written and Law Examination Prep Book © 2017, 2018 • KB Dental Arts – Publisher

The patient will self-administer a prescribed dose of antibiotics prior to treatment and again at the completion of treatment. Premedication prevents the "weaker" areas of the body, such as the heart (if the patient has a heart condition) or the knee (if the patient had a knee replacement), from being attacked by bacteria released into the blood stream during dental treatment. Dental practitioners commonly follow the current standards established by the American Medical Association and the American Dental Association for prescribing pre-treatment prophylaxis to patients.

EFFECTS OF NUTRITION, TOBACCO, SMOKING AND SUBSTANCE ABUSE ON ORAL TISSUES

Proper nutrition is the process of ingesting the appropriate nutrients for the body producing a positive effect on the oral tissues. Food contains water, which has an overall health benefit for the body. Approximately 80% of the human body is water and provides hydration for the body's tissues and organs and helps regulate the body's temperature. Educating the patient on proper nutrition will help prevent tooth decay and enhance their overall oral health.

Smoking puts patients at an increased risk for periodontal disease. Patients who smoke experience increased depth of periodontal pockets, greater bone loss and tooth loss. **Periodontal disease** is a chronic ongoing deterioration of the gingiva, periodontal ligaments and alveolar bone (aka, the periodontium).

One effect of periodontal disease is tooth mobility. **Mobility** creates instability in the adult dentition causing increased sensitivity and pain. Mobility cannot be reversed and eventually leads to tooth loss. The loss of teeth in the adult dentition leads to a collapse of the occlusion. Treatments for periodontal disease are less effective in patients who smoke.

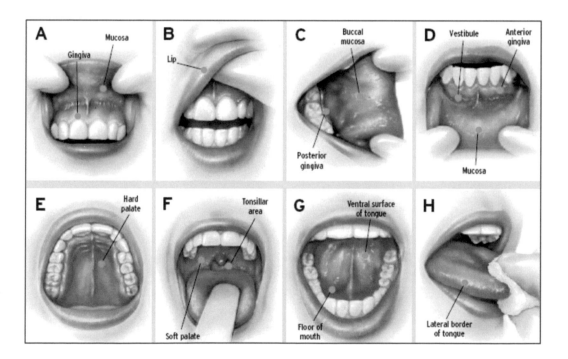

Smokeless tobacco (referred to as "chew") is more dangerous for the oral tissues versus smoking simply because the chemicals in the tobacco are placed directly against the fragile and sensitive soft tissues. The oral tissues can be seriously irritated by the tobacco leading to conditions such as **leukoplakia**. There is an increased oral cancer risk, including cancers of the esophagus, pharynx and larynx, in those individuals who regularly use smokeless tobacco.

The California RDA General Written and Law Examination Prep Book © 2017, 2018 • KB Dental Arts – Publisher

Healthy gingiva should appear pink, firm and smooth. If the tissue looks any different in appearance, especially if the patient has a health history of using tobacco products, the dentist should evaluate the condition of the tissues. Abnormal gingiva can appear as white blotches/marks on the gingiva, redness, puffiness, swelling, exudate (pus), tenderness, bleeding, and any signs or symptoms of oral pathological diseases.

Substance abuse has devastating effects on the teeth, the oral tissues of the mouth and the overall physical condition of the patient. Substance abuse is also called **drug addiction**, which is a physical dependency on a drug. A drug can be alcohol, prescription medications or illegal street/recreational drugs that become habit forming. The body develops a dependency on the drug and eventually will not be able to function without it.

Illegal street drugs, such as methamphetamine, have a more severe effect on the dentition and oral tissues. Teeth will become loose and tooth loss is rampant amongst severe drug users. A drug-abusing patient may present with large carious lesions or large fractured teeth broken down at the gingiva. In severe cases, the hard and soft tissues of the mouth can be destroyed by rampant drug abuse. It is not uncommon to see the hard palate destroyed by an individual with a cocaine addiction. All abused drugs have a negative effect on a patient's overall physical condition.

COMMONLY PRESCRIBED DRUGS IN DENTISTRY

Name of Drug	Purpose	Effect
Tylenol, Advil (analgesic med)	Relieve mild to moderate pain	Raises the pain threshold creating pain relief
Codeine (typically combined with aspirin, acetaminophen or ibuprofen)	For moderate to moderately severe pain	Relieve pain from endodontic or surgical procedures
Antibiotics: Penicillin, Erythromycin	Used to treat and eliminate bacterial infections	Bacterial infection is reduced or eliminated
Valium	Anti-anxiety drug	Reduces/manages stress, anxiety and pain during dental treatment
Vicodin	Prescription narcotic	Relieves severe pain associated with surgery or infections

VITAL SIGNS

Dental assistants are often tasked with recording baseline readings during new patient appointments. Baseline readings are recorded and documented.

Vital signs consist of the following four (4) indicators of the patient's current health status:
1. **Temperature**: normal body temperature for an adult is considered to be 98.6 degrees F but may range between 97.6- and 99-degrees F; temperature readings are usually done with a thermometer, many of which are digital by today's standards and taken orally. The temperature can rise and fall throughout the day as well as with taking in hot and cold drinks. There are differing temperature ranges for children.

2. **Pulse:** the pulse is an expansion of the artery each time the heart beats. When measuring the patient's pulse rate, the dental professional is counting the number of times the heart beats per minute by placing their index

and middle fingers over an artery on the patient's body, careful not to use their thumb – by doing so the clinician will actual measure their own pulse rate, not the patient's.

The most effective arteries used for measuring a pulse rate are the **brachial artery**, located on the inner fold of the arm just below where the arm bends; the **radial artery**, located on the inner wrist closest to the thumb; and the **carotid artery**, located on the neck just opposite to the larynx or "Adam's Apple". The radial artery is the most common location used for measuring a patient's pulse rate.

The rhythm (pattern of the beat) and volume (strength of the beat) of the pulse can be documented as well. A normal pulse rate for an adult is 60 - 100 beats per minute when relaxed. Pulse rate will be higher with physical movement or fright and lower when sleeping or sedated.

3. **Respiration**: is a recording of how the patient is breathing. The patient's respiration rate, rhythm and depth are recorded. A respiration rate is how many breaths per minute that patient is taking. A normal respiration rate for a relaxed adult is 10 - 20 breaths per minute.

    NOTE: Children have an increased respiration of 18 - 30 breaths per minute and babies are even higher. Taking of the patient's respiration rate can be obtained by simply observing the rise and fall the patient's chest.

4. **Blood Pressure (BP)**: this is a measurement of how hard the heart must work to pump blood through the body. There are two readings that are recorded when measuring blood pressure: the **systolic reading** (the higher number) and the **diastolic reading** (the lower number).

An example of a normal blood pressure reading would be 120/80. Blood pressure can be measured using a sphygmomanometer and a stethoscope or with a blood pressure monitor. Blood pressure monitors are quickly becoming the norm in medical and dental offices alike for taking a blood pressure reading.

While not considered a vital sign, pulse oximetry is quickly becoming another item that is recorded when collecting other vital sign readings. **Pulse oximetry** is how the concentration of oxygen in the blood is measured or a measurement of the blood-oxygen level. This reading is obtained by placing a patient's index finger into a machine called a **pulse oximeter**. The pulse oximeter attaches to the patient's finger and shines an infrared light into the capillaries. It then measures the amount of oxygen in the blood. A healthy patient will exhibit a blood-oxygen saturation of 95% - 99%.

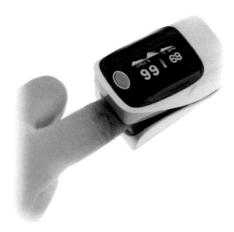

It is important to note that today, aside from measuring a temperature, sophisticated machines can obtain all the above vital signs and pulse oximetry readings. Some machines can record all these vital signs at one time.

MONITORING BLOOD PRESSURE

Patient's will indicate on their medical history form if they have been diagnosed with high blood pressure or hypertension and will indicate the medications, if applicable, currently being used to control blood pressure. There are no contraindications to treating a patient with high blood pressure so long they are following their physician's care instructions to manage their blood pressure; it is, therefore, important to check the patient's blood pressure prior to any dental treatment procedure.

There will be instances when patients are informed, perhaps for the first time while in the dental chair, of their high blood pressure status – dentists must encourage the patient to seek medical attention or contact the physician for further direction in performing dental treatment. Uncontrolled high blood pressure is very dangerous, putting the patient at risk for a heart attack or stroke at any moment.

DENTAL IMAGING – RADIOGRAPHS & INTRAORAL/EXTRAORAL PICTURES

Dental imaging is an important part of obtaining patient information and screening the patient for upcoming care. The term "dental imaging" includes not only dental x-rays but also intraoral pictures and extraoral photographs.

Dental x-rays are performed by the dental assistant who has obtained the proper training and holds a certificate in Radiation Health and Safety issued by a Dental Board-approved provider in California.

Today, there are two (2) radiographic techniques used to produce a dental radiograph:

1. traditional radiology technique using intraoral dental film packets
2. digital radiology technique using a digital dental sensor or imaging receptor

Of the two techniques, digital radiology has become the standard of care of modern dental practices and is far more popular than traditional dental radiology. The ease of use coupled with the decrease in dental supplies and instant viewing of the digital images are only a few reasons why digital radiology is so popular.

The traditional radiology technique is achieved by using dental film and a dental x-ray machine. The assistant will develop the film in an automatic film processor that runs the film through the developer, fixer and rinse stages. It dries the films before dropping them on the other side of the machine. The process of taking the x-rays through the completion of the development phase can take anywhere from 10 – 30 minutes depending on how many dental x-rays are needed for diagnosis for treatment.

The digital radiology technique is the more modern of the two techniques. The digital images are electronic signals captured by sensors and displayed on a computer monitor almost instantly. The **sensor** is connected to the computer and covered with a disposable sheath to prevent cross-contamination from patient to patient.

RADIOGRAPHIC EQUIPMENT

The dental x-ray machine consists of three (3) primary components: the **tubehead**, the **extension arm** and the **control panel**.

The **tubehead** is often referred to as the camera of the x-ray machine. It houses the components needed to generate radiation used to expose the image receptor (film or digital sensor). The tubehead contains a **Position Indicator Device** (PID), often referred to as "the cone", which is the extension of the tubehead used to guide the direction of the primary radiation beam. The PID is lead-lined which helps to reduce the patient's risk of scatter radiation exposure.

The operator will use an image receptor **holding device,** also known as the "ring" system, to help align the tubehead and PID in the correct position extra-orally when exposing the radiograph. The rings are attached to aiming arms and bite devices that hold the image receptor in place. The PID is aligned with the aiming ring to establish proper alignment, avoiding errors such as cone-cutting, elongation or foreshortening.

The **extension arm** provides mobility and allows the tubehead to move around the dental chair and the patient as needed.

The **control panel** is installed outside the immediate treatment area and contains the main power button and various control indicators to allow the operator to adjust the milliamperage or kilovoltage based on the region of the mouth being radiographed.

The **exposure control button** may be housed on the control panel or separate as a wall-mounted button to actually activate the tubehead and expose the image receptor to radiation. Because California Radiation Health and Safety Regulations require the operator to stand at least 6-feet away from the primary beam, the exposure control button is generally located outside the treatment room area to ensure safe operator distance.

TYPES OF RADIOGRAPHIC IMAGES

Radiographs are an integral part of the overall diagnosis and treatment plan for patients. There are three (3) types of radiographic images exposed in a dental practice.

1. **Periapical** X-rays/Images – "PA's"

    - Shows the entire structure of the tooth from the occlusal or incisal surface to approximately five (5) millimeters below the apex to display the periapical bone.

    - This image is commonly used if a patient presents with a toothache or if there is a question in regard to tooth formation and/or eruption.

    - Extremely valuable in endodontics and oral surgery.

2. **Bitewing** X-rays/Images – "BWX"

    - Shows the maxillary and mandibular teeth when in a biting position or closed together.

    - Only the crowns of the teeth and a small portion of the root are visible in the image.

    - Used for diagnosing restorative needs, such as locating recurrent decay, interproximal decay, early periodontal disease and the seal of new crowns or fillings.

3. **Full Mouth** Survey – "FMX"

    - A series of x-rays/images taken on adults as a new patient in a dental office.

    - Only taken once every five (5) years.

    - Series is a combination of periapical images and bitewing images.

    - Consists of 18 – 20 images, 14 periapical images and 6 - 8 bitewing images.

    - Image number can alter depending on the number of teeth present in the mouth.

PANORAMIC IMAGING – "PANO"

A **Panoramic image** (often referred to as a "Pano") is an extraoral image of the skull, jaws, sinuses and teeth. Panoramic imaging, like all dental radiographs, was once only film based. The emergence of digital imaging in modern dentistry is making digital panographs and cone-beam radiography invaluable resource for diagnostics.

INTRAORAL/EXTRAORAL IMAGES/PICTURES

Besides dental x-rays, other intraoral devices can be used to assist with diagnosing and treatment planning, including intraoral cameras. Similar to dental radiographs, the picture images need to be of diagnostic quality in order to be useful.

Intraoral images are obtained by using a wand-like device that contains a small video camera within. This wand is placed into the patient's mouth and up-close images of the tooth can be shown on the computer monitor. This is a good tool to use in educating the patient about findings within their mouth by magnifying the tooth. It is useful for patient case acceptance and legal documentation. These images can also be captured by pressing a button on the wand and turned into a picture. These pictures can also be useful for insurance purposes.

Extraoral images are captured by use of a digital camera with various size lenses. The lenses can be interchanged depending upon what photo is being snapped. The camera can also be used to capture pictures of the teeth with the use of cheek retractors. The camera is useful for before and after pictures such as in orthodontics or in esthetic cases.

PLAQUE AND CALCULUS

Plaque is a colorless, soft deposit found on teeth that contains bacteria. It is easily removed by means of toothbrushing and flossing techniques at home and in the dental setting.

Calculus is mineralized, or hardened, plaque. There is no way to remove calculus at home, therefore, regular dental visits are essential to the health of the mouth. Calculus may only be removed by the Registered Dental Hygienist or Dentist.

The removal of calculus leaves the enamel rough. The roughness of the enamel attracts plaque accumulation; it is recommended that a coronal polishing procedure complete the oral prophylaxis treatment in an effort to smooth the rough areas of the teeth.

A coronal polish procedure is **not a substitute** for a prophylaxis but is actually an **integral part** of the cleaning procedure. When performing coronal polish, the sequence of polishing should be restricted to the anatomical crown, completely avoiding the sensitive cementum as much as possible.

DENTAL STAINS

Dental stains are divided into two (2) categories and two (2) specific types. There are stains that can be removed by mechanical means, or coronal polishing, and others that cannot. It is important for the RDA to be knowledgeable in identifying dental stains for purposes of removal and patient education. The two (2) categories of stains are **endogenous stains** and **exogenous stains**.

Endogenous stains occur within the tooth during development and occur due to systemic disturbances. These disturbances can occur at varying stages of tooth development and can affect both primary and/or permanent teeth. Therefore, when either a primary or permanent tooth erupts into the oral cavity, signs of staining are present. An example of this type of staining results from medication side effects such as tetracycline staining. This type of stain cannot be removed by means of coronal polishing.

Exogenous stains occur outside the tooth and are caused by environmental factors. Exogenous stains are further divided into types of stains depending on whether the stain can be removed by means of coronal polishing or not. The two types of stains are **extrinsic stains** and **intrinsic stains.**

Extrinsic stains occur on the external surfaces of the tooth and can be removed by means of coronal polishing. An effective memory trick for remembering this in a testing situation is to associate the **"ex"** in **ex**trinsic and the **"ex"** in **ex**ternal. Remember, extrinsic stains occur on the external surfaces of the tooth and can be removed by coronal polishing. Depending on the length of time the stain has been on tooth, the stain can be either difficult or easy to remove. Some examples of extrinsic staining are foods, drinks and tobacco. These examples demonstrate stains that are from external sources.

Intrinsic stains occur within the tooth surfaces and are caused by environmental sources. Intrinsic stains cannot be removed by means of coronal polishing because the stain has incorporated itself into the tooth structure. An effective memory trick for remembering this in a testing situation is to associate the **"in"** in **in**trinsic and the **"in"** in with**in**. Again, intrinsic stains occur within the tooth structure itself and cannot be removed by means of coronal polishing.

Examples of intrinsic staining are stains from tobacco products such as chew, cigars or cigarettes that have been on the teeth for lengths of time without being removed. Another example is staining from dental amalgams that have remained in the tooth as a restoration for a number of years. The stain is incorporated into the tooth structure similar to the tobacco products.

HEMOSTASIS

Hemostasis is the process of arresting bleeding by the use of vasoconstrictors to encourage coagulation. **Vasoconstrictors** shrink the capillaries, thereby decreasing the blood flow temporarily to an area. Achievement of hemostasis is generally accomplished using epinephrine and is critical when packing cord for a final impression during crown and bridge and prior to placing a restoration.

Factors that contribute to a lack of hemostasis during intraoral procedures are:

- injury to the gingival tissues.
- certain medications such as blood thinners.
- alcohol present in the bloodstream.
- medical conditions or a lack of anesthetic in the area being worked on leading to an increased blood flow.

Presence of any one factor will result in bleeding during procedures. The dentist will consult with the treating medical doctor to receive authorization for the patient to temporarily discontinue taking any medication that may cause increased bleeding during dental treatment; the manner in which hemostasis is achieved may be adjusted accordingly.

MOUTH MIRROR INSPECTION OF THE ORAL CAVITY

RDAs are allowed to perform mouth mirror inspections in California for basic charting purposes. It is important to note that RDAs never diagnose. The RDA will only chart the findings of the oral cavity inspection for the dentist to review and verify. In performing a mouth mirror inspection, there are specific ways to hold the mouth mirror to properly visualize all areas of the mouth. When looking into a patient's mouth, the operator can use either direct vision or indirect vision.

Direct vision is the task of looking directly at the area being examined without the use of a mouth mirror. **Indirect vision** is the task of viewing the area being examined by using the mouth mirror. Indirect vision is used when the operator is practicing in an ergonomic, comfortable and safe position to provide dental care. The mouth mirror is often used to aid in retraction if the operator moves from indirect vision to direct vision while performing the intraoral inspection.

After assuming the operator position, the overhead patient light is adjusted, using the non-dominant hand, and the patient is asked to adjust their chin up or down or move their head left or right to establish an effective ergonomic position. The operator is now in position to move easily back and forth from direct to indirect vision using the mouth mirror.

The mouth mirror should be held parallel to the working surface to allow for proper viewing of the teeth. It is important to remember that what is being viewed is a mirror reflection, so moving the mirror at an angle will create distortion.

Grasping the mirror handle at the distal half with the thumb, index finger and middle finger will help to create the parallel positioning needed for indirect vision. The mirror does not need to be very close to the teeth, so holding the mirror farther away will allow for movement and positioning.

CARIES DETECTION

As new technology has emerged, dentistry has seen has a shift in the way dental carious lesions ("cavities") are diagnosed by the dental professional.

Today, decay is diagnosed utilizing several different sources, such as:

- Intraoral examination using an explorer
- Visual appearance of the teeth upon intraoral examination
- Radiographs
- Caries indicator dyes
- Caries automated detector devices

Caries detector aides are not meant to take the place of radiographs. It is important to note that the dentist makes the final diagnosis regarding carious lesions. No one method of caries detection, including radiographs, has been found to be 100% accurate in every case.

TYPES OF CARIES DETECTION MATERIALS AND DEVICES

- *Intraoral Exam with Explorer:* The sharp tip of the explorer is valuable when examining the teeth, as it will "stick" into any soft areas of the tooth surfaces. The "stick" alerts the dental professional to more closely examine that area of the tooth. This technique is very useful for the occlusal, buccal and lingual surfaces, but not for the interproximal areas that cannot be reached with the dental explorer.
- *Visual Appearance*: Often, upon examination, the dental professional can visualize areas of decay, broken tooth structure, and/or dark areas on tooth structure. Decay can appear as a grayish, brown tint just under the enamel surface; therefore, care should be taken to not misinterpret decay for stain.
- *Radiographs:* Radiographs are a useful diagnostic tool for the detection of interproximal caries where visual diagnosis is not possible. However, early dental decay is not visible on radiographs. Often the size of the carious lesion is misleading because decay is typically two times larger and deeper than it appears on the radiograph.
- *Caries Indicator Dyes:* Following mechanical removal of a carious lesion, special dyes that are applied to the inside of a cavity preparation may be a useful aide to determine if the carious lesion has been completely removed. The dye will undergo a color change if decay is still present, letting the operator know to continue the preparation.
- *Automated Caries Detector Devices:* At present time, there are several versions of automated caries detection devices available for use in dental offices. While the explorer is still widely used to evaluate a patient for caries, cutting edge caries detection systems are changing the way dental staff screen and treat patients. Capable of detecting and assessing carious lesions earlier and in more locations, caries detection units feature lasers that cause fluorescence of the tooth while others use transillumination to see through the enamel. Regardless of the specific detection technology being used, caries detection systems can help the dental team discover caries at earlier stages when minimally invasive treatment options might be best for the patient. The RDA will need to educate themselves on the various detection technologies; some are integrated into intraoral cameras and other systems are stand-alone units.

As a reminder, the use of caries detection technology is restricted to licensed personnel only – this is not an allowable duty for the unlicensed dental assistant.

CHARACTERISTICS OF AUTOMATED CARIES DETECTION DEVICES

Automated caries detection devices, like many devices used in the profession, have great benefit to the diagnostic process as well as some limitations. It is important to be mindful that automated detectors should not be the only tool utilized when the dentist develops a diagnosis.

The RDA should be fairly knowledgeable as to the characteristics of an automated caries indicator, including the following:

- can indicate any bacterial activity under the enamel
- can be used to diagnose incipient, or early, dental disease (decay)
- cannot locate decay below the gumline or on deeper interproximal surfaces
- cannot detect decay under crowns, bridges or previous restorations
- can give "false positive" reading when not properly calibrated or charged

REVIEWING THE PATIENT'S DENTAL HISTORY AND CHARTING

Recording the conditions in the patient's oral cavity is a technique similar to shorthand – the process involves the use of symbols, numbers and colors to indicate the current condition of the patient's mouth. The dental assistant must be aware of the terms used in the charting process including the types of restorations found in the oral cavity, and their common use in the profession of dentistry. As with all legal documents, the patient's dental history record is maintained regularly and updated as procedures are performed and completed.

CHARTING METHODS

Documentation of dental conditions, new or existing is extremely important for the patient's oral health. A **treatment plan** is created for the patient based upon the findings recorded during the **charting** process of a new patient appointment or recall visit. The charting document becomes part of the patient dental record and is maintained as a legal document.

Charting can be accomplished by using a paper chart with a red/blue pencil or electronically with dental software. The use of the red/blue color designation is the same for both methods. The color red denotes an area needing treatment while blue denotes an area where treatment already exists or has been completed. Symbols are used to note recommended treatments, existing conditions, and/or types of recommended procedures.

There are various styles of charting symbols and every dentist will chart in a slightly different way. For example, a missing tooth can be noted in the dental chart by one or two straight lines through the middle of the pictured tooth. One dental office may use two lines to note a missing tooth while another may use only one line. It is the dentist's preference.

The entire dental team will need to be trained on the dentist's preference, so the charting meets with his/her approval. The assistant should strive to complete the most accurate and legible charting possible. It is important to remember that the dental chart is a form of non-verbal communication. Symbols and colors are being used to communicate the condition of the patient's mouth. Any dental professional should be able to look at a patient's chart and understand the current condition of their oral cavity.

Refer to the charting addendum at the back of this book for a review of commonly used charting symbols.

POST-OPERATIVE INSTRUCTIONS

Post-operative ("post-op") instructions are directions given to a patient following treatment that will aid in healing or encourage patient comfort. There are post-operative instructions for virtually every dental procedure accomplished in a dental practice.

The patient should be provided these instructions prior to treatment and again following treatment. If the patient has a caregiver or someone who may be taking them home following the visit, it is important to let that person know what the instructions are as well. Because some dental procedures can be invasive, like surgeries, it is a good idea to make sure the patient is aware of any post-operative complications or precautions prior to undergoing treatment. All instructions should be presented verbally as well as in written form, so the patient may refer back to them following treatment.

Below are some examples of basic post-operative instructions for the following procedures:

1. care and maintenance of removable appliances
2. care of cemented appliances
3. post-op care following periodontal procedures
4. postoperative care following oral surgery procedures
5. postoperative care following orthodontic procedures
6. postoperative care following restorative procedures

1. **Care and Maintenance of Removable Appliances (retainers, partial/full dentures)**

   - remove appliance from the mouth daily for home care
   - after eating, always remove the prosthesis/appliance from the mouth and brush or rinse the entire piece as well as the soft tissues and/or remaining teeth in the mouth
   - brush appliance with toothbrush and toothpaste; brush and floss abutment teeth and remaining natural teeth to keep them free of debris from food and plaque
   - rinse appliance well under cool running water
   - store appliance in a clean denture or retainer box/container; the container should be airtight and the appliance remain moist
   - a few drops of mouthwash may be placed in the container for freshness (if desired)
   - store appliance in a cool area away from any pets
   - when visiting the dental office, bring appliance so it may be examined, adjusted if needed, professionally maintained and cleaned
   - do not adjust the retainer and/or partial or full denture on own – *NOTE: the patient should be instructed to always contact the dental office if the appliance is causing discomfort rather than attempt to adjust the appliance themselves*

2. **Care of Cemented (Fixed) Appliances (bridges, crowns)**

   - brush and floss all teeth, including the fixed appliance, and gum tissues each day
   - use of a mouthwash is recommended for care of the supporting structures
   - if a new bridge is placed, use a floss or bridge threader to floss under the pontic and alongside the abutment teeth *(instructions on how to use the threader will be provided and demonstrated by the chairside assistant)*

3. **Postoperative Care following Periodontal Procedures**

   - brush and floss the other areas of the mouth as usual
   - use caution around the area just treated for the first 24 hours

The California RDA General Written and Law Examination Prep Book © 2017, 2018 • KB Dental Arts – Publisher

- no vigorous rinsing for the first 24 hours

- limit exercise; no heavy lifting or straining

- rest as much as possible

- residual bleeding is common; apply gauze for 20 minutes with firm pressure to the area; repeat if needed; call the office if the bleeding continues

- no smoking; smoking can have negative effects on the sensitive gum tissue and inhibit the healing process

- take pain medications as prescribed

- discomfort is common after the anesthetic wears off; if discomfort continues, even after taking pain medication as prescribed, call the office

- swelling may occur; if so, use a cold pack for the next four hours in increments of 15 minutes on and 15 minutes off

- a dressing may have been placed around the teeth; the dressing is present to protect the area that was just treated; try to not disturb the dressing; it likely will remain in place until the next appointment, however small pieces may chip off; if a large piece or section comes off prior to your next visit, call the office

- have soft diet the day of the procedure so the area does not become irritated; refrain from eating spicy food or hot beverages; a normal diet may be resumed when the patient feels comfortable again

- home care is important following the procedure; take care the first few days following the procedure; follow the dentist's instructions very carefully; use the prescription mouthwash if prescribed by the dentist

4. *Postoperative Care following Oral Surgery Procedures*

- leave gauze in place for time recommended by the dentist

- change and reapply gauze as needed to control bleeding

- rest as much as possible for the first 24 to 48 hours

- take pain medications as prescribed

- no vigorous rinsing for the first 24 hours following the procedure

- after the first 24 hours, begin gently rinsing with warm salt water to aid in the healing process

- no exercise or heaving lifting for the first 24 to 48 hours

- do not disturb the blood clot; the blood clot is the first step in the healing process and begins to form immediately following the procedure

- no smoking especially in the first 24 hours; smoking creates a suction in the mouth that may disturb the blood clot

- eat soft foods; return to a normal diet when chewing feels more comfortable

- avoid alcohol

- do not use straws; straws create a suction in the mouth that may disturb the blood clot

- swelling frequently occurs following oral surgery procedures; use cold packs for the first 24 hours, 20 minutes on and 20 minutes off; after the first 24 hours use heat packs to encourage circulation and enhance healing

- contact the office if pain is unmanageable, nausea and/or vomiting is occurring, or bleeding continues after the first 24 hours

5. **Postoperative Care following Orthodontic Procedures**

- brush teeth at least twice per day

- use a floss threader to aid in flossing at least once per day

- mouthwash will help the mouth feel fresh and will encourage healthy gum tissue

- rinse mouth frequently with water to remove debris

- avoid sticky foods, such as candies and popcorns, while undergoing orthodontic treatments; gum chewing is not recommended

- use wax over any area of the appliance that may cause irritation to the soft tissues

- keep all scheduled orthodontic appointments so movement of the teeth occurs on the treatment plans schedule

- inspect appliances daily to check for damage and debris that might be present

- contact the orthodontic office immediately if trauma occurs while wearing an appliance or an appliance becomes damaged or breaks

- ibuprofen (Advil) or acetaminophen (Tylenol) may be taken to relieve any discomfort following the procedure

6. **Postoperative Care following Restorative Procedures**

- wait for any anesthetic to wear off prior to eating or drinking any foods or liquids; this may take one to two hours following the completion of the procedure

- the tooth/teeth may be temperature sensitive for the next several days; this is normal; please allow the tooth up to seven days to begin to calm down; if the tooth still feels temperature sensitive longer than seven days, call the office

- if the restoration feels high, contact the office so it can be adjusted by the dentist

- the gum tissue in the area of treatment may be tender or sore; this should dissipate in two (2) to three (3) days

- ibuprofen (Advil) or acetaminophen (Tylenol) may be taken to relieve any discomfort following the procedure

END OF CHAPTER - CRITICAL THINKING QUESTIONS:

1. Do you know the difference between an allergy and sensitivity?

2. When a patient indicates they are "allergic to Novocain", what does this really mean?

3. Do you know the common medical conditions that may require a patient to take pretreatment oral prophylaxis (premedication)?

4. If a patient indicates they are required to take premedication prior to dental treatment and they did not do so for the current appointment, what is the next step the assistant should take?

5. Where fear and anxiety about being at the dental office is present, what steps should an assistant take during the health history and dental review to help alleviate those fears?

6. What is a vasoconstrictor?

7. What common drug used in dentistry is used to act as a vasoconstrictor?

8. What common body fluid is arrested by complete hemostasis?

9. What drug or drugs can a patient take to prevent a vasoconstrictor from working effectively?

10. What are the various methods of charting?

11. Why is it important to create a treatment plan for each patient?

12. Why is it important to provide patients with post-operative instructions?

13. How are caries diagnosed?

14. What is the difference between endogenous and exogenous staining?

15. What do vital signs measure?

16. There are four vital sign measurements. What are they?

17. What is pulse oximetry and why is it important in dentistry?

CRITICAL THINKING QUESTION ANSWERS FOUND IN APPENDIX

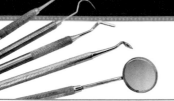

UNIT ONE – PATIENT TREATMENT AND CARE
CHAPTER FOUR: MEDICAL EMERGENCY PREPAREDNESS

EXAMINATION PLAN DATA:

Topic Area	Patient Treatment and Care
Total Weight of Topic Area on Examination	25%
Subject Area	Medical Emergency Preparedness
Percentage of Examination Questions in Medical Emergencies	N/A

MEDICAL EMERGENCY PREPAREDNESS – TASKS AND KNOWLEDGE STATEMENTS

Tasks Associated with Topic Area	Knowledge Statements Associated with Topic Area
Assist in the administration of nitrous oxide/oxygen when used for analgesia or sedation by dentist	Knowledge of procedures for the use and care of equipment used to administer oxygen and nitrous oxide/oxygen
Assist in the administration of oxygen to patients as instructed by dentist	Knowledge of signs and symptoms indicating the need to implement first aid and basic life support measures
Assist in emergency care of patient	Knowledge of signs and symptoms indicating possible allergic reactions and/or sensitivities to medications or materials used in dentistry

SCOPE OF PRACTICE – SPECIFIC TO MEDICAL EMERGENCIES

Unlicensed Dental Assistant	Registered Dental Assistant
Extra-oral duties or procedures specified by the supervising licensed dentist provided that these duties or procedures meet the definition of a basic supportive	Assist in the administration of nitrous oxide when used for analgesia or sedation. A dental assistant shall not start the administration of the gases and shall not adjust the flow of the gases unless instructed to do so by the supervising licensed dentist who shall be present at the patient's chairside during the implementation of these instructions. This paragraph shall not be construed to prevent any person from taking appropriate action in the event of a medical emergency

Licensed Registered Dental Assistant in Extended Functions (RDAEF):

(a) A registered dental assistant in extended functions licensed on or after January 1, 2010, is authorized to perform all duties and procedures that a registered dental assistant is authorized to perform and those duties that the board may prescribe by regulation.

KEY TERMS

Allergy	A hypersensitivity to a substance
Anaphylaxis	A life-threatening allergic reaction affecting the patient's breathing
Antigen	Substance that causes an immune response
EpiPen	Portable device that delivers a dose of epinephrine to the patient exposed to a known allergen
Localized Allergic Reaction	A slow-moving reaction contained to one area of the body
Medical Emergency	An unforeseen set of circumstances which call for immediate action regarding a person who has become suddenly ill or injured while being treated in a dental office
Nitrous Oxide	Tasteless, colorless, sweet smelling gas used with oxygen to relax patients during dental treatment
Sign	Something someone can observe happening with the patient
Symptom	Something the patient is feeling and needs to describe
Syncope	Fainting

A **medical emergency** is an unforeseen set of circumstances that call for immediate action regarding a person who has become suddenly ill or injured while being treated in the dental office. Being prepared for an emergency is essential to the welfare of the patient under the care of the dental team. The dental team (ultimately the dentist) is responsible for the safety of patients under their care. The primary responsibility of the assistant is to ensure the patient is safe. It is important for the RDA to be knowledgeable and ready should such an event occur. The best strategy is to prevent an emergency from happening at all.

The primary step in prevention of an emergency is to know your patient. This entails reviewing the medical history with the patient; ask questions if clarification is needed. A review and updating of the medical history should be done at each recall appointment and before any restorative or major treatment plan commences. Most emergencies that occur in the dental office are due to the patient's apprehension of being at the dental office and the rigors of their daily life converging together. It is helpful to be aware of past negative dental experiences the patient may have experienced while anticipating the extra care this patient may need.

The dental team should discuss how a medical emergency will be handled and which team members will be responsible for alerting 911, staying with the patient, retrieving the emergency kit, and assisting the dentist with the medical emergency. Each team member should be assigned a role. Role playing (practice training) such an event frequently is recommended so all team members feel comfortable and knowledgeable. The dentist and the dental team are responsible for providing care to the patient until EMS arrives and can better assist the patient with their care.

SIGNS VS. SYMPTOMS

One of the many responsibilities of the chairside clinician is to continually scan the patient's overall status during treatment looking for any **sign** the patient may be displaying discomfort, distress or an allergic reaction.

A sign is something the chairside assistant observes, or sees, in the patient. This could be paleness, sweating, shivering, or changes in breathing pattern. It is important for the dental assistant to make the dentist aware of what is being observed. Checking in with the patient allows them an opportunity to let the team know if something is wrong.

A **symptom** is described as what the patient is feeling and experiencing as opposed to what can be observed. Patients are often reluctant to let the dental team know they are not feeling well because they do not want to slow down the procedure or interrupt the dentist. Advising the patient otherwise prior the start of dental treatment may place the patient more at ease to communicate their needs before an emergency situation occurs.

BASIC LIFE SUPPORT

All dental team members are required by regulation of the Dental Board to be certified in Basic Life Support, or BLS, by an American Heart Association or American Red Cross approved provider. Certification must be renewed every two (2) years by all members of the dental healthcare team, regardless of licensure status.

Basic Life Support training contains four (4) critical elements:

1. Immediately recognizing an emergency situation
2. Alerting Emergency Medical Services (EMS)
3. Performing CPR (Cardiopulmonary Resuscitation)
4. Performing defibrillation (if needed)

CARDIOPULMONARY RESUSCITATION (CPR)

CPR is administered immediately in an emergency when it is determined the patient is not breathing and the heart is not beating on its own. The following is a brief synopsis of the 2015 American Heart Association guidelines for CPR performed on an adult patient:

1. Check patient for responsiveness
2. Check patient for respiration and pulse
3. Call 911 (ask someone for help or call first if alone)
4. Begin C – A – B → Compressions – Airway – Breathing

    Compressions: find the lower-half of the sternum and push hard and fast 30 times.

    Airway: establish an airway; tilt the head back, lifting the chin to open the airway.

    Breathing: give two (2) rescue breaths.

Therefore, the ratio is 30 chest compressions to two rescue breaths. Keep repeating this cycle until EMS arrives and takes over or the person starts to breathe.

MEDICAL EMERGENCY KIT CONTENTS

Every dental office, specialty or general, should be equipped with a medical emergency kit, however, this is not required, especially if the office is located near an emergency room facility. In the event a medical emergency kit is present in the office, it is very important that every member of the dental team be aware of the contents of the kit and the location in which it is stored for easy access.

Typically, the dentist will assign the lead chairside assistant in the office the task of keeping the contents current and up-to-date. There are several companies the office can purchase a kit through that will automatically send updated medications along with a letter to the office explaining what to replace in the medical emergency kit. Automated services for replenishment of the kit will occur several times per year.

Dentists will often choose the contents of the emergency kit for the office and may be indicated by the type of dental services rendered. Some of the more common medications and emergency care items are:

Brand/Common Name of Drug	Use	Route
Oxygen and 2-way CPR Mask	Assist with Breathing	Inhalation
Nitrous Oxide	Calming/Analgesic	Inhalation
Cake Icing - Sugar	Hypoglycemia	Orally
Bronchodilator	Asthma Attack	Inhalation
Valium	Seizures	Injection
Ammonia Inhalants	Syncope	Inhalation
Nitroglycerin, tablets/spray	Angina Pectoris	Sublingual
EpiPen	Allergic Reaction	Injection
Benadryl	Allergic Reaction	Oral/Injection
Paper Bag	Hyperventilation	Inhalation
Baby Aspirin	Angina, Cardiac Care	Orally

Oxygen and nitrous oxide are supplied in tanks, or cylinders, with accessory equipment such as hoses and masks that allow for proper delivery. All tanks and supporting equipment are considered an element of an office's emergency kit and should be inspected regularly for needed repairs or replacements. Oxygen is the number one drug utilized in the dental office during a medical emergency. Oxygen tanks/cylinders are always color-coded green.

ALLERGIC REACTIONS

An **antigen** is a toxin or substance that causes an immune response in the body and produces antibodies.

An **allergen** is a type of antigen that produces an abnormally vigorous immune response in which the immune system fights off a perceived threat that would otherwise be harmless to the body. Such reactions are called **allergies or an allergic reaction.**

It is very common for patients to experience an allergy to foods, environmental factors, or ingredients in chemicals. Patients may not be aware they have developed an allergy to a substance or material since allergies can slowly develop over time.

It is extremely important to be aware of any known allergies the patient may list on their health history and perform updates at each dental visit in order to remain current in the event an allergy has developed since their last visit.

When a patient with a known allergy comes into the office, it is important to assess if any part of the procedure could expose the patient to the allergen. This is critical if the patient has a latex allergy, allergy/sensitivity to anesthetic solution or an allergy to acrylate. When treating the patient with these known allergies, it is important to ensure that the dental team takes the proper precautions so as to not cause an allergic reaction.

There are two (2) important factors to consider when evaluating an allergic reaction:

1. Speed with which the symptoms occurred (how quickly a rash, blotchy skin, or itchy eyes developed)
2. Severity of the reaction (the level of symptom severity)

REMINDER: there is a difference between a "sign" and a "symptom."

Allergic reactions can either be localized or systemic, causing anaphylaxis. The onset of a **localized allergic reaction** is slow and typically involves both signs and symptoms such as itching, blotches and hives. A **systemic reaction** known as **anaphylaxis** is a life-threatening allergic reaction that causes patient's breathing to be affected. Depending on the severity of the reaction, the patient could possibly die within minutes of the onset of anaphylaxis.

It is important to note that allergic reactions should be watched very carefully in children. Allergic reactions in children tend to take a turn for the worse faster than adults. We will cover how to respond to a patient experiencing an allergic reaction a bit later in this chapter.

NITROUS OXIDE/OXYGEN ANALGESIA

Nitrous Oxide is a tasteless, colorless, sweet smelling gas that is compressed into a pressurized color-coded blue cylinder. The nitrous oxide is always mixed with oxygen prior to administering to patients. Modern nitrous oxide equipment is equipped with a fail-safe device that ensures the patient is receiving an appropriate mixture of the two gases. The use of nitrous oxide gas and oxygen together is known as **inhalation sedation**. The gases are combined together and are inhaled through a mask also known as a nosepiece. The patient feels the effects of the gases almost immediately.

Inhalation sedation produces a "Stage 1" anesthesia/analgesia state WHEN INSTRUCTED PROPERLY TO BREATHE IN-AND-OUT OF THE NOSEPIECE ONLY. When the patient talks or breaths through their mouth, they will not receive the effective mixture of nitrous/oxygen; therefore, staff should always provide pre-operative instructions to the patient, informing them to remain quiet during the initial stages of inhalation sedation for the most effective results.

NITROUS OXIDE/OXYGEN EQUIPMENT

Dental offices may have a portable nitrous oxide unit or each operatory may be equipped with built-in nitrous/oxygen devices. The following is a list of the nitrous oxide equipment needed to administer the gas safely to the patient:

1. Nitrous oxide and oxygen cylinders or tanks:
   - The cylinders are color coded **green for oxygen** and **blue for nitrous oxide**
   - Can be portable or stored in one central location
   - Should be stored upright, away from a heat source (tanks are explosive)
   - Secured by either a chain or portable cart to prevent cylinders from tipping or rolling

The California RDA General Written and Law Examination Prep Book © 2017, 2018 • KB Dental Arts – Publisher
This book and the individual contributions contained within are protected under Copyright by the Publisher

2. Control valves:
    *   Controls the flow of the nitrous oxide and the oxygen gases
    *   Standard device used on all gas cylinders

3. Flow meter:
    *   Demonstrates the rate of the flow of the gas
    *   There is a standard fail-safe mechanism built in to the flow meter that stops the flow of nitrous oxide, if the oxygen level drops below a certain concentration
    *   Used as a fail-safe mechanism to prevent the patient from inhaling an unsafe level of nitrous oxide

4. Reservoir bag:
    *   Used to combine the two gases; as the patient breathes, the mixed gases are being drawn from the bag

5. Gas hose:
    *   Used to transport the gases from the reservoir bag to the mask or nosepiece where it is inhaled by the patient

6. Masks or Nosepieces (also referred to as nasal hoods):
    *   Masks made of rubber are supplied as disposable (discarded after one use) or reusable after being sterilized (they are autoclavable)
    *   Available in either adult or pediatric patient sizes

REDUCING OCCUPATIONAL EXPOSURE TO NITROUS OXIDE GAS

There are occupational risks associated with working around or directly with nitrous oxide on a routine basis. Therefore, the use of a scavenger system is crucial for protecting the dental healthcare team by reducing the amount of nitrous oxide that may leak from the nosepiece particularly when the patient is not breathing through the nose-only during dental procedures.

Nitrous oxide gas is only used during clinical treatment, not for recreational purposes. The gas is considered a drug and has the potential for abuse. The following precautions should be taken to reduce exposure to nitrous oxide:

1. Use a patient mask (nosepiece) that fits the patient well. Smaller adults may need to use the pediatric size nosepiece; the mask should fit snugly and not lift from the face when the patient is in the supine position. A well-fitting mask reduces the risk of nitrous oxide gas leaking from the sides and feels more comfortable to the patient. The assistant should ensure the mask is placed on the nose correctly and not upside down. The hoses coming off the mask should run along the patient's cheeks.
2. Routinely inspect the nitrous oxide equipment for holes in the tubing, loose connections, and improper flow meters. Ideally, the equipment would be checked every time the nitrous equipment is utilized.
3. Scavenger systems are required to be checked annually by the gas cylinder/tank provider; staff should be aware of the last inspection date performed by the company, the status of the findings of their testing and maintain a copy of the scavenger system report in the office OSHA binder for inspection, if needed.
4. Discourage patients from talking while receiving nitrous oxide. The nitrous can only be absorbed by the patient through breathing so the patient should take deep breaths through their nose. If the patient is talking, nitrous is not being taken into their body and, instead, can be released into the treatment room.

5. The office should have a ventilation system that vents the gas out of the office, not recirculated air.
6. Wear a nitrous oxide monitoring badge system; this is similar to the radiation badge system utilized by many offices.

EXPLANATION OF PROCEDURE TO PATIENT

Before beginning the flow of nitrous oxide gas to the patient, it is important to advise the patient as to how they may feel while inhaling the gas. Nitrous oxide should give the patient a sense of well-being, taking the edge off of the nervousness or fear the patient may be experiencing. Ensure the patient that they are always in control and the nitrous can be stopped at any time during the procedure, if they choose. The assistant should begin by showing the nitrous oxide equipment to the patient and explaining how the system works. Some patients do not like their noses covered due to feelings of claustrophobia, so letting them know in the beginning they need to wear a nosepiece is beneficial.

The assistant needs to educate the patient regarding the feelings or sensations the patient may experience while under nitrous oxide sedation, such as:
- Feelings of well being
- Giddiness
- A floaty, detached sensation
- A slight level of lightheadedness
- An enhanced level of relaxation
- Sensations of warmth in their limbs
- A slight, tingling feeling in the hands or feet – this is an indication the level of nitrous oxide may be too high and should be decreased slightly

Every patient experience differs while inhaling nitrous oxide, therefore, patient education prior to the administration of nitrous oxide is very important and a key responsibility of the chairside assistant.

ASSESSING, ADMINISTRATION AND MONITORING

Prior to offering the patient nitrous oxide during their procedure, a review of the patient's medical history should be completed. Nitrous oxide sedation can affect the patient by enhancing the effect of any medications they may be taking. The patient's vital signs should be recorded before, during and after receiving nitrous oxide. The readings should be compared to the baseline readings taken at the new patient appointment.

To clarify, the assistant may explain the how nitrous oxide gas works and place the nosepiece on the patient but cannot begin the flow of gases until the dentist is present in the treatment area and gives instructions to begin the administration of nitrous oxide/oxygen gases. California regulations are very clear and specific on this issue.

The dentist will begin the flow of gases with 100% pure oxygen, then slowly introduce the nitrous oxide gas into the oxygen. Check-in with the patient to see where their comfort level is; this may take some adjusting of the gases, which is allowable as long as the dentist is at the chairside and gives instructions to do so.

When the procedure is drawing to a close, the dentist will instruct the assistant to eliminate the flow of nitrous oxide and increase the flow of oxygen. At this point, the patient is inhaling 100% pure oxygen only. This process is referred to as "flushing the patient out" by restoring a balance of oxygen into the patient's body. The patient should not rush to remove themselves from the dental chair and should rise slowly to ensure no side-effects from the sedation.

It is recommended that the patient breathe pure oxygen for five to ten minutes. The longer the patient inhales 100% pure oxygen, the less likely they are to experience a post nitrous oxide headache, nausea, a lethargic energy level, and/or dizziness.

The California RDA General Written and Law Examination Prep Book © 2017, 2018 • KB Dental Arts – Publisher

If, after the patient assumes the upright position, they report feeling any symptoms, they should resume inhaling 100% pure oxygen for five additional minutes and then be reassessed. As long as the patient is feeling well and "back to normal", they may drive or return to work.

ADVANTAGES AND CONTRAINDICATIONS OF NITROUS OXIDE SEDATION

Advantages of using nitrous oxide sedation include:
- Creating a relaxing appointment experience for the patient; eases the patient's dental fear and anxiety
- Patient is alert and able to communicate with the dental team
- Can be used with pediatric and adult patients
- Patient can support their own breathing
- There is no need to hire a specialist in anesthesia/sedation
- The patient can resume their daily activities (return to work, drive) after receiving nitrous oxide

There are patients for whom nitrous oxide sedation is contraindicated, including the following:
- Nasal congestion: patient will not receive the full benefit of the nitrous oxide since it must be inhaled through the nose
- Pregnancy: as with most medications, it is not advisable during pregnancy
- Disorders of the lungs or breathing issues: patients with asthma or emphysema have a more difficult time breathing while on nitrous oxide
- Emotional instability: patients may experience a magnified emotional reaction while on nitrous oxide

MEDICAL EMERGENCIES MOST LIKELY TO OCCUR IN THE DENTAL SETTING

No matter how prepared the dental team is, medical emergencies still occur in the dental office. The assistant's role during treatment of these emergencies can be varied depending on the dentist's instructions, however, most assistants are expected to stay with the patient and assist the dentist in treating the patient until EMS arrives. The most common occurrences are:

1. **Syncope (Fainting)**
   - Most common medical emergency
   - Cause: an uneven distribution of blood flow to the brain
   - Signs: paleness, sweaty, jittery appearance
   - Symptoms: nausea, pounding heartbeat, feeling warm, light headed
   - 911 is not usually alerted unless the patient cannot regain consciousness

   Treatment of Syncope:
   - Place patient in the subsupine position with the head lower than the feet allows the blood flow freely to the patient's brain
   - Stay with the patient until they awaken (usually occurs within 30-60 seconds of fainting)
   - Keep an ammonia inhalant ready for use if the patient does not resume consciousness within 60 seconds
   - Instruct patient to remain lying down, taking deep breaths through their nose; place a cool cloth on the forehead and behind the neck
   - Have oxygen ready, if needed
   - Record and monitor the patient's vital signs
   - Call a family member to pick up the patient; do not allow the patient to drive following fainting

2. **Postural Hypotension (altered consciousness; lightheaded or dizziness)**
   - Cause: patient too quickly assumes the upright position following laying back in the dental chair for a procedure causing insufficient blood flow to the brain; the patient usual remains conscious.
   - This is usually very brief, and the patient usually feels better within seconds; however, the patient can lose consciousness or fall.
   - When sitting the patient up, instruct the patient to remain seated in the chair for a few minutes so they can readjust to the upright position.

3. **Angina Pectoris (Chest Pain) vs. Myocardial Infarction (Heart Attack)**
   - Angina is a severe crushing chest pain being caused by insufficient oxygen to the heart. While the pain is severe it usually does not lead to death. Pain caused by angina can be treated with medication and is usually carried by the patient - **nitroglycerin**. A history or incident of angina should be noted on the patient history form.
   - Myocardial infarction is damage to the heart muscle due to a deprivation of oxygen to one particular area of the heart.
   - The signs and symptoms of angina pectoris and a myocardial infarction are very similar.
   - Time is of the essence in responding to either condition as an emergency that is potentially life threatening.

   Treatment of Angina Pectoris:
   - Alert EMS/911 services
   - Place the patient in the upright position
   - Give the patient the nitroglycerin (either from the medical emergency kit or their own supply)
   - Place oxygen on the patient
   - Patient's symptoms should begin to ease within three (3) minutes; another dose of nitroglycerin can be administered, if symptoms persist
   - Monitor and record vital signs; record all treatment, signs, symptoms and dentist's instructions during emergency care

   Treatment of Myocardial Infarction:
   - Alert EMS/911 services
   - Give the patient the nitroglycerin (either from the medical emergency kit or their own supply)
   - Place oxygen on the patient
   - Be prepared to perform CPR should the patient stop breathing
   - Make the patient as comfortable as possible by loosening tight clothing.
   - Monitor and record vital signs

4. **Hyperventilation (increase in respiration)**
   - Hyperventilation occurs primarily as a result of stress and anxiety during dental procedures.
   - Symptoms: breathing too rapidly and an uneven balance of oxygen to carbon dioxide is created within the body.
   - Signs: rapid breathing, fidgeting or uneasiness in chair, frightened appearance.
   - Symptoms: light headedness, fast heartbeat, tightness or pressure in the chest

The California RDA General Written and Law Examination Prep Book © 2017, 2018 • KB Dental Arts – Publisher

Treatment of Hyperventilation:
- Place the patient in a seated upright position
- Speak calmly and quietly to the patient; look them directly in the eye and maintain eye contact
- Hand patient a brown paper bag (from the medical emergency kit) or ask them to cup their hands over both their nose and mouth, and breathe slowly in through their nose and out through their mouth; this WILL force the patient to inhale carbon dioxide, evening the exchange of oxygen and carbon dioxide; eventually the patient's breathing will even out
- Keep the patient calm
- Monitor and record vital signs
- Continue with treatment if patient feels up to it

5. **Asthma Attack (chronic condition that exhibits breathing attacks)**
- Asthma is a pulmonary disorder where patient's airway narrows causing difficulty in breathing and produces a coughing, wheezing sound. Asthma attacks are usually brought on by stress, being ill, or by an allergic reaction.
- Patients with asthma carry a bronchodilator, or inhaler, with them always. The patient should be reminded to bring their inhaler to their dental appointment and placed on the counter during the procedure for easy access while being treated.

If the patient experiences an asthma attack while being treated, the dental team should:
- Remove all materials from the patient's mouth
- Place the patient in an upright seated position. Sitting the patient upright will expand their lungs.
- Hand the patient their inhaler, or if they forgot theirs, the inhaler from the office's emergency kit; allow patient to treat themselves
- If symptoms do not ease or patient begins to lose consciousness, alert EMS/911 services

6. **Cerebrovascular Accident or "CVA" (Stroke)**
- A stroke is an interruption of blood flow to the brain caused by a blood clot, an aneurysm, or uncontrolled high blood pressure. When the brain goes without oxygen to one area for too long, permanent brain damage can occur causing the patient to lose many functional abilities such as speech, walking, or facial expressions.

If the dental team suspects the patient is experiencing a stroke:
1) Alert EMS/911
2) CPR performed, if needed
3) Monitor vital signs and record readings

7. **Hyperglycemia (too much blood sugar)**

- Hyperglycemia is associated with diabetes. The diabetic patient will note the condition in the medical history and the dental team should be aware when treating the patient
- Signs: fruity smelling breath, needing to use the restroom frequently, fast pulse
- Symptoms: very thirsty, dry skin and mouth, blurred vision, headache, low blood pressure

Treatment of hyperglycemia:
- Ask when patient last ate, if conscious, and if they brought along their insulin
- Retrieve insulin and, if able, the patient should treat themselves
- Alert EMS/911, if needed
- If patient goes unconscious, check for breathing using proper protocols, and perform CPR only if patient stops breathing
- Monitor vital signs and record readings

8. Hypoglycemia (too little blood sugar)

Hypoglycemia is also associated with diabetes, but a patient who has not been diagnosed can also suffer from low blood sugar, often the result of not eating. As needed, provide a small snack to ensure the patient's blood sugar remains stable during the procedure.
- Signs: bad mood, anxiety, sweaty appearance
- Symptoms: hunger

Treatment of hypoglycemia (conscious patient):
- Ask when the patient last ate
- Give the patient something sugary to eat or drink such as orange Juice or a sugar cube; this type of food is absorbed quickly into the bloodstream
- If the patient loses consciousness, place cake icing along the facial mucosa on the upper and lower anterior regions of the mouth to absorb quickly into the blood stream; the patient should regain consciousness within one minute
- Alert EMS/911 services
- Monitor vital signs and record readings

9. Allergic Reactions (hypersensitivity to a substance)

Treatment of a localized allergic reaction:
- Signs: itching, hives, redness of the skin (erythema)
- Symptoms: nausea, dizziness, tingling in the mouth
- Locate the rash or area of reaction
- Monitor vital signs and record the readings
- Dispense an antihistamine per dentist's instructions

Treatment of Anaphylaxis:
- Signs: shortness of breath, redness of the skin, itching, hives, loss of consciousness, bluish appearance
- Symptoms: constricted airway, dizziness
- Alert EMS/911 services
- Place patient in the supine position
- Use EpiPen on patient (either their own or from the emergency kit)
- Administer oxygen
- Be prepared to perform CPR if reaction takes a turn for the worse
- Monitor vital signs and record readings

10. Epileptic Seizures

Epilepsy is a neurological disorder where the patient experiences seizures or convulsions of the muscles. Seizures are recurrent and can be frequent. The patient will self-administer medications to lessen the episodes and the severity of seizures; however, medication does not always prevent a seizure from occurring. There are two (2) types of seizures; a grand mal seizure and a petit mal seizure.

- **Grand Mal Seizure:** the patient experiences a temporary loss of consciousness while their muscles involuntarily and uncontrollably contract and relax. This type of seizure has four (4) phases:
    1. Aura: the patient may smell, see, taste, or hear things that are not present and will tell you about them; a "warning" phase of the impending seizure
    2. Loss of consciousness: the patient is not conscious, and the muscles are completely rigid for approximately 10 - 20 seconds
    3. Convulsions: the patient's muscles convulse; convulsions can be extremely physical and wild or mild and hardly noticeable; the patient can injure themselves during the convulsion phase
    4. Muscle relaxation: the patient falls into a deep sleep as the body's systems are recovering.
- **Petit Mal Seizure:** a brief lapse of awareness that can last just a few seconds; the patient may have a blank stare; the patient does not experience the four phases as noted above

Treatment of a seizure:
- Alert EMS/911 services
- Quickly remove all items from the patient's mouth and place in the supine position. Never place anything in a patient's mouth while they are having a seizure
- Protect the patient from injury during the seizure but do not hold them down; allow them to have the seizure while making sure they are safe
- Dispense an anticonvulsant from the emergency kit if dentist instructs
- Monitor vital signs and record the readings

DOCUMENTATION OF A MEDICAL EMERGENCY

General chart documentation is a crucial aspect of being a dental assistant. We have all been taught to the importance of documentation including all activities that occur in the dental office during that patients visit. The saying, "if it's not in the chart, it did not happen", is a correct statement.

The chart is a legal document of the patient's experiences while in the care of the dental office. If a patient experiences a medical emergency, detailed documentation of the event is of the utmost importance.

The following should be recorded:
1. Full explanation of exactly what type of event occurred
2. A description of the emergency care rendered to the patient
3. A description of the patient's condition at the time of release from the office
4. A follow-up phone call should be placed to the patient and/or their family that evening or the next day to inquire about the patient's condition; record discussion
5. The dentist must evaluate all documentation of the incident to ensure accuracy of the information
6. The dentist is responsible to contact the Dental Board in the event the emergency results in the death of the patient

CHAPTER REVIEW COMMENTS:

To prevent a minor office emergency from becoming a serious or perhaps even a fatal event, it is important to have a thorough office emergency routine. Each office differs in how it designates responsibilities to staff; however, there are a few responsibilities that may be delegated to a dental assistant making the dental assistant responsible for ensuring they are knowledge and well-prepared for any situation, including the following steps:

1. ***Notify the dentist of the emergency:*** the dentist must be notified immediately when a situation occurs.
2. ***If necessary, administer basic life support:*** basic life support consists of maintaining an open airway, providing rescue breathing, and providing cardiac compressions; all dental assistants must be able to perform basic life support and is required to maintain a current CPR certification.
3. ***Retrieve the emergency kit:*** once identified as an emergency situation, the emergency kit should be retrieved immediately and ready for use.
4. ***Retrieve the oxygen tank:*** oxygen is necessary in most emergency situations.
5. ***Assist the dentist in administering care:*** although dental assistants cannot legally administer drugs, assisting the dentist during an emergency and ensuring patient comfort is the role of the dental assistant.

END OF CHAPTER - CRITICAL THINKING QUESTIONS:

1. What is a medical emergency?
2. What is the difference between a sign and a symptom?
3. Does a dental professional need to be certified in Basic Life Support (BLS) and CPR?
4. Is it mandatory for every dental office to have a medical emergency kit?
5. What is the number one drug utilized in a dental office during a medical emergency?
6. What is an allergy and what is an antigen? How are they connected?
7. What are the two factors to consider when evaluating an allergic reaction?
8. What state does nitrous oxide usage produce in a patient undergoing treatment?
9. What effects of nitrous oxide should be explained to the patient prior to use?
10. What medical emergency occurs most often in the dental setting?
11. What is a CVA?
12. If a medical emergency occurs, what should be recorded in the patient record?

CRITICAL THINKING QUESTION ANSWERS FOUND IN APPENDIX

Notes

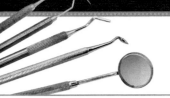

UNIT ONE – PATIENT TREATMENT AND CARE
CHAPTER FIVE: LEGAL REQUIREMENTS AND ETHICAL PRINCIPLES

EXAMINATION PLAN DATA:

Topic Area	Patient Treatment and Care
Total Weight of Topic Area on Examination	25%
Subject Area	Legal Requirements and Ethical Principles
Percentage of Examination Questions in Legal Requirements and Ethical Principles	N/A

LEGAL REQUIREMENTS AND ETHICAL PRINCIPLES – KNOWLEDGE STATEMENTS

Knowledge Statements Associated with Topic Area

Knowledge of the professional and ethical principles related to communicating with and the fair treatment of the patient.

Knowledge of professional and ethical principles regarding patient care.

Knowledge of legal requirements and ethical principles regarding patient confidentiality.

Knowledge of legal requirements and ethical principles regarding mandated reporting (abuse and neglect).

Knowledge of the RDA/RDAEFs legal and ethical responsibilities to report violations of the state dental practice act, administrative rules or regulations to the proper authorities.

KEY TERMS

Abandonment	Discontinuation of a patient/provider relationship once it has been established; discontinuing treatment once begun without cause or notification to the patient
Autonomous	Independent; not controlled by others or outside forces; self-directed; independent in mind and judgment
Beneficence	The state or quality of being kind, charitable and promoting good will
Character	A description of a person's attributes, traits and abilities; the qualities that define a person or group; could be used to define moral or ethical strength
Code of Ethics	A collection of rules or guidelines addressing the ethical standards of a profession or professional entity

Confidentiality	That which is held in confidence; done or communicated in secret; the state of trust placed in a dental assistant by a patient so as not to communicate those items which are privileged
Discrimination	Treatment or consideration placed on class or category rather than individual merit; treating persons differently based on their physical, mental or emotional state, race or gender
Ethics	A set of principles of right conduct; the general nature of morals and of the specific moral choices made by a person
Fiduciary Responsibility	Holding of something of trust to another; a relationship based on the trusted responsibility between patient and health care provider
Implied	A term used when data or knowledge is not specifically stated verbally or in writing; an inferred statement
Implied Consent	By nature of being present in the treatment facility, it is implied that the patient is seeking treatment; a dentist may not communicate the full details of the treatment plan – therefore, treatment may begin with implied consent without agreeing in writing or verbally
Informed Consent	The act of providing information, verbally or in writing, to and ensuring the understanding of the patient, as to the nature of proposed treatment, financial responsibilities, potential risks, options for treatment, potential outcomes, and impact on the patient's physical and oral health
Negligence	Failure to exercise the degree of care considered reasonable under the circumstances resulting in an unintended injury to a patient; lack of reasonable and prudent care of a patient in a healthcare setting
Nonmaleficence	The principle of "doing no harm"; a state of non-injury to a patient during the provision of dental care services
Professionalism	A quality set in standards and methods of performance demonstrating skill, knowledge and professional ability demonstrated consistently
Scope of Practice	The range of duties and functions legally allowable under the defined areas of providership such as type of license, permit or certificate held; set forth by the state Dental Practice Act and the laws of the state
Direct Supervision	A licensed dentist must be physically present in the treatment facility during the performance of the function; the function must be checked and approved by the supervising dentist prior to dismissal of the patient from the office.
General Supervision	The dentist is not required to be physically present during the performance of the function; duties are completed based on instructions given by the supervising dentist.

Patient Autonomy: Autonomy, Consent and Confidentiality

Autonomy: Patients have the right to determine what should be done with their own bodies. Because patients are moral entities they are capable of autonomous decision-making. Respect for patient autonomy affirms this dynamic in the doctor-patient relationship and forms the foundation for informed consent, for protecting patient confidentiality, and for upholding truthfulness. The patient's right to self-determination is not, however, absolute. The dentist and licensed dental healthcare personnel must also weigh benefits and harms and inform the patient of contemporary standards of oral health care as part of the examination, treatment plan and informed consent for treatment process.

The dental professional has a duty to respect the patient's rights to self-determination and confidentiality. This principle expresses the concept that professionals have a duty to treat the patient according to the patient's desires, within the bounds of accepted treatment, and to protect the patient's confidentiality. Under this principle, the dentist's primary obligations include involving patients in treatment decisions in a meaningful way, with due consideration being given to the patient's needs, desires and abilities. It is the responsibility of the entire dental team to safeguard the patient's privacy.

Individual Autonomy and Respect for Human Beings:

The dental assistant has a duty to respect each patient's individuality, humanity, and autonomy in decision making.

- Respect the autonomy of each person to decide from among treatment options, including refusing treatment.
- Respect the legal and personal rights, dignity and privacy of all patients in whose treatment they assist.
- Maintain professional boundaries in relationships with patients.

The dental assistant has a duty to respect each patient's right to confidentiality.

- Maintain patient confidentiality.
- Safeguard all patient and practice information that is confidential in nature.

Patient Records: Dentists are obliged to safeguard the confidentiality of patient records. Dental offices shall maintain patient records in a manner consistent with the protection of the welfare of the patient. Upon request of a patient or another dental practitioner, dentists shall provide any information in accordance with applicable law that will be beneficial for the future treatment of that patient.

Informed Consent: Fully informed consent is essential to the ethical practice of dentistry and reflects the patient's right of self-decision. Except as exempted by state law, a dentist has the obligation to obtain the fully informed consent of the patient or the patient's legal guardian in writing prior to treatment, or the use of any identifiable artifacts (such as photographs, radiographs, study models) for any purpose other than treatment.

Obligation to Inform: A dentist has the obligation to inform patients of their present oral health status.

Nonmaleficence: Harm, Health and Well-Being of Patients

Nonmaleficence ("do no harm"): The licensed dental professional has a principle duty to refrain from harming the patient. Under this principle, the dentist's primary obligations include maintaining currency in scope of practice laws, knowing one's own limitations and when to refer to a specialist or other professional, and knowing when and under what circumstances delegation of patient care to other clinical chairside personnel is appropriate.

The dental assistant also has a duty to refrain from harming a patient and to promote the patient's welfare. The dental assistant has a duty to protect the health and well-being of colleagues.

- Always act in the best interests of each patient.
- Make patient health and safety the first and most important consideration in all actions and decisions.
- Perform only those procedures legally allowed, under supervision, where required, and only by those qualified to perform them competently.
- Respect the health and safety of self, colleagues, and patients.
- Practice without impairment from substance abuse, cognitive deficiency, or mental illness.
- Diligently perform all duties designed to protect themselves and their colleagues from workplace hazards.
- Enhance professional competency through continuous learning, incorporating new knowledge into daily performance of delegated services.
- Refuse to conceal incompetent acts of others and report acts with a potentially dangerous outcome.

Beneficence: Beneficence defined, abuse, neglect and health education

Beneficence ("do good"): The dentist has a duty to promote the patient's welfare. This principle expresses the concept that professionals have a duty to act for the benefit of others. Under this principle, the dentist's primary obligation is service to the patient and the public-at-large. The most important aspect of this obligation is the competent and timely delivery of dental care within the bounds of clinical circumstances presented by the patient, with due consideration being given to the needs, desires and values of the patient. The same ethical considerations apply whether the dentist engages in fee-for-service, managed care or some other practice arrangement.

Beneficence, often cited as a fundamental principle of ethics, is the obligation to benefit others or to seek their good. The dentist refrains from harming the patient by referring to those with specialized expertise when the dentist's own skills are insufficient.

Abuse and Neglect: Dentists, Registered Dental Hygienists, and Registered Dental Assistants are designated by law as **mandated reporters** who are required to report suspected cases of abuse and neglect while in their professional capacities. By taking a proactive role in the detection and reporting of child abuse and neglect, dental mandated reporters may save the lives of young victims and assist agencies in helping families in the community. It is vitally important that mandated reporters become aware of their legal obligations regarding the reporting of abuse and neglect.

Reporting Abuse and Neglect: The public and the profession are best served by dental healthcare personnel who are familiar with identifying the signs of abuse and neglect and knowledgeable about the appropriate intervention resources for all populations. Licensees have an ethical obligation to identify and report the signs of abuse and neglect, including the suspected abuse and neglect involving seniors, children and domestic partners.

Dental professionals have a concurrent ethical obligation to respect an adult patient's right to self-determination and confidentiality while promoting the welfare of all patients. As a matter of ethics, the dental assistant should respect the wishes of an adult patient who asks that a suspected case of abuse and/or neglect not be reported, especially when such a report is not mandated by law. With the patient's permission, other possible solutions may be sought. Dentists should be aware that jurisdictional laws vary in their definitions of abuse and neglect, in their reporting requirements and the extent to which immunity is granted to good faith reporters. The variances may raise potential legal and other risks that should be considered, while keeping in mind the duty to put the welfare of the patient first. Therefore, a licensed healthcare provider has an ethical obligation to identify and report suspected cases of abuse and neglect; beyond the ethical issues of abuse and neglect reporting is the legal requirement.

A mandated reporter shall make a report to any police department or sheriff's department, not including a school district police or security department, any county probation department, if designated by the county to receive mandated reports, or the county welfare department whenever the mandated reporter, in his or her professional capacity or within the scope of his or her employment, has knowledge of or observes a child whom the mandated reporter knows or reasonably suspects has been the victim of child abuse or neglect. The mandated reporter shall make an initial report to the agency immediately or as soon as is practicably possible by telephone and the mandated reporter shall prepare and send, fax, or electronically transmit a written follow-up report thereof within 36 hours of receiving the information concerning the incident. The mandated reporter may include with the report any non-privileged documentary evidence the mandated reporter possesses relating to the incident.

Any mandated reporter who fails to report an incident of known or reasonably suspected child abuse or neglect is guilty of a misdemeanor punishable by up to six (6) months confinement in a county jail or by a fine of one thousand dollars ($1,000) or both imprisonment and fine. If a mandated reporter intentionally conceals his or her failure to report an incident known by the mandated reporter to be abuse or severe neglect, the failure to report is a continuing offense until an agency discovers the offense.

B&P Code Section 1684.5 of the Dental Practice Act states that it is unprofessional conduct for a dentist to allow any treatment to be performed on a patient who is not a patient of record of that dentist. Further, a **patient of record** is defined as a patient who has who has completed a medical and dental history that has been properly reviewed, and who has received a complete oral examination where oral conditions are recorded, and where a complete diagnosis and written treatment plan has been developed and reviewed with the patient by the licensed dentist.

Reporting Violations of the Dental Practice Act: Despite opinion to the contrary, the law is very clear as to the reporting by all licensees, including Registered Dental Assistants, for violations of the scope of practice and additional acts of unprofessional conduct, including, but not limited to:

- A violation of any federal statute, rule, or regulation or any of the statutes, rules, or regulations of this state regulating dangerous drugs or controlled substances.
- Failure to keep the licensee's or registrant's premises and all equipment therein in a clean and sanitary condition.
- Aiding or abetting in any acts that are in violation of any of the provisions of dental practice act, including the aiding and abetting of the illegal practice of dentistry.
- The employment of fraud, misrepresentation, or deception in obtaining the license or registration.

Since 2010, the duties, functions and supervision requirements for all licensed and unlicensed dental assistants were placed into statute (law). The dentist-employer is only legally responsible to perform two specific functions:

- Supervision: Ensure that the proper supervision is used at all times of an allied healthcare professional BASED ON THE LAWS OF CALIFORNIA THAT GOVERN DENTAL ASSISTING, NOT BASED ON THE DENTISTS OPINION AS TO WHAT THEY WANT THE DENTAL ASSISTANT OR LICENSED ASSISTANT TO PERFORM.
- Delegation: It is the responsibility of the Dentist to delegate ONLY THOSE DUTIES AND FUNCTIONS AS DEFINED IN STATUTE (law).

The legal responsibilities of the dentist-employer are very important to understand and commit to memory, not only for the RDA licensure process, but also to understand your professional responsibility to decline a directive to perform an illegal function, and to report to the Dental Board of California any directive at any time from an employer or co-worker to perform a function that is not allowed legally.

The California RDA General Written and Law Examination Prep Book © 2017, 2018 • KB Dental Arts – Publisher

END OF CHAPTER – CRITICAL THINKING QUESTIONS

1. What does the term autonomous mean?

2. Nonmaleficence means _____. Why is this important?

3. What are the responsibilites of a mandated reporter?

4. What is a Code of Ethics? Does Dentistry have a Code of Ethics?

5. Professionalism is _____.

6. Why is informed consent important?

7. What are ethics?

8. What is the difference between general and direct supervision?

9. What does the term Scope of Practice mean? Why is it important to understand this concept?

10. What does negligence mean?

CRITICAL THINKING QUESTION ANSWERS FOUND IN APPENDIX

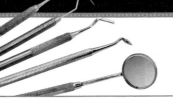

UNIT TWO – DENTAL PROCEDURES
CHAPTER ONE: DIRECT AND INDIRECT RESTORATIONS

EXAMINATION PLAN DATA:

Topic Area	Dental Procedures
Total Weight of Topic Area on Examination	35%
Subject Area	Direct and Indirect Restorations
Percentage of Examination Questions in Direct and Indirect Restorations	30%

DIRECT AND INDIRECT RESTORATIONS – TASK AND KNOWLEDGE STATEMENTS

Tasks Associated with Topic Area	Knowledge Statements Associated with Topic Area
Place bases and liners	Knowledge of types of base and liner materials and the techniques and procedures for their application and placement
Place matrices and wedges	Knowledge of types of wedges and the techniques and procedures for their use
Place temporary filling material	Knowledge of techniques and procedures for using matrix bands with or without band retainers
Apply etchant to tooth surface (tooth dentin or enamel) for direct and indirect provisional restorations	Knowledge of types of temporary filling materials and the techniques and procedures to mix, place, and contour them
Place bonding agent	Knowledge of types of bonding agents and the techniques and procedures for their application and placement
Fabricate and adjust indirect provisional restorations	Knowledge of types of etchants and the techniques and procedures for their application and placement
Place, adjust, and finish direct provisional restorations	Knowledge of irregularities in margins that affect direct and indirect provisional restorations
Perform cementation procedure for indirect provisional restorations	Knowledge of techniques used to eliminate open margins when placing restorative materials
Obtain intraoral images using computer generated imaging system (e.g., CADCAM)	Knowledge of methods for identifying improper occlusal contacts, proximal contacts, or embrasure contours of provisional restorations
Take impressions for indirect provisional restorations	Knowledge of techniques and procedures for mitigating the effects of improper occlusal contacts, proximal contacts, or embrasure contours of provisional restorations

DIRECT AND INDIRECT RESTORATIONS – TASK AND KNOWLEDGE STATEMENTS (CONTINUED)

Tasks Associated with Topic Area	Knowledge Statements Associated with Topic Area
Perform in-office whitening (bleaching) procedures (e.g., Boost, Opalescence)	Knowledge of scope of practice for RDAs and RDAEFs related to applying bases, liners, and bonding agents
Remove indirect provisional restorations	Knowledge of instrumentation and techniques related to the removal of indirect provisional restorations
	Knowledge of equipment and procedures used to obtain intraoral images for computer-aided, milled restorations
	Knowledge of types of impression materials and techniques and procedures for their application and placement
	Knowledge of techniques and procedures used to mix and place provisional materials
	Knowledge of techniques and procedures for bonding provisional veneers
	Knowledge of indications and contraindications for the use of whitening (bleaching) agents
	Knowledge of indications and contraindications for the use of bonding agents
	Knowledge of indications and contraindications for the use of etching agents
	Knowledge of types of whitening (bleaching) agents and the techniques and procedures for their application
	Knowledge of types of cements and the techniques and procedures for their application, placement, and removal
	Knowledge of scope of practice for RDAs and RDAEFs related to applying and activating whitening (bleaching) agents
	Knowledge of RDA and RDAEF scopes of practice related to direct restorations
	Knowledge of RDA and RDAEF scopes of practice related to indirect restorations
	Knowledge of RDA and RDAEF scopes of practice related to final impressions

SCOPE OF PRACTICE – SPECIFIC TO DIRECT AND INDIRECT RESTORATIONS

Unlicensed Dental Assistant	Registered Dental Assistant
Extra-oral duties or procedures specified by the supervising licensed dentist provided that these duties or procedures meet the definition of a basic supportive	All duties that a dental assistant is allowed to perform
Place, wedge, and remove matrices for restorative procedures	Apply and activate bleaching agents using a non-laser light-curing device
	Obtain intraoral images for computer-aided design (CAD), milled restorations
	Place bases, liners, and bonding agents
	Chemically prepare teeth for bonding
	Place, adjust, and finish direct provisional restorations
	Fabricate, adjust, cement, and remove indirect provisional restorations, including stainless steel crowns when used as a provisional restoration
	Remove excess cement from surfaces of teeth with a hand instrument

Licensed Registered Dental Assistant in Extended Functions (RDAEF):

(a) A registered dental assistant in extended functions licensed on or after January 1, 2010, is authorized to perform all duties and procedures that a registered dental assistant is authorized to perform and those duties that the board may prescribe by regulation. In addition:

Registered Dental Assistant in Extended Functions
Extra-oral duties or procedures specified by the supervising licensed dentist provided that these duties or procedures meet the definition of a basic supportive
Take final impressions for permanent indirect restorations
Take final impressions for tooth-borne removable prosthesis
Polish and contour existing amalgam restorations
Place, contour, finish, and adjust all direct restorations

It is essential that the chairside dental assistant working in a general dentistry practice be knowledgeable in the areas of restorative and esthetic dentistry. There are many different dental materials in the dental marketplace these days. Some materials are very sophisticated and easy to use. Other materials have been utilized in dentistry for many, many years, but are still incredibly relevant and important to quality dental work. Every dentist has their own preferences as to the materials they choose to use in the dental office.

KEY TERMS

Base	Placed as a measure of protection for the pulp; protects, insulates and soothes when decay or trauma have disturbed the pulp
Calcium Hydroxide	Main medicament found in a dental liner that is soothing to the pulp
Digital Impression	Picture of the prepped tooth used to design and fabricate a permanent crown
Direct Restorations	Materials placed directly on or in the tooth surfaces
Embrasure	Triangular space, towards the gingiva, between two adjacent teeth
Etchant	An acidic tooth conditioner that aids in roughening up either enamel or dentin in preparation for bonding
Exothermic	Gives off heat when setting
Festooning	Trimming or to trim
Indirect Restorations	Permanent or temporary restorations designed outside the patient's mouth
Liner	A medicament which acts as a barrier against pulpal irritation caused by decay and other stimuli
Polymerization	The process of setting, curing, hardening a dental material
Provisional Coverage	A temporary restoration or temporary crown
Self-Etching Adhesive	A bonding adhesive that has an etchant in it; eliminates the etch step in the bonding procedure
Smear Layer	Secretion created by the layers of the tooth in response to being prepared for a restoration
Temporary Sedative Dressing	A temporary filling; aka Direct Provisional Restoration

TYPES OF DIRECT RESTORATIONS

Direct restorations are materials placed directly on or in the tooth surfaces during treatment. The types of direct restorations include: amalgam, composite, glass ionomers and temporary restorative materials. Direct restorations in dentistry include some esthetic materials, such as tooth whitening materials commonly referred to as **bleach**.

Outlined below are some bulleted facts regarding each type of direct restoration:

1. Amalgam

    - commonly referred to as "silver fillings"
    - used in dentistry for many years
    - researched as a safe restorative material
    - combination of various metals in powder form: silver, copper, zinc, tin
    - silver is the largest metal ingredient giving the mixture a silver appearance
    - metals are held together with mercury forming a soft, easily placed material
    - permanent restoration for posterior teeth via mechanical retention
    - affordable and very strong for patients; can last 20 plus years
    - supplied in capsules to reduce mercury exposure to the dental team

2. Composite

    - also known as "resins" or "composite resin"
    - tooth colored restorative material; supplied in many shades
    - more modern, more desired restorative material
    - permanent restoration for both anterior and posterior teeth
    - not as strong as amalgam restorations; can last 10 plus years
    - filled or unfilled versions work equally well as restorations
    - set with a curing light; no need to wait for material to harden
    - no mercury is needed with composites
    - finished with a dental handpiece and burs

3. Glass Ionomers

    - very versatile material; serves many uses in dentistry
    - restorative uses include: restorations, core buildups and sealants
    - can also be used as: liners, cements and bonding agents
    - releases fluoride after placement
    - bonds chemically to tooth structure
    - supplied in light protected cartridges or tubes

The California RDA General Written and Law Examination Prep Book © 2017, 2018 • KB Dental Arts – Publisher

4. Temporary Restorative Materials – direct provisional restoration

- used to restore tooth function and reduce patient discomfort
- intended to be utilized for a short period of time; not a permanent restoration
- protects the tooth until the permanent restoration can be placed
- IRM (Intermediate Restorative Material) or Cavit are the common temporary materials used in dentistry for direct provisionals

5. Bleaching Material (Tooth Whitening Material)

- placed directly onto the enamel for esthetic purposes
- popular modern product found in gums, toothpastes and mouthwashes
- cost effective and safe
- peroxide based
- can cause sensitivity; important to educate patient on proper use
- may use product at home or in the office; both produce desirable results

TYPES OF INDIRECT RESTORATIONS – PERMANENT AND/OR TEMPORARY

Indirect restorations are permanent or temporary restorations designed outside the patient's mouth and then bonded or cemented to the tooth upon completion. The types of **indirect permanent restorations** include gold and ceramic crowns and bridges, Zirconia crowns, onlays and bridges.

Often, indirect restorations are fabricated in a laboratory, delivered to the dental office upon completion of the fabrication process, and a final delivery appointment is set for the cementation.

Indirect provisional restorations are commonly known as "temporaries". Provisional restorations are most often utilized following a crown and bridge procedure for full coverage of a prepared tooth and are seated in place using a temporary cement.

The types of indirect provisional restorations include: custom acrylic and stainless-steel crowns. Outlined below are some bulleted facts regarding each type of indirect restoration:

1. Gold:

- is too soft to use in the mouth in its pure form so it is combined with other noble metals to create a gold alloy
- considered a high noble metal when mixed with platinum and palladium
- suitable for use in the oral cavity
- resists tarnish and wear
- fabricated into a full gold crown, an inlay, an onlay or a full gold bridge
- cemented into place following fitting and adjusting

2. Ceramic:

- considered a compound because it is combined with a metal and then glazed for strength and durability (example: PFM crowns – porcelain fused to metal)
- dentists like the strength of the metal and the esthetic of the porcelain

3. Custom Acrylic and Stainless-Steel Crown – Provisional Coverage

   - used to restore tooth function, protect the prepared tooth and reduce patient discomfort seated with a temporary cement

   - intended to be utilized for a short period of time; not a permanent restoration

   - protects the tooth until the permanent restoration can be placed

   - seated with a temporary cement

TYPES AND MIXING TECHNIQUES OF BASES

A **base** is placed when the tooth preparation becomes relatively deep as a measure of protection for the pulp. The closer decay gets to the pulp, the more irritated the pulp may become. Additionally, the process of removing the decay can be irritating to the pulp. A base will protect, insulate and soothe the pulp. Bases are always placed on the floor of the tooth preparation creating a protective layer around the nearly or partially exposed pulp. A base will sit in between the pulp and the restoration. Cement materials are used to make the special bases that are under the permanent restorations, so you may recognize the names. However, keep in mind, the material is being used for the purposes of a base and not as a cement material, so the mixing techniques will differ.

The types and mixing techniques of materials used as bases are:

1. ZOE – zinc oxide eugenol

   - serves as an excellent insulating and soothing base due to the oil of cloves in the eugenol

   - cannot be used under composite resin due to the eugenol which inhibits the setting process of the composite resin material

   - supplied as a powder and liquid and is mixed on a paper pad using a cement spatula

   - the ratio for the average size ZOE base is one drop of liquid to one scoop of powder

   - begin mixing by incorporating half of the powder into the liquid; mix for approximately 20 - 30 seconds; incorporate the remaining powder and mix for another 20 - 30 seconds; mixture will be challenging to mix

   - the material will be thick and putty like; roll the material into a ball and place the material onto the end of a condenser and transfer to the dentist for placement

   - have extra powder available for the dentist to place the tip of the condenser into during the placement phase preventing the condenser from sticking to the material

   - the dentist will place the base covering the entire pulpal floor

2. ZPC – zinc phosphate cement

   - ZPC is excellent as a thermal insulating base

   - the phosphoric acid is irritating to the pulp, so a liner needs to be placed prior to the placement of the ZPC base

   - supplied as a powder and liquid; mixed on a cool, glass slab using a cement spatula to slow the setting process and to lessen the materials **exothermic** reaction (exothermic means heat-generating)

- the ratio for ZPC is typically one drop of liquid to four-to-five small mounds of powder

- powder will be incorporated into the liquid in small increments producing a thick material that will be rolled into a ball

- the ball of material is placed on a condenser and transferred to the dentist for placement into the tooth preparation

- have extra powder available for the dentist to place the tip of the condenser into during the placement phase preventing the condenser from sticking to the material

- the dentist will place the base covering the entire pulpal floor

3. Polycarboxylate Cement - **as a base**

- nonirritating to the pulp

- may be placed under all types of restorations

- supplied as a powder and a liquid, mixed on a paper pad with a cement spatula

- the ratio for a polycarboxylate base is typically one-to-two scoops of powder to one drop of liquid – amount of powder is predicated on the size and thickness of base needed

- all powder is incorporated into the liquid at one time; mixing is to be completed within 45 seconds

- once completely mixed, the material will be rolled into a ball, placed on a condenser and transferred to the dentist for placement into the tooth preparation

- the dentist will place the base covering the entire pulpal floor

NOTE: Many dental materials used in dental practices today are auto-mix devices where mixing tips and delivery guns are commonly used, eliminating the need to measure, incorporate and mix powers and liquids together. However, for the purpose of addressing the content of the current RDA examination, we will continue to focus on the concept of materials manipulation as if using traditional powder and liquid products until such time as we see the examination questions change to address more contemporary principles of dental materials.

TYPES AND MIXING TECHNIQUES OF LINERS

A **liner** acts as a barrier against pulpal irritation caused by decay and other stimuli. A very thin layer of a liner is placed at the deepest portion of the preparation only. Tooth decay can be very deep within a tooth, near or possibly even entering the dental pulp. A liner assists in reducing a pulpal response from the affected tooth by protecting the pulp. **Calcium hydroxide** is the main medicament found in a dental liner and works well with all restorative materials. It has the ability to protect the pulp from irritation and stimulates secondary dentin. Some liners contain fluoride that creates a stronger, more caries-resistant layer of secondary dentin while protecting the pulp.

Calcium hydroxide is supplied as a base and catalyst in a two-tube delivery system. A small, even amount of material is dispensed from each tube onto a paper mixing pad. The material is mixed using either a cement spatula or a calcium hydroxide applicator (aka: a Dycal applicator) until the material is homogenous (all one color). Once mixed, the material is handed to the dentist for placement using the calcium hydroxide applicator.

It is important to note that not every tooth requiring a restoration requires a liner and/or a base. The placement of either is at the discretion of the treating dentist and is preceded by a deep tooth preparation. If the tooth preparation is not deep or no additional pulpal protection is warranted, neither a base nor a liner will be placed. In other instances, both a liner and a base may be placed if the dentist deems the treatment necessary. In cases where both a liner and a base are placed, the liner is always placed first, then the base. Remember that the liner is thinner and placed only in the deepest area of the preparation. The liner is placed nearest to the dentin to promote the growth of secondary or reparative dentin. The base is placed over the entire floor of the preparation and acts to protect or insulate the pulp. The restoration is then placed over the medicaments.

USE, TYPES, TECHNIQUES AND PROCEDURES FOR PLACEMENT OF MATRIX BANDS AND WEDGES

A **matrix system** is used when at least one wall of the tooth preparation is missing. In order to properly restore the tooth to its original shape and function, we need to temporarily replace the missing wall. A matrix band helps to create the missing wall so restorative material can be placed and built up. It helps confine material within the prep. It would be used on teeth prepared for a class II, III, or IV restoration. A wedge is used along with the matrix band to provide the anatomic contour needed interproximally.

The most commonly known and widely used matrix system is the Tofflemire matrix system, also known as the Universal matrix system. The parts of this matrix system include the Tofflemire retainer, the matrix band, and the wedge. The Tofflemire retainer holds the matrix band in place. The band is formed into circle and placed into the Tofflemire retainer through the diagonal slot. Once secured, the retained band is placed around the circumference of the tooth, encircling it. The matrix band is creating a temporary wall for the restoration to be placed. A wedge is placed to provide anatomic contour and to hold the matrix band firmly against the gingival margin of the tooth preparation.

The criteria for proper use of a Tofflemire retainer are:

- the diagonal slots holding the matrix band are always positioned towards the gingiva
- Tofflemire is positioned from the buccal surface of the tooth
- handle of the Tofflemire extends out from oral cavity at the corner of the lips
- seated matrix band extends approximately 1 mm below the gingival margin of the prep
- seated matrix band extends no more than 1 – 2 mm above the occlusal surface of the tooth

The parts of the Tofflemire retainer are:

- head with guide slots
- locking vise
- pointed spindle
- outer knob
- inner knob

Wedges are used in combination with matrices to provide anatomic contour to the interproximal surface (in order to replicate a natural tooth interproximally) and to hold the matrix band firmly against the gingival margin of a tooth preparation. The added pressure from the wedge creates a natural contour to occur when the restoration is placed. Wedges are placed lingually, via the lingual embrasure using either locking cotton forceps or hemostats. Depending on the classification of the tooth preparation, more than one wedge may need to be placed. Wedges are made in a variety of sizes, shapes and materials. They may be triangular or round and made from wood or plastic. The commonly used wedge is a triangular wooden wedge. The triangular shape allows it to fit nicely into the triangular embrasure area.

The California RDA General Written and Law Examination Prep Book © 2017, 2018 • KB Dental Arts – Publisher

The criteria for selecting a proper a wedge is as follows:

- Should be wide enough to apply pressure equally to the apical and gingival walls of the tooth preparation
- Presses the band against the tooth and causes a slight separation of the teeth
- Slightly wider than the distance between the cervical portions of the adjacent teeth
- Inserted lingually with locking cotton forceps or hemostat

It is important to avoid creating an overhang; proper wedge selection and placement is crucial to a successful outcome.

To assemble a Tofflemire retainer and matrix band, the following steps are advised:

1. Determine the correct band for use. This is determined by the size and classification of the tooth prep.
2. Burnish the band. The process of burnishing the band creates a thin, contoured area where the contact will be located.
3. Hold the retainer with the diagonal slot facing you while turning the outer knob counterclockwise until the end of the spindle is visible and away from the diagonal slot in the vise.
4. Turn the inner knob until the vise moves next to the guide slots.
5. The Tofflemire is now ready to receive the matrix band.
6. Bring together the ends of the matrix band, creating a circle. You will see one side of the circle being larger than the other. The larger side of the circle will be near the occlusal surface of the tooth being restored. The smaller side of the circle will be placed towards the gingiva of the tooth being restored.
7. With the diagonal slot facing you, slide in the joined ends of the matrix band, with the occlusal side (larger side of the circle) first, into the diagonal slots on the vise.
8. Guide the band into the guide slots. The position of the band in guide slots depends entirely upon if the tooth being restored is maxillary or mandibular and on left or right side of the mouth.
9. Tighten the outer knob on the retainer to hold the matrix in place.

To place a Tofflemire retainer and matrix band with wedge, the following steps are advised:

1. Position and seat the assembled Tofflemire retainer and band around the prepared tooth by looping the band around the width of the tooth, using care to keep assembly of the retainer intact. Once the band is wrapped around the tooth, ensure that the band is 1 – 2 mm above the occlusal surface of the tooth. Double check that the Tofflemire retainer is to the buccal and is parallel to the teeth in the arch.
2. Hold the band securely in place by using finger pressure over the occlusal surface. There is no need to press down – simply holding the band with a bit of pressure will work. While still holding the band, slowly start to turn the inner knob clockwise. This will tighten the band around the tooth. The band tightening can be felt by the finger stabilizing the band in place.
3. Using the mouth mirror and explorer, examine the placement of the band.
4. Use a burnisher to contour the band at the contact area, near the proximal box of the tooth preparation.
5. Place the proper sized and shaped wedge. This depends on the size of the embrasure.
6. Insert the wedge into the lingual embrasure of the prepared tooth next to the matrix band.
7. Using a mouth mirror, check interproximally for the following: there is a seal between the matrix band and the natural prepared tooth, the wedge is not impeding on the gum tissue, and the wedge is near the gingiva to create contour - not an open contact.

To remove a Tofflemire matrix band with wedge, the following steps are advised:

1. When the operator has determined the procedure has ended and is satisfied with the placement of the restoration, removal of the Tofflemire matrix band can begin.
2. Loosen the retainer from the band by placing a finger over the occlusal surface of the band while turning the outer knob of the retainer slowly.
3. The band will appear to "pop" up a bit when released from the retainer. Slide the retainer towards the occlusal surface while leaving the band in place. Remove the Tofflemire retainer from the mouth.
4. Gently lift the band, in an occlusal direction, in a seesaw motion from the tooth.
5. Remove the wedge using locking cotton forceps or hemostat. The wedge stays in place until after the band is removed to help avoid any fracturing of material placed.
6. The restoration can now be finished either by means of carving or by final finishing techniques (depending on the type of restoration being placed).

There are alternative matrix band systems that do not use the Tofflemire/universal retainer; the **AutoMatrix System,** the **Sectional Matrix System** and the **Anterior Matrix**.

The criteria of use for the AutoMatrix system is as follows:

- No retainer used to hold band in place
- Bands are already formed into a circle
- Bands are available in assorted sizes in both metal or plastic
- Each band has a coil-like auto lock loop
- Tightening wrench is inserted into the coil and turned clockwise to tighten the band
- When finished, the tightening wrench is inserted into the coil and turned counterclockwise to loosen the band
- Removing pliers are used to cut the band
- The removing pliers and tightening wrench are both autoclavable while the band can be discarded in sharps container

The Sectional Matrix System is sometimes referred to as "bands and rings" and are used for posterior composite restorations. The system uses tension rings and thin, small, oval shaped matrix bands that look like half-moons. The criteria for the use of the Sectional Matrix system is as follows:

- The band is placed in the area where the interproximal wall is missing using locking cotton forceps or hemostats and a see-saw motion
- The wedge is placed next to firmly close the gingival margin
- The prongs of the tension ring are placed between the band and the wedge closing off the preparation completely

The Anterior Matrix System uses clear/celluloid strips often called **mylar strips**. Mylar strips are used to create a retention wall for composite materials when used in tooth preparations. A retainer is not needed to hold the band in place. Optionally, a wedge may be used for this procedure. The criteria for use of the Anterior Matrix system is as follows:

- Mylar strip is placed between anterior teeth prior to etching and priming to protect adjacent teeth from the material. Wedge can be placed if operator desires. Wedge is placed from the facial for anterior restorations.
- After composite material is placed, the matrix is pulled tightly around the tooth to recreate the tooth's natural contour
- The clear plastic of the mylar allows the material to set completely

The California RDA General Written and Law Examination Prep Book © 2017, 2018 • KB Dental Arts – Publisher

TYPES, MIXING, AND PLACEMENT OF A DIRECT PROVISIONAL RESTORATION

A **direct provisional restoration** is a secondary term for a **temporary filling** that is placed directly into a tooth. A direct provisional restoration is also known as a temporary sedative dressing. These two terms are often used interchangeably, and you may see the term temporary sedative dressing in professional publications. The licensed dental assistant may place this in the dentist's absence or as an emergency treatment by the dental team. Direct provisional restorations decrease patient sensitivity, protect the tooth structure until a more permanent restoration can be placed and maintains tooth function.

There are two types of direct provisional restorations:

- IRM

- Cavit

IRM (Intermediate Restorative Material) is a popular choice for a temporary filling because of its ease of use and durability. It is supplied as a powder and liquid and mixed on a paper mixing pad with a cement spatula. The ratio for IRM is equal amounts, one scoop of powder to one drop of liquid. However, this really depends on the size of the temporary filling needed. One may wish to double the ratio to ensure there is enough material to fill the area if large. The powder should be divided up into three sections on the paper mixing pad. The first section of powder should be incorporated into the liquid, with the second and third sections following quickly, mixing back and forth for approximately ten seconds. It is important that the powder used is incorporated into the mixture and mixing is completed within one minute. The mix will be stiff at the start but will result in a smooth, pliable mixture capable of being rolled into a ball. The mixture can be divided into several "balls" of material to allow for a more evenly placed temporary filling. If an interproximal surface (mesial or distal) is missing in the tooth preparation, then a "ball" of material should be placed there and condensed down with a condenser with additional material placed until the preparation is filled. Attention should be paid to packing the material down to seal any margins that are present. The occlusal surface of the temporary sedative dressing can be contoured using burnishers while the interproximal surfaces can be contoured using a Half-Hollenbeck carver.

Cavit is a premixed temporary sedative dressing that is supplied in a tube or a jar. It can be pink or gray in color depending on the packaging. The material is exactly the same the only difference is the color. Cavit is very easy to use and place. A proper amount of material will be dispensed onto a paper pad depending on the size of the preparation needing to be temporarily filled. The material will be rolled into a ball and placed into the tooth. The material can be condensed down using a condenser and/or finger pressure and contoured using a burnisher and/or Half-Hollenbeck. Attention should be paid to packing the material down to seal any margins that are present. The patient should be instructed to bite down on the material to establish the occlusion. The material is soft enough that it will mold to the patient's bite eliminating the need for adjusting after the final set. Set time of Cavit can be hastened by applying a damp cotton pellet to the area.

It is important to note that direct provisional restorations have irregularities or imperfections along the margins. This is due to the nature of the material used for temporization. The chairside assistant should inform the patient of this and instruct the patient to use care while brushing and to avoid flossing in this area while the temporary is in place.

APPLICATION OF ETCHANT TO TOOTH SURFACES

Etchant is an acidic tooth conditioner that aids in roughening up either enamel or dentin. It is used prior to placing bonding materials onto the tooth structure to enhance the bond and after the tooth has been prepared using the dental handpiece and burs.

Tooth etching is a process whereby the enamel rods or the dentinal tubules are opened up in preparation to receive the bonding material and ultimately the restorative material. In addition, the **smear layer** is removed - the smear layer is a secretion created by the layers of tooth as its response to being prepared with the handpiece and bur. The smear layer is a natural response as the tooth tries to "heal" itself. If the layer remains in place, it will interfere with the bonding process. It can be argued that the etching portion of the bonding procedure is the most important step since it begins the process of bonding different structures (tooth and restoration) together.

A few important facts regarding etchant are as follows:

- very strong acid (37 - 39% phosphoric acid or maleic acid)
- typically, electric blue in appearance
- supplied as a gel or liquid in syringe format; gel form is most popular and easiest to use; the gel is viscous and does not run
- should only be applied to the area of tooth prepared for the restoration
- should not contact the soft tissues (gingiva, lips, cheeks) of the mouth; the soft tissue will suffer a chemical burn resulting in the tissue turning white and sloughing off (peeling)
- etchant remains on the tooth structure for 15 to 20 seconds or consistent with the manufacturer's instructions
- do not over-etch the tooth surface by leaving the etchant in place too long; this causes desiccation, or over-drying, which can harm the tooth
- etching removes the smear layer
- tastes very bad; best to warn patient prior to placing or to use the rubber dam to protect the patient's tongue during the procedure
- etchant must be rinsed off thoroughly using the HVE to suction up the fluid directly off the tooth as it is being rinsed

Steps in applying acid etch to a tooth surface:

1. Preparation is completed by the dentist

2. Ensure that the preparation is clean and rinsed

3. Rubber dam isolation is optional; if not used, ensure that cotton rolls have been placed to help achieve isolation and retraction to place the etchant on the tooth without causing harm to the surrounding soft tissues

4. The preparation should be dried with the air/water syringe. Be careful not to over dry the tooth as this can lead to post-operative sensitivity. The preparation must be kept dry from saliva or water from this point forward

5. Apply the etchant using the supplied syringe only to the areas of the tooth (enamel or dentin) that have been prepared by the dentist with the dental handpiece

6. Leave etchant in contact with the tooth structure for 15 to 20 seconds

7. Rinse the etchant from the tooth structure using the HVE and the air/water syringe for 15 to 30 seconds; dry the tooth with the air/water syringe

8. The etched surface of the tooth will have a chalky appearance after drying; if the tooth does not have this appearance or the area has been contaminated with saliva or water prior to or while the etch was in place then the etching process will need to be repeated

In addition to the acid etchants that are rinsed, there are some products available that include the etching step in the adhesive. This is referred to as a **Self-Etching Adhesive**. This product combines the acid etch step with the next step of the bonding procedure, the dental adhesive. If this product is used, then no rinsing is required as the etching process is taking place simultaneously to the adhesive product being placed. This is a popular method used when placing dental sealants as it eliminates the need for rinsing and then re-isolating the surrounding area which can be time consuming. It is at the discretion of the dentist as to which product they choose to use on their patient, as both have proven safe and effective.

In California, it is legal for the dentist to delegate the placement of etchant to the licensed dental assistant, or RDA, as long as it is part of the bonding procedure necessary for the placement of the restoration or dental sealants. It is not permissible to place etchant as a RDA for the bonding of brackets unless the assistant also possesses an Orthodontic Assistant Permit (OAP). An unlicensed dental assistant, or a DA, is not legally allowed to place etchant.

TYPES, TECHNIQUES AND PROCEDURES OF BONDING PROCEDURES

When a restoration such as a composite or amalgam is being placed, the restoration is bonded to the dentin. If dental sealants or orthodontic brackets are being placed, they are bonding to enamel. Regardless of the tooth surface being bonded, the procedural steps are fairly consistent:

1. Etching: Using etchant (as described previously)

2. Adhesion: Using an adhesive product – there are many varieties available

3. Materials Placement: Using restorative material or placement of sealants or orthodontic brackets

Bonding products, like adhesives and some resin-based restorative materials as well as dental sealants, will set in one of three ways:

1. Light cured: material is cured (set or harden) with an ultraviolet curing light; takes anywhere from 8 to 20 seconds depending on the manufacturer's directions

2. Self-cured: material sets on its own; can take anywhere from one to five minutes

3. Dual cured: material reaches initial set on its own, but needs to be cured with the curing light to reach its final set

The process of setting or curing is referred to as **polymerization**. The terms "cure" and "polymerize" are synonymous for setting or hardening.

Steps in applying a bonding product:

1. Etching process has taken place as previously noted

2. Re-isolate and dry the tooth

3. Adhesive is placed according to manufacturer's directions in the cavity preparation

4. Adhesive is lightly air dried with the air/water syringe

5. Restorative material is placed; sealants or orthodontic brackets are placed

Guidelines for applying a bonding product:

- Follow the manufacturer's directions thoroughly; every bonding product is different

- Some bonding products will have multiple steps while others will only have one step; again, follow the manufacturer's directions closely

- Be generous in the application of bonding agent; ensure the entire surface of the preparation is covered with the bonding agent; it is better to have too much than not enough bonding agent

- Avoid contamination from saliva, water and/or blood while applying the bonding agent

- Do not over dry the tooth; most bonding products work best on a slightly moist tooth surface

PROVISIONAL COVERAGE: TYPES, MATERIALS, FABRICATION, PLACEMENT AND REMOVAL

The term **provisional coverage** is a technical name for a **temporary restoration** meaning short term. A temporary prosthetic device such as a crown, veneer, or a bridge is created to protect the preparation while the dental laboratory is fabricating the permanent restoration or fixed prosthetic. The patient wears a temporary for approximately two weeks.

Provisional crowns, or temporary crowns, are the most common provisionals made in the dental practice, often performed by the licensed assistant (RDA/RDAEF), and made from any of the following types of materials:

- Polycarbonate crowns
- Stainless steel crowns
- Gold anodized crowns
- Strip crowns made from prefabricated plastic used as a mold

The following materials help fabricate two (2) types of provisionals commonly used in dentistry. They are:

1. Custom Temporary

    - most common temporary

    - made from acrylic or composite using an impression from the patient's mouth; acrylic is the most common

    - provides the best fitting temporary

    - looks natural

    - can be used for both anterior and posterior teeth

    - can be used for a single crown temporary, multiple adjacent crown preparations, veneer temps or a bridge temporary

2. Preformed or Prefabricated Temporary

    - comes from the manufacturer already premade into a crown like shape

    - can be used for anterior or posterior teeth

    - best for single crown preparations

    - types of preformed crowns are: polycarbonate crowns, stainless steel crowns and preformed polymer crowns

    - each preformed crown is used in specific areas of the mouth for specific reasons

    - not always the most natural looking

    - do not fit as well as a custom provisional

    - cannot be used for multiple adjacent crown preparations, veneer preps, or bridge preps

The California RDA General Written and Law Examination Prep Book © 2017, 2018 • KB Dental Arts – Publisher
This book and the individual contributions contained within are protected under Copyright by the Publisher

In California, it is legal for the dentist to delegate the fabrication and cementation of either type of provisional to the licensed dental assistant, or RDA. An unlicensed dental assistant, or a DA, is not legally allowed to fabricate and cement provisional restorations.

Fabrication and cementation of a single custom acrylic provisional:

1. Take a preliminary impression of the arch or quadrant prior to the tooth being prepared; later in the procedure the impression will be used to make the custom acrylic temporary.

2. Keep the impression moist by wrapping it in a moist paper towel until needed to prevent distortion.

3. When ready to make the temporary, dry and isolate the prepared tooth.

4. Place a very small amount of Vaseline on the tooth preparation so the acrylic separates easily from the tooth.

5. Unwrap the impression and dry the area where the prep is located in the impression.

6. Hold the gun with the acrylic material cartridge and bury the mixing tip against the impression while expressing the acrylic material into the tooth area of the impression.

7. Grasp the impression with the acrylic material loaded and reinsert into the patient's mouth over the prepared tooth.

8. Wait for the acrylic material to reach its initial set (two to three minutes) and then gently remove the impression.

9. The temporary may be in the impression or in the patient's mouth on the tooth preparation.

10. The temporary should be removed from either location, trimmed and smoothed using the handpiece and an acrylic bur or stone.

11. It is helpful to mark the margin and the contact point with a pencil to aid with the trimming process.

12. The temporary should be tried in and the occlusion checked with articulating paper.

13. If adjustment is needed the temporary should be removed from the patient's mouth and adjusted.

14. Polish the acrylic temporary in the lab using the lathe and rag wheel with pumice to create a smooth, shiny temporary ready for cementation.

15. The preparation should be cleaned, dried and the temporary cement chosen.

16. Cement is mixed and temporary is placed on the tooth.

17. Wait two to three minutes for the cement to reach its initial set.

18. Remove the excess cement using an explorer or a scaler; gently floss both the mesial and distal surface pulling the floss out to the side and not back up.

19. Provide patient with post-operative instructions for caring for the area following treatment.

20. Have the patient return in two weeks for their permanent crown.

Note: Provisional bridges, multiple adjacent provisional crowns and provisional veneers that are custom made using either acrylic or composite are fabricated in the same manner as described above. There will be more crowns to trim, smooth, polish and cement so the process will be more time consuming.

When fabricating a temporary (provisional), it is best to adhere to a few key guidelines:

1. Check for proper contact on the mesial and distal contacts

    *   if the contact is too tight, the temporary will not sit correctly on the tooth

    *   if the contact is insufficient, the adjacent teeth will not maintain a proper contact, causing teeth to drift within two weeks; the permanent crown to not fit properly. Teeth constantly move and must have contacts to create stability.

2. Check the height of the occlusion of the temporary (articulating paper)

    *   the occlusal surface of the temporary should be even with the adjacent natural teeth

    *   if the occlusal surface is too high, the premature biting pressure will cause a tooth ache or breakage

    *   one can take the temporary out of occlusion by reducing the occlusal surface; this protects the prepared tooth from trauma

3. Check the margin for smoothness with a snug fit

    *   the margin of the temporary is the closest to the gingiva

    *   roughness of the margin can cause discomfort to the patient after the anesthesia wears off

    *   smoothness of the margin is essential to prevent gingival irritation

    *   gingival irritation leads to increased bleeding during the final cementation appointment of the permanent crown

4. The provisional is esthetically pleasing

    *   color matches the adjacent natural teeth

5. Temporary does not extend past the margin on the prep

    *   the margin of the temporary meets the margin of the prepared tooth

Provisional Post-Operative Instructions:

*   wait until the anesthesia wears off before attempting to eat or drink anything

*   temporaries have unnatural edges on them so be careful when using floss around the temporary; it is best to avoid flossing around the temporary if possible; if flossing is necessary, carefully insert the floss and then pull out to the side, do not pull back up as temporaries have unnatural edges on them and the floss could pull the temporary off

*   avoid hard food, such as hard bread; the acrylic or composite temporary can break and fracture

*   avoid sticky foods, such as gum or candy; the stickiness will cause the temporary to lift off the tooth

*   if the temporary breaks or comes off, please call the office, and save the temporary so it may be cemented back into place

The California RDA General Written and Law Examination Prep Book © 2017, 2018 • KB Dental Arts – Publisher

The placement and removal of provisional veneers differs from the way other provisionals are cemented and removed. Provisional veneers, by the very nature of the veneer procedure, are not cemented but are instead temporarily bonded into place.

   a)   provisional veneers can be fabricated using acrylic or composite

   b)   the provisional veneers are retained onto the prepared teeth by a bonding technique

   c)   the etchant step is skipped since provisional veneers are in place a short time – often removed within two (2) weeks

   d)   a small spot of bonding agent is placed directly on the middle third of the veneer preparations and a small amount of composite is placed on the provisional veneers

   e)   the provisional veneers are seated into place removing any excess composite prior to curing with the curing light

   f)   to remove the provisional veneers when ready to seat the permanent veneers, they will be cut off by the dentist using the dental handpiece; the temporary veneers are cut down the middle and then peeled back using a spoon excavator

Removal of provisional crowns or bridges will take place approximately two (2) weeks after their initial placement. When removing the temporaries, it is important to do so as gently as possible to ensure it remains in one piece in the event the temporary needs to be re-cemented. This may occur if the permanent crown needs to be sent back to the laboratory for adjustments, additions or a remake.

A provisional is often removed using a hemostat, crown removing forceps or cotton forceps. Once removed, the prepared tooth will need to be cleaned and the excess temporary cement removed using a hand instrument followed by a 2% chlorhexidine gluconate solution which will assist in the successful bonding of the restoration. During the final crown cementation appointment, it is best that the patient not be anesthetized so the patient can communicate with certainty how the bite is feeling and if adjusting is necessary.

PROVISIONAL STAINLESS-STEEL /ALUMINIM SHELL CROWNS

Stainless steel and aluminum shell crowns are used interchangeably in dentistry. Pedodontic practices use stainless steel crowns to restore severely decayed and broken-down primary teeth that need to be retained until they are ready to be exfoliated. Stainless steel and aluminum shell crowns are used as provisional coverage for adult patients awaiting the permanent crown to return from the dental laboratory. This section will focus primarily on stainless steel and aluminum shell crowns as provisional (temporary) coverage.

Outlined below are the steps for preparing a stainless-steel or aluminum shell crown for placement:

   1.   The tooth has been prepared by the dentist; preparation is clean and dried

   2.   Selecting and Sizing:

       •   a crown will be selected from a tray of various sizes for try-in

       •   the fit of the provisional is being checked making sure there are mesial/distal contacts, the provisional covers the entire preparation, is not too big or too small and fits snugly

       •   several crowns may need to be sized in order to select the best fit possible

       •   follow all infection control guidelines during the try-in phase; following selection, disinfect and sterilize all crowns contaminated during the selection process

3. Trimming and Crimping:

    - crown and bridge scissors are used to trim around the margin of the crown which reduces the height of the crown

    - trimming, also known as **festooning**, is continued until the height of the crown matches the adjacent teeth

    - caution should be taken not to remove too much of the crown while trimming and to try the crown in multiple times during the trimming process

    - the crown should be seated with a lingual to buccal roll using firm finger pressure

    - once the correct height of occlusion is achieved, the margin may be smoothed with a green stone

    - contouring and crimping pliers are used to crimp the margin of the provisional to ensure a tight fit and a proper cervical margin

    - crimping pliers should be used carefully so the provisional is not over crimped; if the cervical margin is too tight it will not fit over the preparation

    - crimp the margin all the way around the crown, using overlapping crimps, at approximately the last 2 mm of the length of the crown

4. Cementation:

    - the provisional crown is ready to be cemented into place using a temporary cement

    - the margin of the crown fits to a point 1mm below the gingival margin

ROTARY INSTRUMENTS AND PROVISIONALS

The use of handpieces and burs for the adjustment of provisionals is an acceptable and necessary means of achieving a trimmed, finished and smooth temporary restoration. Temporaries can be trimmed using a high-speed handpiece, a lab handpiece, or a straight slow speed handpiece. Inserted into each of these handpieces are burs that cut or polish the provisional material. The burs of choice when trimming and polishing provisionals are acrylic burs, green stones, or rubber abrasive wheels. Provisionals should be trimmed extra-orally prior to being cemented with temporary cement. If it is determined that additional adjustment is necessary following cementation, the dentist should make those adjustments.

IMPRESSION MATERIALS FOR INDIRECT PROVISIONAL RESTORATIONS

Pre-made or stainless-steel crowns have no need for a preliminary impression since they are already molded and made. A custom temporary will need a preliminary impression prior to tooth preparation. These impressions can be taken with alginate material, AlgiNot material or polyvinylsiloxane material. **Alginate** has been a commonly used impression material used for preliminary impressions and opposing arch impressions. The material is supplied in a powder canister and is mixed with a ratio of water. The water and powder are mixed together in a mixing bowl and placed into a quadrant tray and placed into the patient's mouth. The impression is taken and set aside while the tooth is being prepped. After the preparation, the impression is filled with acrylic material in the area of the tooth prep, placed back into the mouth, creating a custom acrylic crown. Alginate takes a little longer to snap an impression versus some other choices available now. There is more of a clean-up and wait time is a little longer.

AlgiNot is another impression material choice for the creation of an indirect provisional restoration. AlgiNot is supplied in the gun technique. The material is supplied in a cartridge that is loaded into an impression gun. The base and catalyst of the material is mixed in a mixing tip attached to the cartridge and is dispensed directly into an impression tray (quadrant or full tray). The loaded tray is then placed into the patient's mouth prior to the tooth being prepped. The impression is easy to take and sets a little quicker than alginate material. There is not a lot of clean up associated with the AlgiNot material since it is supplied in the gun technique.

Lastly, polyvinylsiloxane material is another excellent choice of impression material for fabricating an indirect provisional restoration. Polyvinylsiloxane is a final impression material used primarily for taking master impressions for crown and bridge procedures. However, much like AlgiNot, it can also be used to take the preliminary impression. It is supplied in the gun technique. A cartridge is placed in an impression gun with a mixing tip attached to the cartridge. The base and catalyst of the impression material is mixed in the mixing tip and dispensed directly into an impression tray (quadrant or full tray). The loaded tray is then placed in the patients mouth prior to the tooth being prepped. This impression, similar to the AlgiNot, is easy to take, is less messy and sets a little faster than the alginate material.

DENTAL CEMENTS – CLASSIFICATIONS, TYPES, MIXING, AND REMOVAL

There are two (2) classifications of dental cements: permanent and temporary cements. Both are considered luting agents. Luting agents act as an adhesive to hold two structures together, ex: permanent or provisional crowns to the tooth structure. Typically, permanent restorations are cemented with permanent cement while temporaries or provisionals are cemented with temporary cement. There may be instances, however, when the dentist chooses to cement a permanent indirect restoration (crown, bridge, inlay) with temporary cement. Some reasons why may include: the tooth is exhibiting signs and symptoms of needing a root canal or experiencing increased sensitivity. As a precaution, the dentist may use a temporary cement to take a "watch and wait" approach to evaluate how the tooth is responding.

Once a permanent restoration is cemented with permanent cement the only way to remove it is to cut it off with a dental handpiece and bur.

Certain types of cements are selected for specific procedures. The types of cements are:

1. Glass Ionomer - permanent

    - primarily used as permanent cements for metal restorations (PFM crowns, gold bridges)
    - special formulas available for use as liners or a restorative material
    - versatile as it can adhere to metals, enamel and dentin
    - powder has a slow release fluoride incorporated which makes the formation of recurrent decay slower
    - adheres to slightly moist tooth structure eliminating the potential for over drying the tooth
    - thin film thickness allowing for a properly seated permanent indirect restoration.
    - less trauma is caused to the pulp of the tooth
    - supplied in: powder/liquid or premeasured capsules
    - available as light cured or self-cured material

2. Composite Resin Cement - permanent

    - designed specifically for: all ceramic/all porcelain crowns, bridges, inlays or onlays, veneers, orthodontic bands and brackets

The California RDA General Written and Law Examination Prep Book © 2017, 2018 • KB Dental Arts – Publisher

- thin film thickness allowing for a properly seated permanent indirect restoration.

- tooth surface needs to be etched and treated with a bonding system prior to cementation

- very common final seating process for veneers

- acts as a permanent bonding

- can be used on dentin and enamel surfaces

- supplied as: powder/liquid or syringe applicators as a base and catalyst

- powder/liquid is mixed quickly with a cement spatula on a paper mixing pad

- syringe base and catalyst are mixed quickly with a nonmetal cement spatula on a paper mixing pad; mixture is paste like

- light cured or dual cured system with bonding agent

3. Zinc Oxide Eugenol (ZOE) Cement – permanent and temporary

- type I and type II ZOE have specific uses

- type I: used for provisional temporary cementation

- supplied with or without eugenol as base and catalyst

- equal lengths of material are dispensed from each tube onto a paper mixing pad mixed quickly using a cement spatula

- type II: used for permanent cementation of cast restorations; cement is ZOE 2200

- least irritating of all the dental cements

4. Polycarboxylate Cement – permanent

- permanent cement for cast restorations, stainless steel crowns as permanent restorations on children and/or cementation of orthodontic bands

- can be used as a base under direct restorations

- supplied as a powder/liquid form, mixed on a paper mixing pad or a glass slab

- liquid is very thick similar to syrup

5. Zinc Phosphate Cement (ZPC)- permanent

- used for final cementation of crowns, inlays, onlays, and bridges as well as a base under direct restorations

- supplied as a powder/liquid

- mixture will be exothermic

- mixed on a cool, glass slab to counteract the exothermic reaction

- increases the working time while mixing

- keeps the mix from thickening too quickly

- powder must be added to the liquid in very small increments

MIXING

The mixing procedure for each type of cement is critical to proper cementation of the restoration to the tooth structure. It is important to read the manufacturer's instructions for the cement, especially if the cement is newly introduced to you or the dental practice. Cements are often improved upon by their manufacturers and mixing instructions may be revised. The instructions included in each package of cement should be reviewed.

Outlined below are some useful guidelines to follow when mixing dental cements:

a) understand what procedure the cement is being mixed for (i.e. restorative, temporary or permanent cement, liner or base)

b) measure out the appropriate ratio for the procedure the cement is being is used and in accordance with the manufacturer's instructions

c) place the powder and liquid on opposite sides of the paper mixing pad or glass slab to allow room for mixing in the middle

d) divide powder into small increments

e) when incorporating powder into the liquid mix thoroughly, making sure all the powder is absorbed prior to introducing more powder into the mix

f) remember that temperature affects the mixture of the cement causing the mix to set faster or slower; this is why a cool glass slab can be used for most cements to delay set time or counteract warm weather affecting the mix

g) be as precise as possible when dispensing the powder and liquid ratios

h) never dispense the cement material ahead of time; always dispense the cement material right when it is needed; this way the material will not be compromised by light, humidity, temperatures, or other factors

After the cement of has been selected, mixed, placed into the indirect restoration and seated, the dentist will instruct the patient to bite down on a cotton roll to allow the cement to reach its initial set. Initial set is usually achieved within two (2) to three (3) minutes.

It is common for there to be some excess cement that spills out from the indirect permanent restoration covering the margin, the adjacent teeth and filling the interproximal areas. Excess cement needs to be removed completely and thoroughly to prevent irritation of the gum tissues. Excess cement can be removed by using a hand instrument such as an explorer or a spoon excavator. The excess cement is easily removed from the adjacent teeth and around the marginal area on the buccal and lingual surfaces.

Removing the excess cement from the interproximal areas is more difficult. Using a piece of floss with a knot tied in the middle of it, insert the floss through the contact area and pull the floss out to the side. The bulk of the knot will dislodge any pieces of cement that are stuck interproximally. The tooth should be rinsed and dried to evaluate complete cement removal.

COMPUTER AIDED INTRAORAL IMAGES – CAD/CAM

Dental labs and dentists are obtaining impressions of tooth preparations for crown and bridge procedures using computer aided design technology. By using a digital camera attached to the computer design system and software installed to assist the operator with designing the crown, the system is sophisticated, capable of snapping pictures, or images creating a **digital impression**. Once the design work is complete, the dentist will check the image, and the final restoration can either be milled in the office unit or the image is sent to a lab electronically and they will fabricate the final restoration.

Only a Registered Dental Assistant is legally allowed to obtain a digital impression by means of CAD/CAM technology and should be completely trained in the process by the manufacturer prior to performance of the procedure.

The RDA may not mill the final restoration on the CAD/CAM machine as this is considered fabrication of a permanent restoration – a procedure only allowed to be performed by an RDAEF (licensed after 1/1/2010) or a dentist.

BLEACHING

Bleaching, also known as tooth whitening, is the process of lightening and brightening discolored, stained or dark teeth. There are three (3) indications for a patient undergoing a tooth whitening procedure:

1. extrinsic stains (food, coffee, tea, smoking)
2. aging teeth
3. intrinsic stains (tetracycline staining or fluorosis)

Contraindications to bleaching include:

1. periodontal conditions
2. existing anterior restorations

Bleaching may be accomplished by using either a professional-grade home-care product obtained through a dental office or a stronger dental-office applied product.

- When using the professional-grade home-care product, the patient will obtain custom bleaching trays fabricated by the dental team. Once fabricated, the patient is sent home with the trays and bleach material after receiving detailed home-care instructions.
- With the stronger in-office treatment, the bleaching material is applied incorporating the use of the curing light to enhance the level of whitening.

Both methods of bleaching have positive results for the patient. The bleach material is usually peroxide based, most commonly a carbamide peroxide. Bleaching material contains 10% to 30% carbamide peroxide, which is very effective on the tooth structure. It is important to note that the higher the percentage of the carbamide peroxide, the stronger the bleaching strength of the material. However, while patients may experience sensitivity with any percentage, increased sensitivity is more common with the higher percentage bleaching material.

Bleaching material is intended for use only on tooth structure and not the soft tissues of the mouth. If bleach material comes in contact with the soft tissues it will create a burn on the tissues. The longer the bleach material contacts the soft tissues the more the tissue will suffer from the burn. The area will turn white and then peel. The area will feel sore for a few days and then will heal. The patient should be advised not to overfill their take-home bleaching trays. The dental team takes extra precautions while performing in-office bleaching by placing a barrier around the gum tissue to prevent the bleach from coming into contact with oral tissues.

CHAPTER REVIEW COMMENTS:

It is essential that the examination candidate understands that the RDA written examination will not ask questions containing product names typically used in the dental office – for example, while the office may use the term Fuji, Duralon or Ketac to identify a certain cement to be used in a procedure, the State examination will only use the technical terms used to identify a type of material, not the product name. Candidates must be critically aware of the technically correct term of a material when studying for the examination; terms such as:

- Polycarboxylate cement

- Glass ionomer

- Zinc oxide or zinc oxide eugenol

- Calcium hydroxide cement or calcium hydroxide liner

- Composite or composite resin

END OF CHAPTER - CRITICAL THINKING QUESTIONS:

1. The term provisional is a technical term used to describe what type of restoration?

2. What is the principal purpose of using a base during a restorative procedure?

3. Is there a difference between a temporary sedative dressing and a temporary filling?

4. What does the term exothermic mean when mixing certain types of dental cement?

5. Zinc Oxide Eugenol is considered to be the least irritating of all dental cements – why?

6. What type of matrix is used for anterior composite resin or glass ionomer restorations?

7. A matrix must be used to create a temporary proximal wall for which classifications of tooth preps?

8. On the Tofflemire retainer, the diagonal slots of the head are always placed towards what surface?

9. A seated band extends no further than _____ above the occlusal surface of the tooth.

10. What is the purpose for using a wedge?

11. What is the consequence of a poorly placed wedge?

12. The wedge is placed from the _____ surface when restoring posterior teeth.

CRITICAL THINKING QUESTION ANSWERS FOUND IN APPENDIX

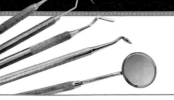

Unit 2 - Chapter 2

UNIT TWO – DENTAL PROCEDURES

CHAPTER TWO: PREVENTIVE DENTAL PROCEDURES

EXAMINATION PLAN DATA:

Topic Area	Dental Procedures
Total Weight of Topic Area on Examination	35%
Subject Area	Preventive Dental Procedures
Percentage of Examination Questions in Preventive Dental Procedures	5%

PREVENTIVE DENTAL PROCEDURES – TASK AND KNOWLEDGE STATEMENTS

Tasks Associated with Topic Area	Knowledge Statements Associated with Topic Area
Perform coronal polishing	Knowledge of scope of practice for RDAs related to coronal polishing and the application of pit and fissure sealants
Prepare teeth and apply pit and fissure sealants	

SCOPE OF PRACTICE – SPECIFIC TO PREVENTIVE PROCEDURES

Registered Dental Assistant

All duties that a dental assistant is allowed to perform

Polish coronal surfaces of the teeth

The application of pit and fissure sealants following completion of a Board-approved program or course

Licensed Registered Dental Assistant in Extended Functions (RDAEF):

(a) A registered dental assistant in extended functions licensed on or after January 1, 2010, is authorized to perform all duties and procedures that a registered dental assistant is authorized to perform and those duties that the board may prescribe by regulation.

A preventive procedure is a measure taken by the dental team in an effort to prevent the development of caries, or dental tooth decay. The most common modern preventive procedures performed by registered dental assistants, and tested on the RDA written examination, are: coronal polishing and pit and fissure sealants, more commonly known simply as **sealants**. There are other preventive procedures such as the placement of topical fluoride treatments; however, since they are not tested on the RDA written examination, we will limit our review in this manual to the previously mentioned procedures. We will look at each of the procedures individually in this chapter.

KEY TERMS

Calculus	Mineralized, or hardened, plaque
Clinical Crowns	Portion of the tooth visible when the patient opens their mouth
Coronal Polishing	A technique used to remove plaque and stains from the coronal portions of the teeth
Dental Sealants	Preventive procedure where the occlusal pit and fissures are sealed with a form of resin to prevent caries on the surfaces of posterior teeth
Disclosing Agents	Coloring agents that temporarily stains and discloses bacterial plaque when applied to the teeth
Filled Resin	Contains fillers making it more resistant to wear
Fulcrum	A finger rest or stabilizing point for the operator
Grit	The texture of a material; refers to polishing agents in this context
Plaque	Colorless, soft deposit found on teeth that contains bacteria
Polishing Agent	An abrasive or dentifrice used in the rubber polishing cup to polish the teeth
Prophy Paste	A mixture of different ingredients that are packaged into round plastic, disposable containers; a type of polishing agent
Sealant Retention	Length of time in which the sealant remains in place and prevents decay
Selective Polishing	Only teeth or surfaces with stain are polished
Supragingival	Above the gum line
Unfilled Resin	No fillers are added

CORONAL POLISHING

Coronal Polishing is defined as a technique used to remove plaque and stains from the coronal portions of the teeth. A coronal polish procedure usually takes place near the end of the debridement, or cleaning, of an adult or pediatric patient's full dentition. Commonly referred to as a "prophy", an oral prophylaxis is defined as the complete removal of calculus, debris, stain and plaque from the teeth.

Plaque is a colorless, soft deposit found on teeth that contains bacteria. It is easily removed by means of toothbrushing and flossing techniques at home and in the dental setting.

Calculus is mineralized, or hardened, plaque. There is no way to remove calculus at home, therefore, regular dental visits are essential to the health of the mouth and is removed by either the dentist or hygienist.

The removal of calculus leaves the enamel rough. The roughness of the enamel attracts plaque accumulation, so it is recommended that a coronal polish completes the oral prophylaxis procedure in an effort to smooth the rough areas of the teeth.

CORONAL POLISH TECHNIQUES

There are two techniques, or methods, of coronal polishing used most frequently today; air-powder polishing and rubber cup polishing. The most common method of coronal polishing is termed "rubber cup polishing" which is primarily used to remove the plaque and stains from the coronal surfaces of the teeth by the use of a rubber cup attachment and prophy angle attached to a slow speed handpiece. A bristle brush attachment may be used in addition to the rubber cup, but only on the occlusal surfaces of posterior teeth and on the lingual surfaces of anterior teeth.

POLISHING AGENTS

A **polishing agent**, or abrasive or **dentifrice**, is typically used in the rubber cup during the coronal polish to reduce the amount of heat being generated onto the tooth surfaces. An empty rubber cup generates more heat on to the surfaces than one with polishing agent. One rubber polishing cup filled with a polishing agent is typically sufficient for up to three teeth. Dental abrasives help to lift stains and plaque from the **supragingival** tooth surfaces. Care must be taken by the dental professional to determine the level of staining the patient presents with at the cleaning appointment. This will assist the RDA in choosing the proper polishing agent for the coronal polish procedure.

Some examples of polishing agents are: prophy paste, pure flour of pumice, silex and even certain toothpastes (known as a dental dentifrice). The most common of all the polishing agents is prophy paste. **Prophy paste** is a mixture of differing ingredients that are manufactured and packaged into round plastic, disposable containers. The base of the prophy paste mixture is pumice; ground up, crushed rock particles. These rock particles then have fluoride, flavoring and glycerin (adds moisture) added to them. Prophy paste comes in a variety of thicknesses based on the grade or level of grit assigned to them.

Grit refers to the coarseness or smoothness of the material. Prophy paste has a grit range of extra coarse, coarse, medium, fine and extra fine. The grit is chosen based on the amount of stain present. The more stain that is present, the heavier the grit of the prophy paste will need to be. The dental professional may try a pure **flour of pumice** mixture to remove the stain. There is no fluoride, flavoring or glycerin added to this mixture. It is pumice in its purist form (it is gray in color and looks like powder) mixed with either water or mouthwash. Pumice is more abrasive than prophy paste so care should be taken in regard to the rate of abrasion and pressure of the rubber cup on the tooth surfaces.

DISCLOSING AGENTS

Disclosing agents are coloring agents (dyes) that make plaque visible when applied to the teeth. As discussed earlier, plaque is a colorless, soft deposit found on teeth that contains bacteria. Dental professionals can use disclosing agents as a means of patient education showing the patient the areas of the mouth being missed during brushing.

The California RDA General Written and Law Examination Prep Book © 2017, 2018 • KB Dental Arts – Publisher

Disclosing agents are supplied as tablets or as a solution. In the tablet method, the patient is instructed to chew the tablet completely, allow for the dye to mix with their saliva, and swish the mixture around their mouth without swallowing. The patient is then instructed to spit out the mixture, but not to rinse. The teeth will be stained a pink to purple color with the areas of plaque appearing darker in color.

In the solution form, an adequate amount of solution is dispensed from the container into a disposable cup. A cotton tipped applicator is used to dip into the solution in the cup and then is painted onto the patient's teeth. Similar to the tablet method, the patient's teeth become stained a pink to purple color with the areas of plaque appearing darker in color.

Either method is acceptable and becomes operator preference. Some offices choose not to use disclosing agents at all. Care should be taken when using disclosing agents on patients because the agents can stain clothing, sinks, and equipment.

FULCRUM AND HANDPIECE GRASP

A **fulcrum** is another dental term for a finger rest or stabilizing point. Whenever one is using an instrument in the patient's mouth, it is proper and safe to establish a fulcrum to stabilize the operator's hand while working. The oral cavity is a warm and moist environment making the possibility of slipping with the instrument very likely. This could harm, and/or even worse, injure the patient. Therefore, a fulcrum is considered a standard of care whenever working as the operator in the patient's mouth. Either an intraoral or extraoral fulcrum is acceptable.

When performing a coronal polish, the prophy angle is attached to a slow speed handpiece. The handpiece functions by the operator stepping on the rheostat, or foot pedal, located directly behind the back of the dental chair. The operator holds the slow speed handpiece in the pen grasp, allowing the longer part of the handpiece to rest between the thumb and the index finger in the "V" section of the hand. The operator's thumb and index finger are secured as close as possible to the working end of the handpiece for better control.

EQUIPMENT, SUPPLIES AND MATERIALS USED FOR CORONAL POLISHING

Armamentarium:
- Mouth mirror (disposable or traditional)
- Explorer
- Cotton forceps
- Prophy angle (traditional or disposable)
- Slow speed handpiece
- Rubber cup and bristle brush attachments or prophy angles with these attachments (disposable)
- Prophy paste or other dentifrice
- Disclosing agent with cotton tipped applicator (optional)
- Saliva ejector or HVE tip
- Air/water syringe tip (disposable or traditional)
- 2 x 2 cotton gauze
- Floss and floss aides, if needed (floss threader)
- Hand mirror (optional – to assist with patient education)

CORONAL POLISHING PROCEDURE SEQUENCE

When performing coronal polishing, it is important to follow a sequence or pattern of polishing to ensure all surfaces are treated. The procedural steps for coronal polishing are as follows:

1. Follow the established pattern of polishing
2. Begin with the most posterior tooth in the quadrant chosen; place the filled rubber cup on the most distal surface of the tooth prior to stepping on the rheostat; establish a comfortable fulcrum
3. Apply gentle pressure, enough to flare the rubber cup, and engage the rheostat to begin the polishing stroke
4. The polishing stroke should follow along the gingival third of the tooth towards the incisal/occlusal third of the tooth using a lifting, sweeping motion – do not scrub
5. Use overlapping strokes to confirm complete coverage of the tooth
6. Each tooth surface should take approximately three to five seconds to complete
7. This should be repeated until the midline is reached at which time the patient should be rinsed with the air/water syringe and the saliva ejector or HVE tip
8. Polishing is then resumed at the midline reaching into the next quadrant. This sequence is followed until all teeth and surfaces have been polished
9. Using the air/water syringe and the saliva ejector, rinse the mouth to remove the polishing agent
10. With dental floss, floss each interproximal area, using remnants of polishing agent to help remove stain from the proximal surfaces; flossing also removes any abrasive agent or debris that may be lodged in the contact areas
11. Perform a final thorough rinse of the oral cavity

SELECTIVE POLISHING

Selective polishing is a procedure in which only those teeth or surfaces with stain are polished. The purpose of selective polishing is to avoid removing even small amounts of surface enamel unnecessarily. In some individuals, stain removal may cause dentinal hypersensitivity during and after the appointment. Selective polishing can help reduce such sensitivity.

PRECAUTIONS AND TIPS

It is important for the operator to keep the following in mind when performing a coronal polish procedure:

- Retraction of the lips, cheeks and tongue is important to avoid injury during the coronal polishing procedure. To accomplish retraction, utilize a mouth mirror as well as the head of the prophy angle while polishing.
- Avoid polishing the gingiva, causing soft tissue damage and injuring the patient. The stroke should come close enough to the gingiva to cause blanching, a temporary whitening of the gingiva along the gumline, but should not be directly polished.
- Caution should be taken when polishing esthetic restorations; use appropriate polishing agents based on the type of restorative materials used.
- Do not polish in one location of a tooth for longer than three (3) to five (5) seconds. The longer an area is polished, the greater the effect of abrasion.
- Watch the speed of the handpiece - it is not a race. A slow, even speed is needed to accomplish polishing safely and effectively for the patient.
- Do not forget to re-establish a fulcrum when moving from location to location while polishing.

- Do not be afraid to ask the patient to help in gaining greater visibility into the oral cavity. The patient can easily be repositioned in the dental chair. They can also move their head from side to side or raise their chin up or down to help the operator.
- Do remember key points in operator positioning such as: feet are flat on the floor, thighs parallel to the floor, arms at waist level and even with the patient's mouth.

INDICATIONS FOR CORONAL POLISHING

Coronal polishing is indicated for the following:

- Prior to cementation of crowns and/or bridges
- Prior to cementation of orthodontic bands
- Prior to the placement of dental sealants (if the manufacturer recommends)
- Prior to the placement of the rubber dam
- Prior to the use of dental acid etchant material (if the manufacturer recommends)

Some benefits of coronal polishing include:

- Smooth, mirror like tooth surfaces for greater ease in keeping the teeth clean
- It is more difficult for plaque to adhere to smooth, clean tooth surfaces, slowing the formation of new plaque deposits
- Patients enjoy their appearance and the feel of smooth, clean teeth
- The teeth are nicely prepared for the placement of dental sealants, if indicated
- The teeth are nicely prepared for the placement of orthodontic brackets and/or bands, if indicated

CONTRAINDICATIONS TO CORONAL POLISHING

Coronal polishing is contraindicated for the following:

- There is no stain present on the tooth surfaces
- Patients with newly erupted teeth
- Patients with sensitive teeth
- Patients at high risk for dental caries or in demineralized areas
- Patients with exposed cementum

Coronal polishing can be damaging to gingiva, tooth surfaces and restorations. If care is not taken regarding the speed of the handpiece and specified areas, such as those mentioned above, damage can be done by the polishing procedure.

PIT AND FISSURE SEALANTS

A **dental sealant** is a protective plastic (resin) coating that is placed where a pit of fissure is found to be weak or vulnerable to dental disease. A sealant can be placed on patients of any age but are most commonly placed during the caries active phase, ages 6 to 15 years old. Children typically have deeper grooves than adults simply because they have less wear on their teeth. It is very difficult for children to properly clean deep grooves and often the grooves are deeper than the toothbrush bristles can even reach. This sets the stage for food and debris to remain trapped in the grooves starting the caries cycle in motion. Sealants prevent food and other bacteria from becoming trapped in deep occlusal grooves, thus placing a physical barrier, preventing decay from forming. As long as the sealant is properly placed and remains intact, the occlusal surface of the tooth is protected from decay. It is important to note that sealants protect the occlusal surface only. The interproximal surface is still susceptible to decay. Therefore, sealant placement does not eliminate the need for proper home care (toothbrushing and flossing techniques are still important!) or regular dental visits. Sealants are a part of a preventive program.

INDICATIONS FOR PIT AND FISSURE SEALANTS

Dental sealants may be indicated for children and/or adults who:
- Demonstrate a moderate or high risk of developing dental caries
- Have incipient carious lesions
- Have deep pits and fissures
- Have teeth that are fully erupted that may be susceptible to dental caries

CONTRAINDICATIONS TO PIT AND FISSURE SEALANTS

Dental sealants may be contraindicated for children and/or adults who:
- Have shallow pits and fissures or very little occlusal anatomy present
- Have deciduous teeth that will be exfoliated soon
- Have overt carious lesions present; a restoration is needed instead of a sealant
- Have the presence of interproximal decay
- Have a partially erupted tooth
- Lack the ability to cooperate with the dental team during placement

TYPES OF SEALANT MATERIALS

There are hundreds of dental sealant products on the market today. There is not one product that is superior over another. It simply comes down to operator preference. There are several sealant materials that have gained popularity mainly due to their ease of use and operator satisfaction. All sealant materials work if used and placed properly.

It is very important to read the manufacturer's instructions for each sealant kit - not all sealant kits are created equal. It is never a good idea to mix sealant products from multiple kits based on the varied content from one kit to another.

For example:
- Some sealant kits contain an etchant material, while others do not.
- Some sealant kits require a priming step using a priming agent, while others do not.
- Some sealant kits contain sealant material that appears colored for ease of placement and then turns opaque following curing. NOTE: In some cases, a clear sealant may be more difficult to evaluate.
- Some sealant materials are filled while others are unfilled – see description below.
- Some sealant materials release fluoride while others do not.
- Some sealant materials have a thicker viscosity than others.

Each of the described characteristics will differ depending upon the sealant brand. The dental assistant must always read the manufacturer's instructions before any dental material is utilized.

FILLED VS. UNFILLED DENTAL SEALANT MATERIALS

Dental sealant materials are a form of resin or plastic. Sealants are available as **filled or unfilled** resins. The manufacturer chooses whether their sealant material will contain fillers. Fillers are added to the resin to make it more resistant to wear. However, filled and unfilled resins are equally successful at penetrating the pits and fissures of occlusal anatomy, have similar retention rates and show no difference in microleakage. Simply stated, there is no difference in the quality of the sealant being placed using a filled versus an unfilled sealant material. It ultimately ends up becoming operator preference.

The California RDA General Written and Law Examination Prep Book © 2017, 2018 • KB Dental Arts – Publisher

One important note - a filled sealant material will require the operator to check the patient's occlusion following placement of the sealant. If the sealant appears too high, it will need to be adjusted with a handpiece and bur. This is not a necessary step when using an unfilled sealant material as the patient's natural bite will establish the occlusion.

POLYMERIZATION

Polymerization is a dental term for describing the process of curing, or hardening, of a material. There are many products in dentistry that undergo a polymerization process and sealant materials are just one example. There are three (3) types of setting processes:

1. **Light-Cure:** a process of polymerization of resin-based materials including dental sealants and composite restorations. There is no mixing of materials required with light-cured sealants.
2. **Self-Cure** (also called Auto-Polymerization): the process is achieved by placing the material and then waiting the specified amount of time for a chemical reaction to occur with the material that leads to its setting. Sealant materials using the self-cure method require the mixture of a base and catalyst that typically sets within one (1) to two (2) minutes.
3. **Dual-Cure:** the process is achieved by placing the material and then waiting a specified amount of time for an initial cure to occur (based on manufacturer's instructions). The polymerization process is completed by using the curing light for one (1) to two (2) minutes.

Of the three (3) polymerization methods discussed, the light-cure process is the most common and popular with today's dental sealant materials. Due to the flowable nature of the sealant materials, operators prefer to cure the material as quickly as possible.

STORAGE AND USE

Guidelines for storage and use of sealant materials:

- Always replace caps on syringes and bottles immediately after use
- Do not expose the materials to high temperatures
- Most etchant and sealant materials are designed to be used at room temperatures
- Check the manufacturer's instructions
- The shelf life of most sealant materials stored at room temperature range from 18 to 36 months

ETCHANT MATERIALS

The enamel surface is prepared for sealant placement by using a 37% phosphoric acid called **etch or etchant gel**. The gel appears light to dark blue in color and serves to roughen the enamel, opening the enamel rods, which dehydrates or desiccates the enamel. The etchant material opens up these "pores" (rods) allowing the resin sealant material to mechanically interlock with the enamel. The etch remains on the tooth structure for 15 to 20 seconds (or the manufacturer's recommended time) followed by rinsing.

Care should also be taken not to touch the lips, cheeks, tongue or gingiva with the etching material. It is unhealthy, and possibly damaging for soft tissue to come in contact with the etchant. It also tastes very bitter, so avoiding the tongue is of particular importance, especially if working on children. It is recommended that the flow of the etchant material be tested by the operator on a piece of 2 x 2 gauze prior to dispensing in a patient's mouth to ensure a smooth flow free from air bubbles.

Additionally, a **self-etch adhesive** is an etchant, primer and adhesive all together in one step. The materials are activated by mixing all together and placing directly onto the enamel to be sealed. A scrubbing motion is used when placing the material onto the tooth surface. Following placement, the surface is simply air dried. The area is not rinsed or cured. While this is a different technique of etching, it is still considered an etching process as the enamel rods are being roughened and opened up to allow for mechanical interlocking of the soon to be placed sealant material and the enamel.

ISOLATION, SEALANT RETENTION AND SEALANT FAILURE

Isolation and moisture control are the most important steps in sealant placement. As the operator, it is extremely important to prevent moisture from contaminating the tooth structure especially following the etching process. Cotton rolls are the quickest, most efficient form of isolation and moisture control for the oral cavity. Moisture contamination is the number one reason why sealants fail.

Sealant retention refers to the length of time in which the sealant remains in place and prevents decay. A properly placed sealant can be effective for 10 years.

DENTAL SEALANT ARMAMENTARIUM, EQUIPMENT AND SUPPLIES

The following is essential to a successful dental sealant procedure:
- Protective eyewear for patient and operator/personal protective equipment
- Basic set-up
- Etchant material
- Sealant material
- Applicator tips/syringes
- Prophy angle with cup/brush and handpiece
- Abrasive agent: pumice and water
- Cotton rolls
- Curing light with shield
- HVE/saliva ejector/air-water syringe tips (disposable)
- Articulating paper and holder
- Floss
- Adjusting materials (if needed)
- Caries detection device (optional)

DENTAL SEALANT PROCEDURAL STEPS

The following is a generalized guide to sealant procedure steps. Each sealant kit will differ slightly in its step placement. Please remember to review the manufacturer's instructions for that particular sealant kit. The key technique-point to remind oneself when placing sealant material is to make "a river, not a lake." Think of the cusps as being mountains and the central groove as being a river that runs along the valley floor. The goal of sealant placement is to place a thin protective barrier; therefore, we want to create a small river along the central groove on occlusal surfaces. In other words, do not overfill the grooves with sealant material as it will interfere with the patient's occlusion and ultimately cause the sealant to fail.

Prepare room for treatment of patient. Be certain to check the following:
- light curing device – turn device on and test for accuracy of ultraviolet light;
- air/water syringe – test on a paper tray liner or glove to be certain water is not leaking into air flow (water contamination will cause failure in retention);

The California RDA General Written and Law Examination Prep Book © 2017, 2018 • KB Dental Arts – Publisher

- place all necessary barriers including curing light sleeve;
- tray/instrument set-up;
- personal protective equipment ready;
- clean patient/operator goggles; and
- advise patient of the procedure and all post-operative instructions, including oral hygiene review.

Step 1 – Isolation:

Cotton roll or rubber dam isolation is essential to successful sealant placement. If rubber dam isolation is utilized, be certain that the clamp does not impinge on the tissue surrounding the tooth or teeth being isolated. Should this procedure be uncomfortable to the patient, cotton-roll isolation is adequate.

Be certain to place a saliva ejector as close to the cotton rolls as possible and secure the device to avoid movement or slipping. If necessary, ask the patient to hold the saliva ejector tubing.

Step 2 - Clean:

Once isolated, the occlusal surface of the tooth being sealed may be cleaned thoroughly with a prophy paste, a dry brushing, or wetted pumice to remove abundant or residual plaque. Although most sealant manufacturers no longer recommend pre-cleaning the surface, it is easy to find that large particles of food debris are not removed via the etchant process and hampers adhesion. At one time it was recommended not to use fluoridated paste; however, prophy pastes contain a small percentage of fluoride.

In a comparison of different cleaning pastes with or without fluoride, used before composite restorations and sealant procedures, no difference was found between bond strengths.

In the event an air abrasion/air polishing device is used for cleaning, it is imperative that a rinse of hydrogen peroxide be applied to the abraded surface prior to acid etching due to the use of sodium bicarbonate in the air device. Peroxide should be flushed directly onto etched/air abraded surface (using a syringe) for no less than 15 seconds, followed by a thorough drying for another ten seconds, followed by acid etchant procedures. This three-step process should be repeated to remove the base of sodium bicarbonate. For this reason, it is not recommended to use an air abrasion device.

Step 3 – Etch:

Apply an etchant (phosphoric acid) to the enamel surface using a syringe tip or application device. The manufacturer's instructions should be followed.

The use of a colored etching solution (such as blue) allows for targeted product application into the fissure. The acid results in a porous or roughened surface that allows the sealant material to mechanically interlock with the enamel to facilitates a stable, long-term bond.

Step 4 – Rinse:

The operator uses a combination of water and HVE to gently remove the etchant gel. Place the HVE close to the tooth to remove all rinse water prior to the fluid contacting the patients tongue and to avoid fluid/etchant from flooding the patient's mouth.

If saliva should come in contact with the newly etched tooth, re-etch for 5 to 10 seconds only.

Once irrigated, dry the etched surface for a full ten seconds, keeping the high-volume suction close to the surface being dried. Be certain the air from the syringe does not contain moisture droplets or oily particles. Make certain the rest of the mouth is dry so that you are not blowing saliva or moisture onto the newly etched surface. The dried

The California RDA General Written and Law Examination Prep Book © 2017, 2018 • KB Dental Arts – Publisher

surface should appear "sanded" or abraded, as if a light rub of sand paper were used on the surface. There should be no appearance of a shine to the etched surface.

Step 5 – Apply Sealant Material:

If using an applicator device or syringe tip, test the flow of the product before entering the patient's mouth. This small test of the material will allow for accurate placement and eliminate any air bubbles that may be present.

Following the manufacturer's directions, apply sealant material using an applicator or syringe tip, slowly placing material into the pits and fissures of the tooth. Do not allow material to seep beyond the etched areas of the tooth. Do not allow the sealant material to completely fill the pit or fissure where it may interfere with occlusion. Overfilling will cause failure of the sealant. Accuracy of material placement is essential to the overall success of the sealant.

An explorer may be used to run through the placed material, gently manipulating bubbles or voids in the material. The use of a microbrush applicator will remove overflow or excess material.

Step 6 – Cure Sealant Material:

Polymerize using a suitable ultraviolet light source for 20 seconds unless otherwise indicated by the product instructions. The cure tip should be placed as close as possible to the sealant without touching it. Curing lights emitting light within the wavelength range of 350–450 nm and a light intensity of over 300 mW can cure the range of sealant materials available.

The blue light in a traditional curing light has appropriate filtration at the light source to eliminate any stray ultraviolet radiation. Although there is minimal potential for radiation damage, caution and eye protection should always be used by the operator to protect/prevent damage to the retina of the eye. All curing lights should be checked routinely to confirm their output and to avoid under-curing.

Step 7 – Evaluation:

Check the sealant for:

- accuracy of placement
- potential voids (missing areas) and bubbles
- overfill of product within the margins of the etched area

The product should not look like a traditional restoration but rather small filler within the fissure of the occlusal surface.

Once isolation is removed, be certain to check the interproximal spaces with floss to ensure product has not leached into the contact areas. Using a water-dampened cotton-tip applicator, wipe the surface of the sealant to remove any residual film or residue of uncured resin, as this may be sticky and noticeable to the patient when occluding. Check the occlusion using articulating paper and adjust if required.

NO ETCH SEALANT MATERIAL & PROCEDURAL STEPS

The "no-rinse" sealant placement technique uses a self-etching dental adhesive to bond the sealant to the tooth.

Unidose L-Pop delivery system

Indications for Use:
- Bonding light-cured composite and compomer materials to dentin and enamel
- Desensitization of exposed root surfaces
- Bonding of light-cure resin-based pit and fissure sealants

<u>Self-etch Adhesive Clinical Technique</u>
- Thoroughly clean the teeth to remove plaque and debris from the enamel surfaces and fissures
- Do not use any cleaning medium that may contain fluoride or oils as it may affect the adhesion value
- Rinse thoroughly with water and dry
- Isolate the tooth (e.g. with cotton rolls, rubber dam)
- Dry the surface to be sealed
- Activate the L-Pop

Self-Etch Adhesive: L-Pop Activation

Squeeze the material from the red reservoir into the yellow (middle) reservoir.

The middle reservoir will expand indicating proper transfer of fluid.

Fold back the red reservoir until it meets the flat face of the yellow reservoir.

Keep the red reservoir tightly squeezed while bending the package to prevent the material from flowing back.

Squeeze the liquid from the yellow reservoir into the blue reservoir.

Apply a churning or spinning motion to the applicator for five seconds to mix the adhesive and fully coat the applicator tip.

A lightly yellow-tinted applicator tip indicates proper activation. If a yellow color is not obtained unfold the L-Pop, reactivate, and apply a spinning motion to the applicator for five seconds to mix the adhesive.

Apply adhesive onto the surface to be sealed; scrub for 15 seconds applying moderate finger pressure. Do not shorten this time.

Proper bonding will not occur if the solution is simply applied and dispersed.

Use a gentle stream of air to thoroughly dry the adhesive to a thin film (approximately 10 seconds).

If the stream of air is too forceful, the adhesive will be blown off the tooth.

The tooth surface will not appear frosty as in the "traditional" technique.

Apply a light-cured sealant material.

Light-cure the sealant and adhesive together with a halogen, LED or plasma light for the amount of time specified to cure the sealant.

Check sealant coverage, occlusion, and wipe the surface of the sealant material clean using a wet cotton-tipped applicator; this removes the "smear" layer or tackiness of the material used.

BENEFITS OF NO-RINSE TECHNIQUE

- No rinsing involved (means no bitter taste, which can increase salivary flow and affect isolation)
- Adper Prompts are simple to use and will etch any uncut enamel surface
- Sealant is actually being bonded to the tooth (same concept as bonding a composite)
- Less micro-leakage compared to the traditional technique means less chance of recurrent decay/better retention
- Decreases challenge of patient management
- Saves time compared to the traditional technique

PRECAUTIONS WHEN PLACING DENTAL SEALANTS AND ETCHANTS

Be careful of the following pitfalls when placing dental sealants:

- Take care when using phosphoric etchant to avoid soft tissues, skin and eyes
- Wear PPE at all times when placing sealants
- Use both operator and patient protective eyewear
- Know the sealant material being utilized; refer to manufacturer's instructions
- Review the patient's medical history for acrylate allergies; sealants should not be used on patients with this reported allergy
- Use isolation techniques
- Keep the area as free from moisture contamination as possible
- Do not seal a patient's contact! Remember that sealant material is placed in the pits and fissures only; check all contacts with floss prior to dismissal

CHAPTER REVIEW COMMENTS:

The RDA state examination includes questions pertaining to coronal polishing and sealants although the candidate may have already completed certification courses in these two areas; however, the Dental Board wants to ensure competency in the theoretical aspects of both of these preventive procedures – each being technique-sensitive procedures.

Only licensed Registered Dental Assistants can perform these two preventive procedures even if certification course completion has been accomplished. Dental Assistants certified in Coronal Polish and Sealants will need to wait to perform these two procedures, even if delegated by the employing dentist, until RDA licensure is obtained.

END OF CHAPTER - CRITICAL THINKING QUESTIONS:

1. What is a preventive procedure?
2. What are the two common preventive procedures performed by RDA's?
3. When may a dental assistant perform the function of Coronal Polishing?
4. Why is a fulcrum important when Coronal Polishing?
5. Who may legally place a dental sealant?
6. What is the difference between a filled and an unfilled sealant material?
7. What does polymerization mean?
8. What is the life expectancy of a properly placed sealant?

CRITICAL THINKING QUESTION ANSWERS FOUND IN APPENDIX

The California RDA General Written and Law Examination Prep Book © 2017, 2018 • KB Dental Arts – Publisher

Notes

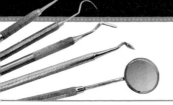

Unit 3 - Chapter 1

UNIT THREE – DENTAL SPECIALTY PROCEDURES
CHAPTER ONE: ENDODONTIC & PERIODONTAL PROCEDURES

EXAMINATION PLAN DATA:

Topic Area	Dental Specialty Procedures
Total Weight of Topic Area on Examination	10%
Subject Area	Endodontic Procedures
Percentage of Examination Questions in Endodontics	2%

ENDODONTIC PROCEDURES – TASKS AND KNOWLEDGE STATEMENTS

Tasks Associated with Topic Area	Knowledge Statements Associated with Topic Area
Test pulp vitality	Knowledge of techniques and procedures for testing pulp vitality
Dry canals with absorbent points	Knowledge of techniques and procedures for measuring canal length and size
	Knowledge of scope of practice for RDA's and RDAEF's related to initial pulp vitality testing and other endodontic procedures

SCOPE OF PRACTICE – SPECIFIC TO ENDODONTIC PROCEDURES

Registered Dental Assistant	Registered Dental Assistant in Extended Functions
Pulp vitality testing and recording of findings	Size and fit endodontic master points and accessory points
Dry endodontically treated canals using absorbent paper points	Cement endodontic master points and accessory points

KEY TERMS

Abscess	An infection within the bone commonly found at the tip of the root; referred to as the apical abscess
Apex	The clinical tip of the root
Apicoectomy	Surgical endodontic procedure involving the removal of the tip of the root
Dental Dam	Rubber sheet used to isolate a tooth or series of teeth; prevents materials from entering the oral cavity; prevents salivary contamination of the working area

Endodontist	A dentist with advanced education specializing in endodontic therapy
Gutta Percha	Plastic-like final canal filling material used to replace the removed pulp from the root canal space(s)
Necrotic	Dead tissue; term used to describe a dead pulp
Obturate	Fill the canal with gutta percha
Paper Points	Used to dry canal(s) of the tooth after final filing, shaping and irrigating; used prior to the placement and cementation of the gutta percha
Pulp/Pulpal	The nerve of the tooth; pulpal refers to the area of the tooth that is the pulp
Pulpectomy	Complete removal of the tooth pulp
Pulpitis	Inflammation of the tooth pulp (nerve)
Pulpotomy	Partial removal of the tooth pulp
Radiographic Apex	The visual tip of the root; used to visually measure the length of the canals before, during and after endodontic treatment
RCT	Root Canal Therapy or Root Canal Treatment
Sodium Hypochloride	Bleach solution used to irrigate and disinfect canal spaces during the filing and shaping process
Vital	Live tissue; a positive response to stimuli indicates that the tooth is still alive

Endodontics is a specialty of dentistry focused on the prevention, diagnosis and treatment of the dental pulp. Endodontics is usually associated with performing root canal treatment or therapy, also referred to as **RCT**.

The **pulp** is often referred to as the nerve of the tooth. It is helpful think of the pulp as the "heart" of the tooth. If the "heart" becomes damaged or irritated, it will become sick and can die. If pulp tissue dies, or becomes **necrotic**, root canal therapy is needed.

The need for educated, knowledgeable dental assistants is crucial when performing endodontic procedures. There are several key points during endodontic procedures, such as pulp testing and drying the canals, where a qualified dental assistant can be fully utilized.

The California RDA General Written and Law Examination Prep Book © 2017, 2018 • KB Dental Arts – Publisher
This book and the individual contributions contained within are protected under Copyright by the Publisher

There are two (2) main causes of pulpal damage to a tooth. They are:

1. Extensive **dental decay** that reaches the pulp. Dental decay contains bacteria and therefore destroys the pulp.
2. **Trauma** such as a fall or car accident; the teeth or surrounding tissues are damaged and traumatized by the forces of external trauma. Internal trauma can affect pulp vitality as well – biting into an olive pit or foreign substance causing a tooth to fracture or chip.

Each patient will experience pulpal discomfort and symptoms differently; however, some commonly reported symptoms are:

1. Pain while chewing or biting
2. Sensitivity to temperatures of food and drink
3. Swelling of the face

The symptomatic patient will call the dental office for an appointment. At the appointment, the dental team will investigate what is causing the patient's discomfort by performing two types of examinations on the patient, the subjective and the objective examination.

1. Subjective Examination

   The patient explains their symptoms to the dental assistant; the dental assistant should be knowledgeable of what questions to ask to gather needed information for the dentist.
   - Establish the chief complaint – identify the tooth or area causing the pain
   - Establish a description for the type of pain experienced and for what length of time
   - Establish the cause of the pain – identify the stimuli causing the pain
   - Establish the presence of both thermal and masticatory pain – heat, cold, chewing, biting pressure

The dental assistant will note the patient's chief complaint in the chart and report all findings to the endodontist or general dentist. If an additional radiograph is needed, the clinical assistant will perform while the objective examination begins.

2. Objective Examination
   - The endodontist/dentist considers the information gathered from the subjective exam, the radiograph and what they visually see regarding the health of the tooth.
   - The endodontist is looking for the following:
     ○ Swelling of the face or gingival tissues around the questionable tooth
     ○ Present decay and its extent around the questionable tooth
     ○ Tooth mobility
     ○ Periodontal issues with the questionable tooth
     ○ A recently placed large restoration in the questionable tooth
     ○ Pulpal exposure of the questionable tooth

There are several methods for testing pulp vitality. The dentist or endodontist will explain each of the tests that will be performed helping the patient understand the process. The dentist will typically pick one or two pulp vitality tests to assist in arriving at a proper diagnosis. It is important to note that with each method of pulp testing a control tooth is utilized for comparison.

A **control tooth** is a healthy tooth, similar in size to the suspect tooth, selected from the opposite quadrant on the same arch to test and determine a "normal" response. For example, the suspect tooth is #3, the maxillary right first molar; therefore, the control tooth would be #14, the maxillary left first molar.

PULP VITALITY TESTING

1. Palpation

The dentist/endodontist uses his/her index finger and applies pressure at the apical area of the suspect tooth looking for the presence of swelling or discomfort.

2. Percussion

The dentist/endodontist uses the end of a mouth mirror to gently tap on the occlusal or incisal surface of the tooth parallel to the long axis of the tooth. The dentist is noting any patient discomfort, sensitivity and/or swelling.

3. Thermal Testing

The dentist utilizes cold and hot temperatures to determine the health status of the pulp. If the pulp is necrotic, or dead, it will not respond to hot or cold temperatures. If a tooth is in the process of necrosis (the process of dying) it may respond to either hot or cold depending on the disease level of the pulp.

Ice or dry ice is used for the cold test. The cold is placed on the cervical third of the control tooth and then placed on the cervical third of the questionable tooth. The patient's responses are noted and compared. The heat test is performed by using a small amount of heated gutta percha on the end of an instrument.

Gutta percha is the filling material used for obturating, or filling, the root canals during an endodontic procedure, but is useful for this diagnostic test as well. The heated gutta percha is placed on the cervical third of the control tooth and then placed on the cervical third of the questionable tooth.

The patient's responses are noted and compared. It is important for the dental assistant to be aware that thermal testing should not be placed on a restoration or on gingival tissue. This could cause damage to tissue and an inaccurate response from the tooth. The most accurate responses will come from placing the temperatures against enamel.

4. Electric Pulp Testing

Electric pulp testing is performed by using a wand attached to a machine or handheld device called a **pulp tester** or **vitalometer**. A **necrotic pulp** will not respond to electric pulp testing. Like the other tests, the results are supported by other findings during the subjective and objective examinations. Vitalometers, or pulp testers, deliver a low electrical current or stimulus to the tooth. The patient will feel a warmth or tingling sensation.

The vitalometer is tested on the control tooth first, then the suspect tooth is tested. Below are general steps in using the vitalometer:

1. The tooth is isolated and dried
2. Apply a small amount of toothpaste to the tip of the tester as a conductor
3. The dial is set to "0" (zero) and the tip of the tester is placed on the middle third of the tooth (the control tooth will be tested first and then the suspect tooth)
4. Increase the dial level slightly until the patient responds
5. Record the number reading

RADIOGRAPHS

Radiographs are extremely important when working endodontically on a tooth. Since the dental team cannot see through the tooth to the canal(s), dental radiographs are the principle tools used during the procedure, assessing the progress at each key step. Of primary use is the **periapical** image – the only radiograph used in endodontic procedures to diagnose, treat and follow-up on the root and apex of each tooth.

A series of five (5) periapical x-rays are taken while performing a root canal:

1. Initial x-ray:
    *   This film is taken when the dentist/endodontist diagnoses the condition of the pulp. The dentist may request the dental assistant take this x-ray after the subjective exam but prior to the objective examination.
2. Working length x-ray:
    *   Once the access to the pulp has been gained, this film helps the endodontist/dentist determine the length of the canal(s). Typically, the dentist will leave a file in place while the x-ray is taken as a measurement guide. The assistant should warn the patient not to bite down or close.
3. Final instrumentation x-ray:
    *   This x-ray is taken when treatment is nearing completion. The final size files are left in place while this x-ray is taken as a guide. Again, the assistant should warn the patient not bite down or close all the way if the rubber dam is removed.
4. RCT final x-ray:
    *   A final radiograph is taken when the canals have been filled with gutta percha and the tooth has been temporized. The RCT is complete.
5. Post treatment x-ray (sometimes called the recall x-ray):
    *   This film is taken approximately six months after treatment. The purpose is to evaluate how the area is healing especially if an abscess was present at the time of treatment. An abscess creates a hole in the alveolar bone.

Endodontic radiographs should be free from elongation or foreshortening errors as they can interfere with the dentist's ability to accurately measure the canal(s). Periapical radiographs must show the apex and surrounding tissues and bone clearly; a minimum of 8 – 10 millimeters of periapical bone is considered an endodontic-quality radiograph.

ROOT CANAL LENGTH AND SIZE

The endodontist or general dentist determines canal length and size by utilizing the initial and working length radiographs. Endodontic files, either hand or rotary style, are used to clean (debride) and shape the canals along with irrigating solution.

The irrigating solution (commonly sodium hypochloride) helps to destroy bacteria present along the root canal walls and flush debrided canals during treatment. Rubber stops are used on endodontic files to prevent the dentist from working beyond the apex, perforating (puncturing) the apex or the side of the root. The dental assistant will set the stoppers on the files to the millimeter (mm) length determined by the dentist. Additionally, the canal length and size are important for measuring the absorbent paper points.

ABSORBENT PAPER POINTS

After the canal(s) have been instrumented, cleaned and shaped thoroughly, a final irrigation is performed by the dentist, followed by drying of the canals with absorbent paper points prior to filling the canal(s). The RDA can complete this portion of the procedure for the dentist, if delegated.

– 117 –

Paper points range in size from extra-fine, fine, medium, coarse and extra-coarse. The paper point is measured approximately 1mm shorter than the working length of the canal. Several points should be pre-measured and set before needed. The measured paper point is placed into the canal using cotton pliers. The wet paper point is discarded; additional points are used until a paper point emerges from the canal dry. Once the canal(s) is dry, the assistant should count the number of paper points used and record in the chart.

EXAMINATION PLAN DATA:

Topic Area	Dental Specialty Procedures
Total Weight of Topic Area on Examination	10%
Subject Area	Periodontal Procedures
Percentage of Examination Questions in Periodontal	1%

PERIODONTAL PROCEDURES – TASKS AND KNOWLEDGE STATEMENTS

Tasks Associated with Topic Area	Knowledge Statements Associated with Topic Area
Place periodontal dressings at surgical site	Knowledge of scope of practice for RDA's and RDAEF's related to the placement of periodontal dressing materials
	Knowledge of types of periodontal dressings and techniques for their application

SCOPE OF PRACTICE – SPECIFIC TO PERIODONTAL PROCEDURES

Unlicensed Dental Assistant	Registered Dental Assistant
Remove periodontal dressings	Place and remove periodontal dressings

Licensed Registered Dental Assistant in Extended Functions (RDAEF):

While there is nothing specifically listed for periodontal procedures under the RDAEF category, it is important to note the following, as taken from the table of allowable duties for a RDAEF:

(a) A registered dental assistant in extended functions licensed on or after January 1, 2010, is authorized to perform all duties and procedures that a registered dental assistant is authorized to perform and those duties that the board may prescribe by regulation.

KEY TERMS

Periodontal Dressing	A pliable material placed directly over the surgical site while the area heals
Periodontics	Specialty of dentistry focused on the health of the periodontium
Periodontist	Dental specialist with an advanced education in periodontics
Periodontium	Consists of the alveolar bone, periodontal ligaments and gingiva

Periodontal and Post-Extraction dressings are used following surgical procedures. The dental specialty of **Periodontics** is focused on the health of the periodontium. The **periodontium** consists of the alveolar bone, periodontal ligaments and the gingiva, commonly referred to as the supporting structures of the teeth. Periodontal surgery is typically recommended when treatments such as scaling and root planing, increased dental cleanings and more aggressive home care and/or gingival curettage do not succeed in halting the disease process. When surgery is indicated, a periodontal dressing needs to be placed prior to patient dismissal.

A **periodontal dressing**, commonly referred to as Perio Pak, is a pliable material that is placed directly over the surgical site serving as protection for the area during healing. Periodontal dressing is often referred to as a "bandage" for the surgical area.

TYPES OF PERIODONTAL DRESSINGS

1. ZOE Dressing (Zinc Oxide- Eugenol)
   - Supplied as a powder/liquid
   - Provides excellent protection of the surgical site
   - Is mixed on a paper pad
   - Difficult to mix
   - Slow set allows for longer working time
   - Material is rolled into "worm" like strips
   - Can be mixed, rolled and stored (in refrigerator) ahead of time

2. Non-Eugenol Dressing
   - Most commonly used Perio Pak
   - Supplied two ways: Two (2) tubes (Base & Catalyst) and Auto Mix Gun Technique
   - Easy to mix and place on patient
   - Enhanced patient comfort
   - Is mixed on a paper pad with a tongue depressor with two-tube method
   - Sets quickly if exposed to warmth
   - Material can be rolled into "worm" like strips with two-tube method
   - Material is mixed and dispensed directly from auto mix tip onto surgical area with the auto mix gun technique
   - Cannot be mixed, rolled or stored ahead of time

PREPARATION METHODS OF PERIO PAK

Since non-eugenol Perio Pak is the most common and modern type, we will focus on the two-tube method of preparation and the auto mix gun technique.

Coe Pak – Two-tube Perio Pak – Base and Catalyst
1. Place out armamentarium: Base and Catalyst, tongue depressor, large paper mixing pad, disposable cup with room temperature water, and water.
2. On the paper pad, dispense equal lengths of base and catalyst.
3. With tongue depressor, mix the base and catalyst together until homogeneous (all one color; no streaks should be present).
4. When the material is no longer tacky, scoop up with tongue depressor and place into the cup of water.
5. Get gloved fingers moist with water and remove mixture from cup.
6. Roll the paste into strips, approximately the thickness of a "worm" and the length of the surgical area.

The California RDA General Written and Law Examination Prep Book © 2017, 2018 • KB Dental Arts – Publisher

7. Roll two (2) strips, one for the buccal and one for the lingual; set aside a small amount of material for the interproximal spaces.

Auto mix gun technique-cartridge contains base and catalyst – auto mix tip
1. Place out armamentarium: dispensing gun, Perio Pak Cartridge, auto mix tip.
2. Assemble the gun, cartridge and the auto mix tip (the base and catalyst are mixed in the auto mix tip eliminating the need for hand mixing).
3. Prepare patient for placement (the material is placed directly from the auto mix tip to the surgical site).

PLACEMENT TECHNIQUES

Placement of the Coe Pak Dressing:
1. Following material preparation, the surgical area should be prepared by gently drying the area with sterile 2 x 2 gauze.
2. Place a small triangle shaped piece of periodontal dressing into the interproximal spaces (on both the buccal and lingual surfaces) using the set aside material.
3. Taking one of the rolled strips, press one end around the most distal surface of the last tooth on the buccal/facial surface in the surgical area.
4. The rest of the strip will be placed along the buccal/facial aspect of the surgical area moving mesially towards the anterior.
5. Once adapted to the small pieces of dressing already inserted into the interproximal areas, repeat the same steps on the lingual.
6. Interlock the periodontal dressing by making sure the ends of the dressing are adapted together and the strips from the buccal and lingual surfaces are touching through the interproximal. When the periodontal dressing sets the material will set or "lock" together.

It is important to note that periodontal dressing should be placed on the gingiva along the surgical site and not sit lower than the gingival third of the teeth. The dressing should not interfere with the patient's occlusion and should not extend into the mucco-buccal fold or floor of the mouth. This will cause irritation and the patient will likely pick at the dressing causing it to break off. The patient should be instructed not to brush or floss the surgical area. Periodontal dressing frequently covers sutures without harming or displacing the suture.

PLACEMENT OF THE AUTO MIX GUN TECHNIQUE:
1. The cartridge containing the dressing material should be bled prior to inserting the auto mix tip to ensure a smooth flow during placement.
2. The auto mix tip is placed on the cartridge and the base and catalyst are mixed through the tip.
3. The surgical area is gently dried with sterile 2 x 2 gauze.
4. The auto mix tip dispenses the periodontal dressing directly onto the surgical site beginning with the most distal surface of the last tooth on the buccal/facial surface in the surgical area moving mesially towards the anterior.
5. The material is adapted as quickly and efficiently as possible gently pressing material into the interproximal and along the surgical area.
6. This is repeated on the lingual surface.
7. Interlock the periodontal dressing by making sure the ends of the dressing are adapted together and the strips from the buccal and lingual surfaces are touching through the interproximal. When the periodontal dressing sets, the material will "lock" together.

END OF CHAPTER – CRITICAL THINKING QUESTIONS

ENDODONTIC PROCEDURES CRITICAL THINKING QUESTIONS:

1. What is the definition of endodontics?

2. What are the two main causes of pulpal damage?

3. What is the difference between a subjective exam and an objective exam?

4. Give an example of a question a dental assistant could ask during the subjective exam.

5. What is a control tooth? Why is a control tooth important?

6. Name and describe the four pulp vitality tests utilized for endodontic testing.

7. Why are radiographs important while performing an endodontic procedure?

8. How does the dentist determine canal length?

9. What is the purpose of paper points? Why are they an important step?

10. Name the conditions a dentist is searching for relating to the health of the tooth during the objective exam.

PERIODONTAL PROCEDURES CRITICAL THINKING QUESTIONS:

1. The specialty of periodontics is concerned with what?

2. What structures of the oral cavity make up the periodontium?

3. What is Perio Pak? What purpose does it serve?

4. Name and describe each type of periodontal dressing.

CRITICAL THINKING QUESTION ANSWERS FOUND IN APPENDIX

The California RDA General Written and Law Examination Prep Book © 2017, 2018 • KB Dental Arts – Publisher

Notes

Unit Three

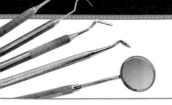
UNIT THREE – DENTAL SPECIALTY PROCEDURES
CHAPTER TWO: ORTHODONTIC PROCEDURES

EXAMINATION PLAN DATA:

Topic Area	Dental Specialty Procedures
Total Weight of Topic Area on Examination	10%
Subject Area	Orthodontic Procedures
Percentage of Examination Questions in Orthodontics	3%

ORTHODONTIC PROCEDURES – TASKS AND KNOWLEDGE STATEMENTS

Tasks Associated with Topic Area	Knowledge Statements Associated with Topic Area
Place orthodontic separators	Knowledge of scope of practice for RDA's and RDAEF's related to the placement of orthodontic materials
Place and remove ligature ties and arch wires	Knowledge of techniques for placement and removal of orthodontic separators and bands, arch wires and ties
Place elastic ties to secure arch wires	Knowledge of techniques for placement and removal of orthodontic appliances
Remove orthodontic bands	Knowledge of types of materials for taking impressions for removable orthodontic appliances and the techniques for their application
Take impression for fixed and removable orthodontic appliances	

SCOPE OF PRACTICE – SPECIFIC TO ORTHODONTIC PROCEDURES

Unlicensed Dental Assistant	Registered Dental Assistant
Perform measurements for the purposes of orthodontic treatment	All DA duties
Place and remove orthodontic separators	Place ligature ties and archwires
Examine orthodontic appliances	Remove orthodontic bands
Cure restorative or orthodontic materials in operative site with a light-curing device	
Remove ligature ties and archwires	
After adjustment by the dentist, examine and seat removable orthodontic appliances and deliver care instructions to the patient	

A registered dental assistant may only perform the following additional duties if he or she has completed a board-approved registered dental assistant educational program in those duties, or if he or she has provided evidence, satisfactory to the board, of having completed a board-approved course in those duties.

>   (1) Remove excess cement with an ultrasonic scaler from supragingival surfaces of teeth undergoing orthodontic treatment.
>   (2) The allowable duties of an orthodontic assistant permit holder.

Licensed Registered Dental Assistant in Extended Functions (RDAEF):
While there is nothing specifically listed for orthodontic procedures under the RDAEF category, it is important to note the following, as taken from the table of allowable duties for the RDAEF:

(a) A registered dental assistant in extended functions licensed on or after January 1, 2010, is authorized to perform all duties and procedures that a registered dental assistant is authorized to perform and those duties that the board may prescribe by regulation.

NOTE: Please remember that the category of Orthodontics has its own Permit entitled the **Orthodontic Assistant Permit** (OAP). The OAP holder is allowed to perform an array of orthodontic procedures not allowable under the DA, RDA, and RDAEF categories. This exam prep book is focused only on preparation for the blended RDA Written Examination.

KEY TERMS

Malocclusion	Improper contact of the teeth when they contact
Occlusion	Contact between teeth when they bite closed
Orthodontics	Dental specialty interested in the prevention, diagnosis, interception and treatment of malocclusion
Orthodontist	Dental specialist with advanced education in orthodontics
Archwire	A wire shaped to conform to the dental arch that can be used with dental braces as a source of force in correcting irregularities in the position of the teeth; archwires can also be used to maintain existing dental positions
Bracket	Small metal or ceramic attachments used to fasten or secure an archwire. These attachments are soldered or welded to an orthodontic band or cemented directly onto the teeth
Orthodontic Bands	Pre-formed stainless-steel bands fitted around the teeth and cemented into place; used to anchor an appliance to the teeth or secure an archwire to the molars
Separator	Elastomeric or spring devices that assist in creating 1 mm of separation between contacts, so the orthodontic band can be properly seated.
Ligature Tie	An elastomeric tie or wire tie that encircles the bracket around the tie wings securing the arch wire to the fixed appliance

Orthodontics is the specialty of dentistry interested in the prevention, diagnosis, interception and treatment of malocclusion. Orthodontists are concerned with correcting function first and then esthetics. **Occlusion** means simply the contact between teeth. More technically, it is the relationship between the maxillary and mandibular teeth when they approach each other. **Malocclusion** refers to teeth not properly meeting due to a variety of reasons. Malocclusion interferes with proper function.

Angle's three classifications of malocclusion are:

1. **Class I:** normal molar relationship, but the anterior teeth are crowded or rotated
2. **Class II:** known as the "bucktooth" appearance, the maxillary anterior teeth protrude over the mandibular anterior teeth excessively; molars are not in proper alignment; also referred to as distoclusion
3. **Class III:** known as the "bulldog" appearance, the mandibular anterior teeth protrude over the maxillary anterior teeth excessively; molars are not in proper alignment; also referred to as mesioclusion

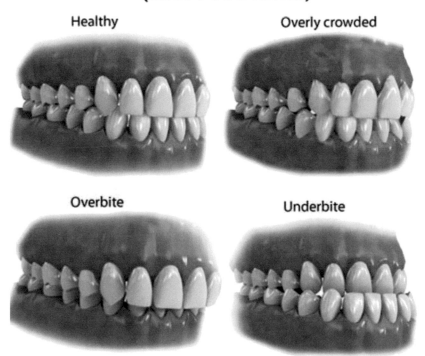

Malocclusions
(Bite Problems)

Healthy   Overly crowded

Overbite   Underbite

These functional malocclusions will be addressed prior to esthetics; however, esthetics is an important concern in Orthodontics. The Orthodontist at the initial examination will discuss these issues. A treatment plan will be created, and the patient may need to wear full braces or the "fixed appliance". The following information will be useful as it may appear on the RDA written examination and is part of the RDA written exam plan.

– 125 –

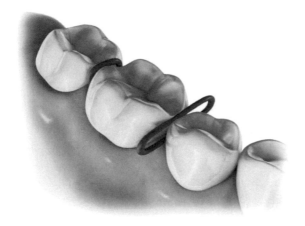 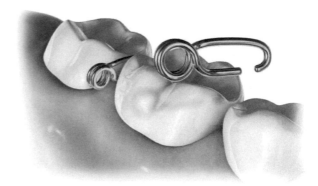

ORTHODONTIC SEPARATORS

The first step in proceeding with placement of the fixed appliance is to evaluate the tightness of the interproximal contacts around the molars where the orthodontic bands will be cemented in place. The bands act as an anchor for the entire fixed appliance and must be properly seated. However, due to tight interproximal contacts in the molar area on some patients, the teeth must be separated slightly prior to seating a proper band. This is accomplished using an orthodontic separator.

There are two (2) types of separators commonly used for posterior teeth: **steel separating springs** and **elastomeric separators**. Of these two types, the elastomeric separators are the most popular. **Elastomeric separators** are placed using **orthodontic separating pliers**, a specialized orthodontic instrument designed specifically for placement of separators.

The patient should be instructed not to pick at, floss or eat anything sticky while the separators are in place. If the separator becomes dislodged or falls out, the patient should be instructed to call the office promptly for its replacement. If the separator does not stay in place, the molars will not separate thus delaying the placement of the bands. Separators stay in place for approximately one week. At the next appointment, the separators will be removed, and the bands will be immediately properly seated (cemented) into place.

Removal of the separators is accomplished using either the orthodontic scaler or the orthodontic separating pliers. The assistant should refer to the patient's chart regarding how many separators were placed; the same number of separators should be removed.

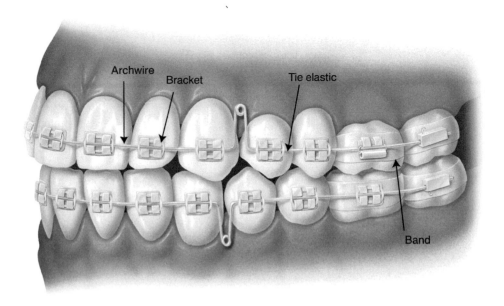

Archwire Bracket Tie elastic Band

TYPES OF ORTHODONTIC BANDS

An **orthodontic band** is a prefabricated circular stainless-steel ring that encircles a tooth, usually a first and/or second molar. These bands are made in a variety of sizes and, after being fitted for size, are cemented in place. The bands are a cornerstone of the fixed appliance, or braces, along with the brackets, auxiliary attachments and arch wires. The orthodontic bands are worn permanently while the fixed appliance is in place.

Bands are designed for specific teeth to accommodate the anatomical differences of each tooth. Therefore, bands are supplied for the maxillary and mandibular arches along with being designated for the right and left sides of the mouth. For example, #3 needs a band, so one would look for a band designated for the upper right (UR). The bands are stored in a covered tray with multiple labeled compartments where they are selected from for use on a patient.

Some orthodontic bands have auxiliary attachments while others are plain. Auxiliary attachments are items such as tubes, cleats, buttons, and hooks that are soldered to the band by the manufacturer. When ordering orthodontic bands, they can be ordered with or without as many auxiliary attachments as desired for proper patient treatment.

Auxiliary attachments either assist with the arch wire placement and retention or are used during the course of treatment for power products. Power products are items such as elastics, or "rubber bands" which exert extra force on the arch, or specific teeth in the arch, to create increased movement.

REMOVAL OF ORTHODONTIC BANDS

Orthodontic band removal occurs at the end of treatment when the fixed appliance is being removed or during the course of treatment if the band becomes loose. The **posterior band remover pliers** are the preferred instrument of use when performing this procedure on a patient.

This instrument is capable of safely and effectively removing the band without harming the tooth or causing patient discomfort. Orthodontic bands are removed quite simply. The plier has a "can opener" effect on the stainless steel orthodontic band basically crushing the occlusal top and gingival bottom of the band between its beaks. This causes the band to lift free from the tooth. The underlying cement is also crushed. Band removal is typically accomplished from the buccal surface allowing for adequate movement and space of the posterior band remover pliers.

An **orthodontic scaler** can be utilized to remove the underlying cement particles from the tooth. This instrument is useful particularly if there is cement adhering to the tooth structure.

THE ORTHODONTIC ARCH WIRE

The most important part of the fixed appliance is the arch wire. The arch wire is the part of the fixed appliance that initiates and establishes tooth movement in the arch. The remaining features of the fixed appliance (the brackets, the bands, the auxiliary attachments) are all present to support the arch wire and help the arch wire move the teeth.

The arch wire begins as a smooth piece of wire designed for placement in a patient's mouth. The orthodontist places a "pattern" into the archwire. The pattern is a design created by the orthodontist (based on the patient's treatment plan) that twists and bends the arch wire in various directions. The orthodontist then places the patterned arch wire into place. The patient will be seen again in approximately one (1) month.

During the next month, the arch wire will attempt to untwist and undo the "pattern" placed by the orthodontist. The untwisting of the pattern is what helps move the teeth in the direction desired by the orthodontist. The arch wire places force on the teeth will cause some necessary discomfort for the patient. Force is necessary to allow for movement in the arches by stretching and pulling the periodontal ligaments of each tooth. With each orthodontic appointment, the orthodontist will evaluate the amount movement that has taken place and establish a new prescription or pattern.

SIZES, SHAPES AND TYPES OF ARCH WIRES

Different sizes and types of arch wire are used during varying points in treatment or at the discretion of the treating orthodontist. The size of an arch wire refers to its gauge, or thickness. There are various gauges used in dentistry and the orthodontist will select the gauge they are comfortable working with. Additionally, arch wires come in two (2) shapes:

1. Square or rectangular
    - Positions the tooth in its correct occlusal relationship
    - Used during the final stages of treatment
    - Applies greater force on the teeth
    - Provides stability for the tooth while the root positions itself in its new location

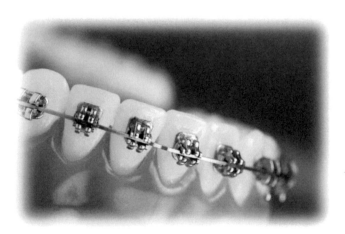

2. Round Wires
    - Corrects crowded, crooked teeth
    - Levels the arch
    - Assists in closing diastimas
    - Used during beginning and middle phases of treatment

There are four (4) types of arch wires. They are:

1. Optiflex
   - Newest of the arch wire types
   - Esthetically pleasing (no wire appearance)
   - Made from composite material
   - Provides light force
   - Used at the initial phase of positioning teeth

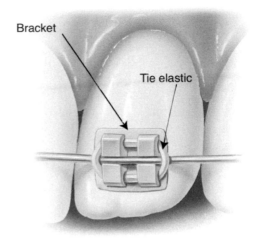

Bracket

Tie elastic

2. Stainless Steel Wire
   - Applies increased force to the teeth
   - Very stiff
   - Provides stability during tooth movement
   - Can withstand the environment of the oral cavity very well
   - Strongest of all the arch wires
3. Nickel Titanium (aka "NiTi")
   - Very flexible
   - Useful in movement of the teeth
   - Use to create movement for crowded teeth
4. Beta Titanium (aka "TMA")
   - Offers a combination of strength, flexibility and memory

PLACEMENT OF THE ARCH WIRE

The arch wire is placed into the middle of each bonded bracket and inserted into the edgewise tube on the band. The edgewise tube is an auxiliary attachment located on the buccal surface of a band. It is square and receives the end of the arch wire. The arch wire is then bent towards the gingiva, securely locking the arch wire in place. The arch wire is trimmed with either a **wire cutter** or a **distal end cutter plier**.

The **wire cutter** is used outside the patient's mouth just prior to placement while the distal end cutter is used intraorally just after placement.

The **distal end cutter** is unique in that it cuts and then holds the trimmed the end of the arch wire so it does not fall into the patient's throat.

The **Howe Pliers** or the **Weingart Utility Pliers** are used to place and/or remove the arch wire into the brackets and tubing. Either of these instruments assists in sliding the wire into the tubing as well as positions the wire into the brackets. The orthodontist may have marked the position of the midline in the arch wire further assisting with proper placement and positioning of the arch wire in the brackets.

LIGATING THE ARCH WIRE

The arch wire has been secured in the edgewise tube and now must be ligated, or tied down, at each bracket. Ligating the arch wire at each bracket creates the external force necessary for tooth movement basically forcing the pattern against the teeth. Brackets can be ligated with either wire ligature ties or elastomeric ligature ties. Wire ligature ties are thin, pliable wires that wrap around each bracket to secure the arch wire in place. Elastomeric ligature ties are made from elastic, or rubber, and are shaped like "O" rings. The elastic is stretched over the bracket securing the arch wire in place.

The elastomeric ligature ties are very popular by today's standards because ligation is very quick with this technique. However, wire ligature ties are often indicated or preferred by the orthodontist. A patient can also have a combination of wire and elastomeric ligature ties at the same time. The operator will start with the most posterior tooth on either the right or the left side and work towards the midline.

For placement of wire ligature ties the following armamentarium is needed:
- Wire ligature ties – multiple, thin 0.01-gauge wires
- Hemostat – instrument used to twist the wire around the bracket
- Ligature Tying Pliers - instrument used to twist the wire around the bracket; can be used with or in the place of the hemostat
- Pin and Ligature Cutter – instrument used intraorally to trim the excess wire ligature once it has been ligated to the bracket
- Ligature Director – instrument used to tuck the cut end of the wire ligature behind the bracket

For placement of elastomeric ligature ties the following armamentarium is needed:
- Elastomeric ties – one for each bracket being ligated
- Hemostat – instrument used to place elastomeric ties on bracket
- Orthodontic scaler – instrument used to help stretch elastomeric ligature tie over one wing of the bracket, using finger to secure in place, while stretching with the Ortho scaler to hook the tie over the remaining wings on the bracket.

REMOVABLE ORTHODONTIC APPLIANCES

The purpose of **removable orthodontic appliances** is to assist in stabilizing teeth in their new corrected position. Teeth have a memory and will want to return to their previous location in the mouth. Therefore, they must be trained to remain in their new desired location.

The two (2) removable orthodontic appliances commonly used are the Hawley retainer and the orthodontic positioner.

Hawley Retainer:
- Most common
- Made of clear acrylic; acrylic covers the palate on the maxillary
- Contains a molar clasp to secure in place
- Has an anterior facial wire
- Retains teeth in their new position
- Allows some tooth movement if indicated

The California RDA General Written and Law Examination Prep Book © 2017, 2018 • KB Dental Arts – Publisher

Orthodontic Positioner (Tooth Positioner):
- Made of a rubber material
- Completely covers the patient's dentition on upper, lower or both
- Allows the bone time to rebuild support around the teeth before the patient wears a retainer
- Retains the teeth in their new position
- Massages the gingiva

END OF CHAPTER - CRITICAL THINKING QUESTIONS:

1. Describe Angle's classifications of malocclusion.
2. Per California law, who is allowed to place orthodontic bands? Who is allowed to remove orthodontic bands?
3. What is a fixed appliance?
4. What is called the "cornerstone" of the fixed appliance?
5. What is placed into the wire by the orthodontist?
6. Name and describe the instruments that assist in arch wire placement.
7. What does ligating, or ligation, mean?
8. What items can be used to accomplish ligation?

CRITICAL THINKING QUESTION ANSWERS FOUND IN APPENDIX

Notes

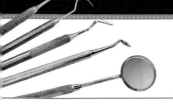

Unit 3 - Chapter 3

UNIT THREE - DENTAL SPECIALTY PROCEDURES
CHAPTER THREE: IMPLANTS, ORAL SURGERY & EXTRACTIONS

EXAMINATION PLAN DATA:

Topic Area	Dental Specialty Procedures
Total Weight of Topic Area on Examination	10%
Subject Area	Surgical Procedures
Percentage of Examination Questions in Implants, Oral Surgery and Extractions	3%

SURGICAL PROCEDURES – TASKS AND KNOWLEDGE STATEMENTS

Tasks Associated with Topic Area	Knowledge Statements Associated with Topic Area
Remove post-extraction and post-surgery sutures as directed by dentist	Knowledge of techniques for removing post-extraction and post-surgery sutures
Place and remove dry socket dressing as directed by dentist	Knowledge of methods for treating dry socket

SCOPE OF PRACTICE – SPECIFIC TO SURGICAL PROCEDURES

Unlicensed Dental Assistant	Registered Dental Assistant
Remove post-extraction dressings after inspection of the surgical site by the supervising licensed dentist	All DA duties
Remove sutures after inspection of the site by the dentist	Place post-extraction dressings after inspection of the surgical site by the supervising licensed dentist

Licensed Registered Dental Assistant in Extended Functions (RDAEF):
While there is nothing specifically listed for this subject area under the RDAEF category, it is important to note the following, as taken from the table of allowable duties for the RDAEF:

(a) A registered dental assistant in extended functions licensed on or after January 1, 2010, is authorized to perform all duties and procedures that a registered dental assistant is authorized to perform and those duties that the board may prescribe by regulation.

NOTE: The category of Dental Sedation Assistant has its own Permit entitled the Dental Sedation Assistant Permit (DSAP). The DSAP holder is allowed to perform specified tasks regarding surgical monitoring and procedures not allowable under the DA, RDA, and RDAEF categories. This exam prep book is focused only on preparation for the blended RDA Written Examination.

Alveolitis	Inflammation of the alveolar bone; aka, "dry socket"
Blood clot	Body's natural way of stopping bleeding from the socket
Needle Holder	Surgical Instrument used to hold the suture needle
Oral Surgeon	Dental surgical specialist with advanced education in oral surgery
Suture Scissors	A surgical scissor designed with shorter, very sharp blades, with a half-moon shape in the blade to ensure grasp of the suture material prior to cutting.

REMOVAL OF POST-EXTRACTION AND POST-SURGERY SUTURES

A suture is what is more commonly known as a stitch, or a sewing up of a surgical site. In dentistry, this can be performed after an extraction to help protect the socket or after a surgery where a scalpel is used to make an incision. It is usually used to control bleeding and promote healing to begin. The suture(s) are placed by the dentist but can be removed by the DA or RDA. The assistant should make note of how many suture(s) are placed at the surgical site in the patient chart.

There are two (2) types of suture materials a dentist can place in a surgical area - absorbable or non-absorbable. **Absorbable sutures** dissolve on their own as the area heals. They are made of natural materials, such as catgut, that are absorbed accordingly by the body. **Non-absorbable sutures** are made of a synthetic material, such as silk or nylon, and will need to be removed after healing has occurred. They will not dissolve on their own and usually stay in place for five (5) to seven (7) days.

When a patient returns for their post-operative "post-op" appointment, the surgical/extraction site will be checked by the dentist. If the area has not healed enough, the patient will return for another examination in one week. If the area has healed adequately, the sutures can be removed. The dentist may delegate this duty to the DA or RDA. The steps to follow in suture removal are as follows:

1. Dentist checks the area and delegates suture removal to the assistant.
2. Using the cotton forceps, the assistant gently holds the knotted end of the suture.
3. Holding the knotted portion of the suture up and away from the gum tissue, the assistant uses suture scissors to cut the suture material just under the knot.
4. _NEVER_ cut the knot; always cut just under the knot and away from the gum tissue.
5. Gently pull the suture material through the gum tissue using the cotton forceps.
6. Place the removed suture on a 2 x 2 gauze.
7. Repeat the above procedure for each remaining suture in the patient's mouth.
8. The assistant should count all sutures once they are removed to ensure the number of sutures removed matches the number of sutures placed as previously recorded in the patient chart. This is a safety precaution to ensure no suture is accidentally left behind.

POST EXTRACTION DRESSING

Placement of **post extraction dressing** is also known as "packing the socket." The medication in the pack soothes the inflammation in the area relieving the intense discomfort the patient experiences. The medicated gauze pack acts as the blood clot while encouraging clot formation.

A **blood clot** is the body's natural way of stopping the bleeding from the socket, protecting the alveolar bone and closing off the environment of the oral cavity to the rest of the body. If this blood clot is disturbed or never forms, the patient can experience a condition called Alveolitis.

Alveolitis, better known as "dry socket", is the inflammation of the alveolar bone and is extremely painful. The oral surgeon will instruct the patient to take specific medication, either over-the-counter or prescription, which commonly includes anti-inflammatories as well as pain medications, in an attempt to control the discomfort level.

The patient will return to the dental office where treatment of Alveolitis will include:
1. Cleaning and irrigating the socket to remove any debris that may have entered the socket.
2. Placing a medicated gauze pack, or post extraction dressing, into the socket area to promote healing.
3. Instructing the patient to return to the office within 24 to 48 hours to have a fresh post extraction dressing placed.
4. Instructing the patient to rinse the socket (using a disposable syringe) at least three (3) times per day with a warm salt-water rinse to encourage healing and remove food debris from the socket.

In reviewing post-op instructions with the patient, increased emphasis is placed on not dislodging or disturbing the blood clot that is forming at the base of the socket via activities such as sucking through straws, chewing gum or eating foods that are sticky, all of which can disrupt clot formation.

The patient may return several times for fresh dressings until symptoms are relieved and healing is underway.

END OF CHAPTER - CRITICAL THINKING QUESTIONS:

1. What is a post extraction dressing?
2. What is alveolitis?
3. What is done if a patient is experiencing alveolitis?
4. What are the two types of suture materials?
5. What should never be cut when removing sutures from a patient's mouth?
6. Once the suture is removed, what should the assistant do as a safety precaution?

CRITICAL THINKING QUESTION ANSWERS FOUND IN APPENDIX

Notes

Unit Three

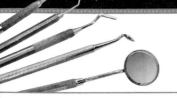
UNIT THREE – DENTAL SPECIALTY PROCEDURES
CHAPTER FOUR: PROSTHETIC APPLIANCES

EXAMINATION PLAN DATA:

Topic Area	Dental Specialty Procedures
Total Weight of Topic Area on Examination	10%
Subject Area	Prosthetic Appliances
Percentage of Examination Questions in Prosthetic Appliances	1%

PROSTHETIC APPLIANCES – TASKS AND KNOWLEDGE STATEMENTS

Tasks Associated with Topic Area	Knowledge Statements Associated with Topic Area
Adjust prosthetic appliances extraorally	Knowledge of methods for identifying pressure points (sore spots) related to ill-fitting prosthetic appliances
	Knowledge of materials, equipment and techniques used for adjustment of prosthetic appliances
	Knowledge of scope of practice for RDA's and RDAEF's related to the adjustment of extraoral prosthetic appliances

SCOPE OF PRACTICE – SPECIFIC TO PROSTHETIC APPLIANCES

Unlicensed Dental Assistant	Registered Dental Assistant
N/A	Adjust dentures extraorally

Licensed Registered Dental Assistant in Extended Functions (RDAEF):
While there is nothing specifically listed for this subject area under the RDAEF category, it is important to note the following, as taken from the table of allowable duties for the RDAEF:

(a) A registered dental assistant in extended functions licensed on or after January 1, 2010, is authorized to perform all duties and procedures that a registered dental assistant is authorized to perform and those duties that the board may prescribe by regulation.

KEY TERMS

Edentulous	A mouth without teeth
Full Denture	Removable prosthesis that replaces all of the teeth in one arch
Partial Denture	Removable prosthesis that replaces a certain number of teeth in one arch
Pressure Points	Specific areas on a partial or full denture that may apply pressure or rub against the underlying soft tissue.
Sore Spot	A pressure point(s) on the soft tissue caused by the partial or full denture that has progressed into causing discomfort on the underlying soft tissue.

DENTURE POST DELIVERY APPOINTMENT

The fabrication process of a full or partial denture is a methodical, step by step, multiple appointment journey for both the dentist, the assistant and the patient. The DA or RDA will assist the dentist in the multiple steps along the way in the fabrication process. After the denture is delivered, the patient is scheduled to return for post-delivery appointment. This appointment is very important as the underlying soft tissue is checked for any needed denture adjustments. The patient may feel the "sore spot" caused by the new denture rubbing or pushing against the soft tissue. The denture is fabricated from a hard acrylic, so it may withstand the varying temperatures and bite stresses experienced in the mouth. While the acrylic material allows for strength, it can often impede upon the underlying soft tissue. The best analogy is a pair of new shoes that rub against one area of your foot until you are able to break them in. A blister develops on the foot in the area where the rubbing or pressure occurs. While the shoes break in and eventually feel more comfortable, the denture will need to be adjusted in order to feel better to the patient. If the denture is not adjusted, the patient is more likely to avoid wearing the denture causing the denture to eventually not fit properly.

Post-delivery adjustments, or "sore spot" adjustments, is where the RDA is able to assist both the dentist and the patient with direct services. There is a material utilized in sore spot adjustment called Pressure Indicating Paste, or PIP. The PIP is painted on the inside base of the denture and then the denture is placed back into the patient's mouth. The denture is once again removed from the mouth and the PIP is inspected for any areas where it has been rubbed away. The areas that are free of the paste are adjusted with an acrylic lab bur and a straight handpiece extraorally. It is important to note that the denture should always be adjusted extraorally – never inside the patient's mouth. The denture should be held firmly in the assistant's hand using care not to drop or otherwise harm the denture. The area on the denture should be adjusted a little at a time, no big adjustment "chunks" should be taken out of the denture. The assistant does not want to cause a food trap area under the denture or create an ill-fitting denture by over adjusting. The denture is now tried in and out of the patient's mouth using this same method over and over until the PIP and the patient both indicate the area feels relieved of soreness and pressure.

It is important to use a disposable brush for painting on the PIP onto the denture to avoid cross-contamination to the next patient. Disclosing wax is alternative material that can be used other than the PIP to indicate areas needing adjustment. However, PIP is the most popular material utilized at this time. The office will request the patient return in approximately one week or sooner for another post-delivery check, especially if any soreness or pressure returns. After a new denture is delivered it is common to have several sore spot adjustment appointments until the patient and their soft tissue ridge become accustom to the denture.

END OF CHAPTER - CRITICAL THINKING QUESTIONS:

1. What is a full denture?

2. What is a partial denture?

3. What is a sore spot?

4. Why does a sore spot need to be adjusted?

5. What are the two materials used to indicate sore spots on the base of the denture?

6. What equipment is utilized to adjust sore spots?

7. How should the denture be adjusted?

8. Who is legally allowed to adjust a denture?

CRITICAL THINKING QUESTION ANSWERS FOUND IN APPENDIX

Notes

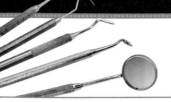

Unit 4 - Chapter 1

UNIT FOUR - SAFETY
CHAPTER ONE: INFECTION CONTROL

EXAMINATION PLAN DATA:

Topic Area	Safety Procedures
Total Weight of Topic Area on Examination	30%
Subject Area	Infection Control
Percentage of Examination Questions in Infection Control Procedures	24%

INFECTION CONTROL PROCEDURES – TASKS AND KNOWLEDGE STATEMENTS

Tasks Associated with Topic Area	Knowledge Statements Associated with Topic Area
Wear personal protective equipment during patient-based and non-patient-based procedures as specific to the tasks	Knowledge of laws and regulations pertaining to infection control procedures related to "Dental Healthcare Personnel" (DHCP) environments
Purge dental unit lines with air or water prior to attachment of devices	Knowledge of protocols and procedures for purging dental unit waterlines and hand pieces (DUWL)
Use germicides for surface disinfection (e.g., tables, chairs, counters)	Knowledge of procedures and protocols for the disposal of biological hazardous waste and Other Potentially Infectious Materials (OPIM)
Use surface barriers for prevention of cross-contamination	
Perform instrument sterilization in compliance with the office's infection control program	
Disinfect and sterilize laboratory and operatory equipment in compliance with the office's infection control program	
Use hand hygiene procedures	
Conduct biological spore testing to ensure functioning of sterilization devices	
Dispose of biological hazardous waste and Other Potentially Infectious Materials (OPIM)	
Dispose of pharmaceuticals and sharps in appropriate container	

SCOPE OF PRACTICE – SPECIFIC TO INFECTION CONTROL PROCEDURES

According to the *Dental Practice Act,* the Dental Board of California's *Minimum Standards for Infection Control Regulations* are the guidelines by which all dental healthcare personnel shall be required to adhere:

> *CCR §1005(b: All DHCP <u>shall comply</u> with infection control precautions <u>and enforce</u> the following minimum precautions to minimize the transmission of pathogens in health care settings mandated by the California Division of Occupational Safety and Health (Cal/OSHA).*

Infection control is the primary means of disease containment in all healthcare settings, including the dental office. Dental assistants who have an understanding of disease transmission and the methods of containing potentially infectious microorganisms help to play a key role in reducing the potential for spreading disease. All members of the clinical dental team are responsible for maintaining proper infection control techniques. The dentist is ultimately responsible for introducing, maintaining, updating, and managing all training and records associated with staff training; however, this duty is often delegated to another member of the dental team, usually the dental assistant.

KEY TERMS

ADA	American Dental Association
Aseptic Technique	Employing all forms of washing, sanitizing, disinfecting, and sterilization of items that come in contact with patients
CDC	Centers for Disease Control and Prevention
DHCP	Dental Healthcare Personnel
EPA	Environmental Protection Agency
HBV	Hepatitis-B Virus
HCV	Hepatitis-C Virus
HIV	Human Immunodeficiency Virus
Microorganisms	Those living things too small to be seen by the naked eye
Mycobacterium Tuberculosis var Bovis	Tuberculosis
OPIM	Other Potentially Infectious Materials
OSHA	Occupational Safety and Health Administration
Pathogens	Harmful disease-causing microorganisms
PPE	Personal Protective Equipment

Spatter	(large-particle spatter) Made up of water, saliva, blood, microorganism, and other debris.
Spores	Bacteria with an outer covering that protects them from chemical disinfectants
Standard Precautions	A group of infection prevention practices that apply to all patients, regardless of suspected or confirmed infection status

PRINCIPLES OF INFECTION CONTROL

Infection control is based upon the principle that transmission of infectious disease will be prevented when any of the steps in the chain are broken or interrupted. The six (6) steps in the chain of infection control are:

1. Infectious Agent:

    a. Cleaning

    b. Disinfection

    c. Sterilization

2. Reservoir of Source:

    a. Hygiene

    b. Dressing changes

    c. Disposal of fluid containers

    d. Change soiled linen

3. Portal of Exit from Reservoir or Source:

    a. Clean dressing over wounds

    b. Cover mouth and nose when coughing or sneezing

4. Mode of Transmission:

    a. Handwashing

    b. Proper disposal of contaminated objects

    c. Wear PPE

5. Portal of Entry to Host:

    a. Proper disposal of needles or sharps

    b. Sterile technique

6. Susceptible Host:

    a. Skin integrity

    b. Balanced nutrition

    c. Exercise

    d. Intact immune system

The California RDA General Written and Law Examination Prep Book © 2017, 2018 • KB Dental Arts – Publisher

Bacteria, viruses, and some fungi cause infectious diseases. Sterilization is the process that destroys all biologic material capable of reproduction. In other words, an item that has no living bacteria, viruses, yeast, or other biologically active material in or on its surfaces is sterile. Sterilization kills all forms of microbial life.

In contrast, disinfection means the reduction or elimination of disease-causing microorganisms from surfaces and does not kill. A disinfectant will kill some pathogens, many viruses and bacteria, but many living microbes could remain.

CALIFORNIA DENTAL BOARD REGULATIONS FOR INFECTION CONTROL

The State Board examination for the RDA contains questions specific to the regulations for infection control. Many assistants who have been trained "on-the-job" may not have received a copy of the regulations or were not trained to the regulations; therefore, this chapter will spend time going through each regulatory requirement, explain the intent of the requirement, and standard operating procedures in each area so that assistants preparing for the examination are doing so with the knowledge of how the regulations are intended to be used in the office setting and not what may actually be happening in the office setting.

Remember, the examination is based on "textbook" criteria, not necessarily what the office is doing!

Each regulation is identified in *italics* below and the numbers indicate where in the regulations to find each section. A copy of the full text of the regulations is available at the end of this chapter. The regulations begin with definitions of specific terms in infection control, so that is where we will begin:

REGULATIONS

The regulatory language begins with definitions:

(1) **"Standard precautions"** *are a group of infection prevention practices that apply to all patients, regardless of suspected or confirmed infection status, in any setting in which healthcare is delivered. These include hand hygiene, use of gloves, gown, mask, eye protection, or face shield, depending on the anticipated exposure, and safe handling of sharps. Standard precautions shall be used for care of all patients regardless of their diagnoses or personal infectious status.*

The term "universal precautions" has been used for years nationally to refer to the OSHA Bloodborne Pathogens Standard. Universal precautions are based on the concept that all human blood and body fluids, including saliva in dental procedures, are to be treated as if known to be infected with HIV, Hepatitis or other bloodborne diseases. The concept is based on the fact that patients are not always honest about their health history, may not disclose certain information, or simply may not know their specific health status if an undiagnosed disease should be present.

Eventually, the CDC expanded the concept and changed the term to "Standard Precautions" and incorporated all diseases, not just those transmitted by blood. Saliva has always been considered a potentially infectious material in dental procedures; the list of potentially infectious materials now includes:

- Blood
- All body fluids, including saliva in dental procedures, secretions, and excretions regardless of whether they contain blood (visible blood or not visible blood)
- Mucous membranes (oral tissues)
- Non-intact skin (cracked lips, ripped cuticles)

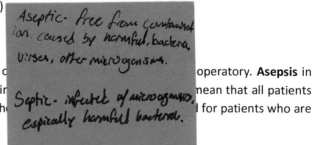

Aseptic techniques are required to eliminate the spread of [...] operatory. **Asepsis** in the operatory requires physical tasks and an understandin[...] mean that all patients must be thought of as potentially infectious. Therefore, th[...] for patients who are

- 144

known to harbor infectious diseases must be the same procedures applied universally for all patients seeking treatment.

California regulations require that standard precautions be used for all patients, regardless of health history, and the dental assistant is to consider all patients infectious as they prepare, handle, clean and disinfect/sterilize dental instruments and equipment.

INSTRUMENT CLASSIFICATIONS

A major concern of most patients is the passage of diseases from previous patients through the use of contaminated instruments. In healthcare, we use a national standard for ranking devices, instruments and equipment used in the provision of patient care – the **Spaulding Classification System**.

Spaulding's Classifications, originally established in 1957, is a widely used system for matching the disinfection and sterilization of surfaces, particularly those of re-usable medical/surgical devices, with available processes. It presents a ranking, from simple disinfection through to sterilization, that should be considered in the reprocessing of instruments and devices based on the risks associated with their use, ranging from 'critical' (presenting a high risk), through 'semi-critical' to 'non-critical' (presenting a low risk).

The Dental Board adopted those same classifications in the 2011 regulations, as follows:

(2) *"Critical items" confer a high risk for infection if they are contaminated with any microorganism. These include all instruments, devices, and other items used to penetrate soft tissue or bone.*

(3) *"Semi-critical items" are instruments, devices and other items that are not used to penetrate soft tissue or bone, but contact oral mucous membranes, non-intact skin or other potentially infectious materials (OPIM).*

(4) *"Non-critical items" are instruments, devices, equipment, and surfaces that come in contact with soil, debris, saliva, blood, OPIM and intact skin, but not oral mucous membranes.*

What is considered a critical instrument? All items that penetrate skin, mucous membranes, or bone which include all surgical devices, scalers, and burs. These instruments are considered to carry the greatest risk of transmitting infections.

What are semi-critical items? Typically, items included in this category are handpieces, mirrors, amalgam condensers, x-ray holders, and reusable impression trays. Sterilization is required for all items that may touch saliva or intact mucosal tissues.

Noncritical items come in contact with intact skin surfaces, soil, debris, saliva, blood or other potentially infectious materials, and include surfaces, devices and equipment as well as instruments. Intermediate-level disinfection is required for operatory surfaces such as light handles, counter tops, x-ray heads, and dental chairs.

DISINFECTION CLASSIFICATIONS

Disinfection is intended to kill disease-causing microorganisms, but only after the surface is pre-cleaned to remove soil, debris, or bio-burden. Pathogenic spores cannot be killed using disinfectants. Disinfection and sterilization are not to be confused with each other in that disinfection is not able to kill all forms of microbial life.

The Environmental Protection Agency (EPA) registers and regulates disinfectants and chemical sterilants according to the products use instructions and its ability to kill viruses, spores, fungi, bacteria and mycobacteria. There are three (3) categories of disinfectants used in dentistry based upon their effectiveness: **low level, intermediate level** and **high-level**.

The three (3) categories of disinfectants are further defined in the regulations, as follows:

The California RDA General Written and Law Examination Prep Book © 2017, 2018 • KB Dental Arts – Publisher

(5) **"Low-level disinfection"** is the least effective disinfection process. It kills some bacteria, some viruses and fungi, but does not kill bacterial spores or mycobacterium tuberculosis var bovis, a laboratory test organism used to classify the strength of disinfectant chemicals.

(6) **"Intermediate-level disinfection"** kills mycobacterium tuberculosis var bovis indicating that many human pathogens are also killed. This process does not necessarily kill spores.

(7) **"High-level disinfection"** kills some, but not necessarily all, bacterial spores. This process kills mycobacterium tuberculosis var bovis, bacteria, fungi, and viruses.

The principle factor that determines the level of each disinfectant product is its ability to kill the benchmark illness our profession deals with regularly – Tuberculosis.

In addition, the term germicide is also defined in the regulations:

(8) **"Germicide"** is a chemical agent that can be used to disinfect items and surfaces based on the level of contamination.

Regardless of the product selected for disinfection, be certain to follow exactly all of the manufacturer's directions for use, proper application shelf life, activated use-life and reuse-life, and all safety warnings.

DISINFECTANT TYPES

Choosing the best disinfectant for a particular task is difficult for dental healthcare workers, especially because of exaggerated or distorted claims made by some manufacturers. All available disinfectants are not ideal; therefore, dental healthcare workers must compare and decide which product will best serve the specific needs of the practice.

Microbial destruction by disinfectants typically involves chemical reactions between the disinfectant and vital contents of the cell. When a disinfectant actually kills an organism, they are called bactericide, fungicide, or germicide agents.

- **Alcohols**: Ethyl and isopropyl alcohols have been used for years as disinfectants. The alcohols work over a large spectrum of microbes, including most viruses and hardy bacterial cells. The most effective concentration of alcohol is 70%. Unfortunately, alcohols have little, if any, effect on endospores, are not effective cleansing agents, and do not leave an antimicrobial residue. Because of these shortcomings, the ADA and CDC do not accept alcohols for use as a surface disinfectant in the dental office.

- **Detergents**: Detergents are chemicals that form bridges between water-loving solutions and water-insoluble molecules, such as fats. Because fats are necessary for the cell to function, altering cells with detergents usually results in death of the cell. The most common group of disinfecting detergents is the quaternary ammonium compounds.

IODINE AND IODOPHORES

Although iodine is ideal as an antimicrobial, it has several negative properties, including irritation and staining of skin and corrosion of metal instruments. Solutions of iodophores do not store well after dilution and must be prepared daily.

Iodophor solutions have minimal toxicity for human tissues and are often used as antiseptics. They are often the active agent in surgical scrubs and can be used on skin and mucosal surfaces. After the surfaces are scrubbed, the iodophores residual antimicrobial activity remains strong even when rinsed with water.

GLUTARALDEHYDES

Glutaraldehydes are the most widely used disinfectants in the dental profession. They have a wide antimicrobial range, including hepatitis viruses and M. Tuberculosis var Bovis (TB) cells. In addition, glutaraldehydes have good cleaning characteristics because of their ability to penetrate biological materials, such as blood.

Some accept the fact that because glutaraldehydes kill spores, they can be used to sterilize equipment. But the ADA no longer accepts these cold sterilants based on a number of reasons, including the product's inability to inactivate microbes.

STERILIZATION

*(9) **"Sterilization"** is a validated process used to render a product free of all forms of viable microorganisms.*

The three (3) acceptable processes of sterilization in California are:

- Autoclave – steam under pressure
- Dry heat
- Unsaturated chemical vapor

The goal of sterilization is to kill all forms of microbial life (the killing of disease causing, or pathogenic, microorganisms). Microbial kill allows for all contaminants to be killed including spores which carry disease and are not killed by traditional disinfectants.

Microbial kill requires three (3) specific environments to occur at once:

- ✓ Time
- ✓ Heat
- ✓ Pressure

AUTOCLAVE

Autoclaves use saturated steam at a temperature of 121° C or 250° F to create sterile conditions. The microbes are killed when their proteins are denatured. The 121° C temperature is higher than what can be achieved by boiling a pan of water on the stove. The laws of physics dictate that water at 100° C (212° F) at sea level will produce steam. The only way to raise the temperature of steam is to allow the steam to build pressure. The chamber of an autoclave is strong and allows the steam to build pressure. As a result of the pressure, the temperature increases to 121° C. Once this temperature is reached, most manufacturers of autoclaves recommend a 15-minute exposure of instruments. The time should be extended to 20 or more minutes if the autoclave contains a large mass of instruments.

The autoclave has proven to be a very effective and rapid means of sterilizing dental instruments. A drawback to the use of the autoclave is that the steam may react with metal instrument surfaces causing discoloration and dulling the cutting surfaces. Autoclaved items may also retain water from condensation of the steam. In addition to the traditional autoclave, effective high-temperature autoclaves are available that operate at 132° C (270° F). Because of the increased temperature, the recommended cycle time is reduced to between four (4) and eight (8) minutes – this is commonly referred to as **flash sterilization** and is not a recognized method of sterilization in California. Although flash sterilization is much quicker than conventional autoclave settings, the dental assistant may find greater rates of instrument corrosion.

NOTE: The sterilization-times indicated for machines are for the sterilization portion of a cycle only and do not include the time to heat the unit to the desired temperature or the time for the unit to reduce the internal temperatures to a safe level at the end of a run as part of the sterilizing time. Instrument packages and cassettes should be completely dried before removing them from the sterilizer.

The California RDA General Written and Law Examination Prep Book © 2017, 2018 • KB Dental Arts – Publisher

DRY HEAT

Sterilization can also be achieved by placing instruments into a dry-heat sterilizer that is heated to 150° C to 170° C. This oxidizes microbes. FDA-approved dry-heat sterilizers use forced-air circulation within the sterilizer. In these systems, a load of instruments will be sterilized in one hour at 170° C (340° F).

CHEMICAL VAPOR

The chemical vapor sterilizer was developed to reduce the instrument corrosion caused by the saturated steam of an autoclave. It is physically similar to an autoclave, but operationally, the chemical vapor sterilizer uses a mixture of alcohol, water, formaldehyde, and other trace chemicals to create a non-saturated vapor inside the chamber.

Microbial killing occurs due to the reaction with the formaldehyde. The operating temperature of the unsaturated chemical vapor sterilizer is 132° C (270° F), and the recommended exposure time is 20 minutes. The manufacturer's instructions to use porous instrument wraps and careful loading techniques must be observed for effective sterilization to occur. Fabrics and plastics absorb the vapors and should not be used for 24 hours after sterilization to avoid skin irritations.

CLEANING

> *(10) **"Cleaning"** is the removal of visible soil (e.g., organic and inorganic material) debris and OPIM from objects and surfaces and shall be accomplished manually or mechanically using water with detergents or enzymatic products.*

As it relates to surfaces, equipment and nonsterilizable items in the dental office, precleaning of these surfaces and items must occur before disinfection. Even if no blood is visible on the surface, it must be precleaned because even a thin layer of bioburden, saliva or other potentially infectious material can reduce the effectiveness of the disinfectant (germicide) used. Precleaning reduces the number of microbes and removes other bioburden to allow surface disinfectants to perform according to their intended use.

CONTROL OF OPERATORY SURFACE CONTAMINATION

A quick look at the front of a protective face shield or eye glasses worn during routine work in the operatory will reveal significant spatter following most dental procedures. The generation of sprays containing potentially infectious microorganisms is virtually impossible to eliminate from the dental operator. Therefore, all surfaces in an operatory must be considered contaminated. Continual handling of air and water syringe lines, saliva ejectors, and light handles with gloved hands inadvertently leaves these surfaces/items contaminated. Because the equipment cannot be sterilized, disinfection of these surfaces must be accomplished using a low to intermediate-level, hospital-grade germicide.

Surface disinfection requires pre-cleaning of all surfaces not covered by impervious barriers with the same low to intermediate-level disinfectant used for other contact surfaces, preferably an intermediate-level product with a tuberculocidal kill time of less than five (5) minutes. Today, most dental offices use a combination of surface disinfection and barrier protection to accomplish proper infection control protocols.

All surfaces are required to be pre-cleaned before disinfection using the **"SPRAY-WIPE-SPRAY-WAIT"** method to ensure proper disinfection. The purpose of precleaning is to remove all contamination, both seen and unseen, as well as any bioburden that may be on clinical contact or housekeeping surfaces. Change all surface disinfectants according to manufacturer's directions.

The first "spray and wipe" is to clean = this can also be accomplished using properly labeled wipes with detergent properties or labeled as a germicide capable of cleaning and disinfecting. Wipe the wet areas with a disposable paper towel to dry – now the surface is CLEAN but not yet disinfected.

The second "spray and wait" is to disinfect = following the manufacturer's instructions, re-spray or re-wipe the surfaces with a fresh disinfection wipe, making sure all areas are moist and stay wet for the required amount of time for proper germicidal kill.

INSTRUMENT CLEANING

Once a procedure is complete, the operatory must be prepared for the next patient. Instruments must be gathered and prepared for sterilization. The dental healthcare worker must wear proper personal protective equipment including utility gloves during this operation.

Using mechanical devices for instrument debridement is required by regulation. Refer to the specific manufacturer's recommendations regarding the type of ultrasonic cleaning detergents or enzymatics to use and the length of time needed to clean a typical load.

After cleaning, rinse the instruments with generous amounts of tap water. The operator must take care to remember that these cleaned instruments harbor infectious microorganisms; therefore, personal protective equipment must be used in accordance with regulations. The rinsed instruments are dried and are then ready for packaging.

PERSONAL PROTECTIVE EQUIPMENT – (PPE)

*(11) **"Personal Protective Equipment"** (PPE) is specialized clothing or equipment worn or used for protection against a hazard. PPE items may include, but are not limited to, gloves, masks, respiratory devices, protective eyewear and protective attire which are intended to prevent exposure to blood, body fluids and OPIM, and chemicals used for infection control. General work attire such as uniforms, scrubs, pants and shirts, are not considered to be PPE.*

The dental healthcare worker is at risk of infection by pathogenic microbes from the patient. Several experiments have been performed using colored or dyed saliva and looking for the dye after a procedure. In virtually all cases, the dentist and assistant were contaminated with patient saliva from the waist up, including their hair. For the dental staff, obviously sterilization is not possible and most high- and intermediate-level disinfectants are not compatible with human tissues.

Both Federal and California OSHA regulations indicate that long-sleeved gowns, gloves, a face shield with mask or protective eyewear with mask are required as the minimal level of personal protection. Masks and gloves _must_ be changed after each patient or when saturated with liquid or punctured during a procedure.

Washing gloved hands is not allowed. Gloves need not be sterile but should fit well and be comfortable. Similarly, masks must be comfortable and fit well, especially up over the bridge of the nose and under the chin. Protective eyewear must shield against spatter from the sides and front.

OTHER POTENTIALLY INFECTIOUS MATERIALS

*(12) **"Other Potentially Infectious Materials"** (OPIM) means any one of the following:*

(A) Human body fluids such as saliva in dental procedures and any body fluid that is visibly contaminated fluids;

(B) Any unfixed tissue or organ (other than intact skin) from a human (living or dead); and,

with blood, and all body fluids in situations where it is difficult or impossible to differentiate between body

(C) Any of the following, if known or reasonably likely to contain or be infected with HIV, HBV, or HCV:

> *(i) Cell, tissue, or organ cultures from humans or experimental animals;*

> *(ii) Blood, organs, or other tissues from experimental animals; or*

> *(iii) Culture medium or other solutions.*

The California RDA General Written and Law Examination Prep Book © 2017, 2018 • KB Dental Arts – Publisher

Although OSHA's Bloodborne Pathogens Standard is a separate regulatory requirement and compliance area for the dental team, the Dental Board of California has adopted the content of the Standards and requires all dental healthcare workers to comply with the Standards. Included is the term **OPIM** (Other Potentially Infectious Materials) as seen in the above stated regulation.

Simply put, the definition of OPIM is any item or material considered contaminated that may have the potential to transmit disease, not just visible blood or invisible saliva.

DENTAL HEALTHCARE PERSONNEL – DEFINED IN REGULATION

In the latest edition of the Board's Infection Control Regulations (adopted 8/2011), the Board defined the term DHCP and in doing so used the term DHCP throughout the regulations to identify who the regulations were to adhere to and who was required to follow and be compliant with the regulations. The regulatory language states the following:

(13) *"Dental Healthcare Personnel"* (DHCP) are all paid and non-paid personnel in the dental health-care setting who might be occupationally exposed to infectious materials, including body substances and contaminated supplies, equipment, environmental surfaces, water, or air. DHCP includes dentists, dental hygienists, dental assistants, dental laboratory technicians (in-office and commercial), students and trainees, contractual personnel, and other persons not directly involved in patient care but potentially exposed to infectious agents (e.g., administrative, clerical, housekeeping, maintenance, or volunteer personnel).

In addition, the Board established the following regulatory language for all DHCP:

(b) All DHCP shall comply with infection control precautions and enforce the following minimum precautions to minimize the transmission of pathogens in health care settings mandated by the California Division of Occupational Safety and Health (Cal/OSHA).

(1) Standard precautions shall be practiced in the care of all patients.

(2) A written protocol shall be developed, maintained, and periodically updated for proper instrument processing, operatory cleanliness, and management of injuries.

(3) The protocol shall be made available to all DHCP at the dental office.

PERSONAL PROTECTIVE EQUIPMENT

(4) All DHCP shall wear surgical facemasks in combination with either chin length plastic face shields or protective eyewear whenever there is potential for aerosol spray, splashing or spattering of the following: droplet nuclei, blood, chemical or germicidal agents or OPIM. Chemical-resistant utility gloves and appropriate, task specific PPE shall be worn when handling hazardous chemicals. After each patient treatment masks shall be changed and disposed. After each patient treatment, face shields and protective eyewear shall be cleaned, disinfected, or disposed.

(5) Protective attire shall be worn for disinfection, sterilization, and housekeeping procedures involving the use of germicides or handling contaminated items. All DHCP shall wear reusable or disposable protective attire whenever there is a potential for aerosol spray, splashing or spattering of blood, OPIM, or chemicals and germicidal agents. Protective attire must be changed daily or between patients if they should become moist or visibly soiled. All PPE used during patient care shall be removed when leaving laboratories or areas of patient care activities. Reusable gowns shall be laundered in accordance with Cal/OSHA Bloodborne Pathogens Standards (Title 8, Cal. Code Regs., section 5193).

PPE INCLUDES GLOVES

Significant risks exist for dental healthcare personnel and patients when gloves are not used. Ungloved hands are the mechanism by which dental personnel have acquired HBV infections from their patients. Transmission of infectious agents including herpes virus from ungloved provider to patient has also been documented. Gloves must be worn whenever you anticipate contact with blood, saliva, mucous membranes, or blood-contaminated objects or surfaces. Two (2) categories of gloves routinely used in the dental clinic include:

(1) thin latex, synthetic, nitrile or vinyl exam gloves used during patient treatment, and

(2) general-purpose heavy-duty or utility gloves used for cleaning operations.

General-purpose utility gloves are thicker gloves that are only appropriate for use during cleanup and disinfection procedures. Chemical-resistant utility gloves are required for use when disinfecting operatories and puncture-resistant utility gloves are required for handling instruments during cleaning and sterilization procedures. Unlike medical exam gloves used during patient care, utility gloves can be washed and reused and, in many cases, can be sterilized in a steam autoclave. However, be sure to replace them if they become cracked, worn, or show other evidence of deterioration.

In the event medical exam gloves should rip or tear during a procedure, the dental healthcare provider must remove the glove, wash and dry hands, and place on new gloves.

PPE INCLUDES MASKS

Spatter containing blood and saliva is generated during dental procedures from equipment such as the handpiece, air-water syringe, or ultrasonic scaler. A mask must be worn to protect the mucous membranes of the nose and mouth from exposure to the airborne blood and saliva.

Several guidelines for the use of masks include the following:

1. Choose a style that can be adjusted to fit your face comfortably and tightly.

2. Men: Keep your beard and mustache groomed so that the mask fits well and can be worn effectively.

3. Always change the mask between patients and if it gets wet during a procedure.

4. Remove the mask when treatment is over. Do not leave it dangling around your neck; either wear it properly or take it off.

5. Never leave the operatory with a mask in place or around your neck.

6. When removing a mask, handle it only by the elastic or cloth tie string; never touch the mask.

PPE INCLUDES PROTECTIVE EYEWEAR

Protective eyewear must be worn to protect the mucous membranes of the eyes from projectiles and spatter of blood and saliva. The risk of exposing the tissues of the eyes to blood and body fluids is well documented. Viruses such as hepatitis B and herpes simplex have been transmitted to dental staff whose eyes were spattered with saliva or blood.

Choice of eyewear depends on the nature of the procedures that are being performed. However, prescription or safety glasses equipped with side shields are considered to be the minimal acceptable protective eyewear. Goggles afford the greatest eye protection. As an alternative to protective glasses or goggles, a face shield with a mask may be worn by the clinician. Because many dental procedures produce flying objects from materials such as amalgam restorations or crowns, protective eyewear for the patient should also be considered.

PPE INCLUDES PROTECTIVE ATTIRE – GOWNS AND LAB COATS

Lab coats and disposable gowns provide protection from possible exposure to blood and other body fluids. When selecting a gown, consider those with the greatest coverage for your body. The isolation gown is ideal and recommended because it fits closely around the neck and the long-cuffed sleeves cover the arms. Gloves should overlap the cuffed sleeves of the lab coat or gown. Lab coats and gowns must be changed daily or more often if they have been sprayed with saliva or blood or are visibly soiled.

Like masks and gloves, protective attire may only be worn in areas of patient care activities – clinical activities – and are not allowed in nonclinical settings or staff support areas such as staff lounge, doctor's office or behind the front desk.

The appropriate sequence a dental healthcare worker should utilize when removing or donning each PPE item:

> On – (MEG) mask first, eyewear second, gloves last
>
> Off – (GEM) gloves first, eyewear second, mask last

HAND HYGIENE

(6) All DHCP shall thoroughly wash their hands with soap and water at the start and end of each workday. DHCP shall wash contaminated or visibly soiled hands with soap and water and put on new gloves before treating each patient. If hands are not visibly soiled or contaminated an alcohol based hand rub may be used as an alternative to soap and water. Hands shall be thoroughly dried before donning gloves in order to prevent promotion of bacterial growth and washed again immediately after glove removal. A DHCP shall refrain from direct patient care if conditions are present that may render the DHCP or patients more susceptible to opportunistic infection or exposure.

(7) All DHCP who have exudative lesions or weeping dermatitis of the hand shall refrain from all direct patient care and from handling patient care equipment until the condition resolves.

HANDWASHING

Hand washing is one of the most important functions clinicians perform to prevent transfer of contaminants from one person to another. Every dental team member should begin the day by washing hands with soap and water. The thumbs, fingertips, and areas between and around the fingernails should receive particular attention.

Following hand hygiene regulations, hands must be washed before gloving and after glove removal. Alternatively, an alcohol-based hand rub may also be used in lieu of soap and water in the event hands are not contaminated or visibly soiled.

When washing times are too short or technique is poor, the opportunity for disease transmission may occur for the following reasons:

1. Fingertips, thumbs, and the areas between the fingers are washed poorly or may be skipped entirely.

2. The dominant hand is generally washed less effectively than the non-dominant hand.

3. The microbial count under fingernails will be higher than normal.

Soap containers and sink equipment will become contaminated; therefore, soap dispensers and faucets controls should be mechanical or "touchless."

GLOVES

(8) Medical exam gloves shall be worn whenever there is contact with mucous membranes, blood, OPIM, and during all pre-clinical, clinical, post-clinical, and laboratory procedures. When processing contaminated sharp instruments, needles, and devices, DHCP shall wear heavy-duty utility gloves to prevent puncture wounds. Gloves must be discarded when torn or punctured, upon completion of treatment, and before leaving laboratories or areas of patient care activities. All DHCP shall perform hand hygiene procedures before donning gloves and after removing and discarding gloves. Gloves shall not be washed before or after use.

Many types of exam gloves are on the commercial market. Factors to consider when choosing gloves include the type of procedure, tactical sensitivity required for the procedure, and comfort of the wearer.

Nonsterile medical examination gloves provide an adequate level of protection for operative or general dentistry procedures. Gloves must be changed between patients and whenever they are torn or breached during treatment.

NEEDLE AND SHARPS SAFETY

(9) Needles shall be recapped only by using the scoop technique or a protective device. Needles shall not be bent or broken for the purpose of disposal. Disposable needles, syringes, scalpel blades, or other sharp items and instruments shall be placed into sharps containers for disposal as close as possible to the point of use according to all applicable local, state, and federal regulations.

The most common incident for the dental professional is the parenteral wound such as cuts on the hands by sharp instruments and needle sticks. The OSHA guidelines cover these areas, but two aspects of the guidelines need reinforcement for the dental profession. OSHA prefers that all injection needles be discarded after a single use; however, most dentists retain the anesthesia syringe at the chairside throughout a procedure. If this is done, the needle must be resheathed using either a one-handed scoop technique or mechanical manipulation of the sheath. Both systems remove the hand and fingers from the proximity of the exposed needle.

Sharp instruments/items/devices such as needles, burs, broken glassware and scalpel blades should be placed intact into OSHA-approved, puncture-resistant containers (sharps container). Never remove sharps with anything other than forceps. All sharps containers are required to be located at the point-of-use (operatory).

Handle sharp items carefully. Appropriate procedures for handling sharp instruments during operatory recycling include the following:

1. Wear puncture-resistant utility gloves when handling and cleaning contaminated instruments or other sharp items.

2. Ensure all PPE are worn when processing operatory.

3. Keep a log of injuries that should include the date of injury, person injured, cause of injury, patient's name (if involved), description of situation, witness, action taken, outcome, and follow-up if necessary.

Another problem is the safe handling, cleaning and sterilization of handpieces following use on patients. Often contaminated burs are left on the handpiece chuck and in some operatory settings workers are in danger of being scrapped or punctured by these burs as they move around the operatory.

A major problem during patient treatment is that the level of mental concentration on the procedure by the clinical staff is quite high, and the proximity of potentially dangerous sharps is forgotten. Therefore, observe the following:

1. Keep hands away from rotating instruments.

2. Dispose of needles and other sharp items promptly and appropriately.

3. Avoid any quick motions that would bring one hand toward the other or the instrument across the plane of any part of your body when handling sharp instruments.

4. Point sharps away from you.

5. Use the proper technique at all times when passing sharp instruments. The point should be held away from everyone.

STERILIZATION AND DISINFECTION

(10) All germicides must be used in accordance with intended use and label instructions.

(11) Cleaning must precede any disinfection or sterilization process. Products used to clean items or surfaces prior to disinfection procedures shall be used according to all label instructions.

(12) Critical instruments, items and devices shall be discarded or pre-cleaned, packaged or wrapped and sterilized after each use. Methods of sterilization shall include steam under pressure (autoclaving), chemical vapor, and dry heat. If a critical item is heat-sensitive, it shall, at minimum, be processed with high-level disinfection and packaged or wrapped upon completion of the disinfection process. These instruments, items, and devices, shall remain sealed and stored in a manner so as to prevent contamination, and shall be labeled with the date of sterilization and the specific sterilizer used if more than one sterilizer is utilized in the facility.

(13) Semi-critical instruments, items, and devices shall be pre-cleaned, packaged or wrapped and sterilized after each use. Methods of sterilization include steam under pressure (autoclaving), chemical vapor and dry heat. If a semi-critical item is heat sensitive, it shall, at minimum, be processed with high level disinfection and packaged or wrapped upon completion of the disinfection process. These packages or containers shall remain sealed and shall be stored in a manner so as to prevent contamination, and shall be labeled with the date of sterilization and the specific sterilizer used if more than one sterilizer is utilized in the facility.

(14) Non-critical surfaces and patient care items shall be cleaned and disinfected with a California Environmental Protection Agency (Cal/EPA)-registered hospital-grade disinfectant (low-level disinfectant) labeled effective against HBV and HIV. When the item is visibly contaminated with blood or OPIM, a Cal/EPA-registered hospital-grade intermediate-level disinfectant with a tuberculocidal claim shall be used.

INSTRUMENT HANDLING/PROCESSING

Instruments are NOT to be submerged in a surface disinfectant solution – this is NOT STERILIZATION. The solution is contained in spray bottles or wipes, properly labeled, and is to be used for surface disinfection only.

Submersion solution may be used solely for pre-soaking of contaminated instruments that are waiting for ultrasonic cleaning. Holding baths are to be utilized for the presoaking of instruments using a detergent or enzymatic cleaning solution. Solutions should be mixed and changed according to manufacturer's directions.

Following mechanical cleaning, instruments are prepared for sterilization by packaging or wrapping. Many different ways of packaging instruments for sterilization exist; however, certain principles must be applied to the process. First of all, use only bags, pouches, or wraps that have been designed for the sterilizer you are using. For example, paper bags work well in an autoclave but char and disintegrate in dry heat sterilizers. Specially designed sealing plastic packages work well in autoclaves and dry heat sterilizers but are not recommended for unsaturated chemical vapor units, because the vapor cannot readily penetrate through the plastic.

When using metal or plastic cassette systems, the dental assistant should place the cleaned instruments into the cassette and keep it closed. Wrap the entire unit with specially designed wrap (eg: CSR blue wrap) or cloth and secure the edges with indicator autoclave tape. This will provide excellent protection against contamination once the cassette is removed from the sterilizer and stored.

Secondly, tightly capped containers should never be used because steam and chemical vapors cannot penetrate into the interior of the container. Similarly, biohazard bags should not be tightly closed when sterilizing the contents.

Many sterilizer bags and tapes have chemical markers that change colors following sterilization. These should be checked daily to confirm that the packages were subjected to sterilizing conditions. Only the weekly biologic monitor is sufficient to verify that the conditions were maintained sufficiently to achieve sterility. Chemical indicators cannot be used as substitutes for biologic indicators. Because of the open space within cassettes, stacking them flat in the sterilizer is acceptable.

When loading the sterilizer, follow the manufacturer's recommendations. In general, placing individual packages on edge rather than flat is better. But be careful not to overload the unit, and make sure the minimum exposure times are achieved. Wrapped cassettes may be placed flat in the sterilizer.

THE CASSETTE SYSTEM TO MANAGE INSTRUMENTS

An increasing need occurs in dental offices to develop more effective ways to organize, clean, sterilize, and store dental instruments. Cassettes are designed to hold complete procedural set-ups and can provide easy organization for all smaller items. This allows the dental assistant to have organized and sterile set-ups ready for immediate use.

CLEANING AND STERILIZING HANDPIECES

> *(15) All high-speed dental handpieces, low-speed handpieces, rotary components and dental unit attachments such as reusable air/water syringe tips and ultrasonic scaler tips, shall be packaged, labeled and heat-sterilized in a manner consistent with the same sterilization practices as a semi-critical item.*

The Board's Infection Control Regulations state that all handpieces and rotary devices must be sterilized between each patient. In use, handpieces rarely contact open wounds and should be considered semi-critical. However, the spray generated readily covers the handpiece and, because of its construction and inner workings, the inside of the handpiece is often contaminated.

A visible spray is created during the use of rotary dental and surgical instruments (e.g., handpieces, ultrasonic scalers) and air-water syringes. The dental handpiece spray contains two specific elements: **splatter and aerosols**.

Spatter is defined as being primarily large-particles of water, saliva, blood, microorganisms, and other debris that makes up the bulk of the spray from handpieces and ultrasonic scalers. Spatter travels only a short distance and settles out quickly, landing either on the floor, nearby operatory surfaces, the dental health care personnel providing care, or the patient. Spatter is commonly seen on face shields, protective eyewear, and other surfaces immediately after the dental procedure, but after a short time it may dry clear and not be easily detected.

Aerosols take considerable energy to generate, consist of particles less than 10 microns in diameter, and are not typically visible to the naked eye. Aerosols, like a mist, can remain airborne for extended periods of time and may be inhaled.

To prevent contact with splashes and spatter, dental health care personnel should position patients properly and make appropriate use of barriers (face shields, surgical masks, gowns), rubber dams, and high-volume evacuators.

The California RDA General Written and Law Examination Prep Book © 2017, 2018 • KB Dental Arts – Publisher

SINGLE-USE ITEMS – DISPOSABLE ITEMS

Several single-use items are used in dentistry today. Because these items are used on only one patient and then discarded, they help to reduce the chance for patient-to-patient contamination. It must be clear that the act of immersing single-use items in a cold chemical solution is not allowed in California.

Single-use items are addressed by the Board as follows:

> *(16) Single use disposable items such as prophylaxis angles, prophylaxis cups and brushes, tips for high-speed evacuators, saliva ejectors, air/water syringe tips, and gloves shall be used for one patient only and discarded.*

Items considered single-use are:
- Gloves
- Masks
- Autoclave packages, bags, wraps and tapes
- Cotton products, paper products, and non-autoclavable plastic items

- Non-sterilizable irrigation items
- Needles, sharps and glassware
- Items marked by the manufacturer as being single-use or disposable only

BIOLOGICAL SPORE TESTING - WEEKLY

> *(17) Proper functioning of the sterilization cycle of all sterilization devices shall be verified at least weekly through the use of a biological indicator (such as a spore test). Test results shall be documented and maintained for 12 months.*

A consideration in any sterilization cycle is verification that the sterilizer worked properly. Only using biologic monitors can do this. The CDC and ADA recommend weekly monitoring of sterilizers using biological monitors – The Dental Board of California requires all autoclaves and mechanical sterilization units, regardless of type, to be spore tested weekly.

Chemiclaves (chemical vapor device) use a different type of spore testing device than steam or dry heat autoclaves; however, the testing procedure is exactly the same regardless of type. Unlike steam autoclaves that use water, the primary active agent in the solution used for chemical vapor sterilization is formaldehyde that requires a different type of spore testing strip to be used.

Once the testing process is complete, the spore test is sent to an authorized laboratory for evaluation. Spore test laboratory reports are to be kept available in the facility for no less than 12 months – one year.

If the results are unsatisfactory, the laboratory will call the office and notify the staff or doctor of the results. If the problem is thought to be the testing method, the test is repeated. If the problem is defective equipment, the sterilizer is rendered "non-functional" until checked/repaired by the dental repair service or manufacturer.

Dental assistants need to consider the following reasons as to why a spore test could produce negative or failing results:

a. Make sure sterilizer is being operated using correct time, temperature, and pressure and correct solutions

b. DO NOT overload chamber

c. DO NOT interrupt sterilizing cycle

d. DO NOT stack instruments or over crowd instrument packs

e.   If any problem, redo sterilization cycle

f.   DO NOT test the first load of the day – the machine has not had a chance to properly warm-up prior to testing

g.   Never test in an empty machine – always place spore testing device in the center of the chamber

IRRIGATION

(18) Sterile coolants/irrigants shall be used for surgical procedures involving soft tissue or bone. Sterile coolants/irrigants must be delivered using a sterile delivery system.

The Board's regulations address the use of sterile-only coolants or irrigants during procedures such as surgery by using sterile delivery systems or devices such as a sterile disposable syringes or sterile bulb syringe.

NEW LAW:

On September 19, 2017, Governor Brown signed Assembly Bill (AB) 1277 into law, which requires the Dental Board to amend (change) the regulations on the minimum standards for infection control to require water or other methods used for irrigation to be sterile or contain recognized disinfecting or antibacterial properties when performing dental procedures that expose dental pulp.

All DHCP should be aware of the new law and the basis for the new ruling. In 2015 and 2016, two states, California and Georgia, reported dental patients contracting a bacterial infection *(M. Abscessus)* found to be caused from dirty dental unit waterlines. In total, more than 75 pediatric dental patients were hospitalized with this very serious bacterial infection that, historically, causes leprosy and tuberculosis. In both cases, the treatment being performed involved pulp-capping.

FACILITIES

(19) If non-critical items or surfaces likely to be contaminated are manufactured in a manner preventing cleaning and disinfection they shall be protected with disposable impervious barriers. Disposable barriers shall be changed when visibly soiled or damaged and between patients.

(20) Clean and disinfect all clinical contact surfaces that are not protected by impervious barriers using a California Environmental Protection Agency (Cal-EPA) registered, hospital-grade low- to intermediate-level disinfectant after each patient. The low-level disinfectants used shall be labeled effective against HBV and HIV. Use disinfectants in accordance with the manufacturer's instructions. Clean all housekeeping surfaces (e.g. floors, walls, sinks) with a detergent and water or a Cal-EPA registered, hospital-grade disinfectant. Products used to clean items or surfaces prior to disinfection procedures shall be clearly labeled and follow all material safety data sheet (SDS) handling and storage instructions.

Every dental healthcare worker should ensure that each patient is protected against risk of infection from contamination. To accomplish this, the dental operatory and adjacent support areas must be processed for infection control between each patient.

Three (3) major steps regarding infection control in the dental operatory include:

1.   Aseptic preparation of the operatory.

2.   Control of contamination generated during treatment.

3.   Disposal of consumable products and sterilization and disinfection of reusable materials.

Clinical contact surfaces are considered to be countertops, dental carts, patient chairs, and operator stools to name a few. Housekeeping surfaces are considered to be floors, walls and sinks and require, at minimum, a low-level hospital grade surface disinfectant to use when cleaning and disinfecting.

DENTAL UNIT WATER LINES AND VACUUM SYSTEMS

> *(21) Dental unit water lines shall be anti-retractive. At the beginning of each workday, dental unit lines and devices shall be purged with air or flushed with water for at least two (2) minutes prior to attaching handpieces, scalers, air water syringe tips, or other devices. The dental unit lines and devices shall be flushed between each patient for a minimum of twenty (20) seconds.*

A plastic, disposable or autoclavable metal syringe tip is used for each patient and either discarded or sterilized. Plastic barriers cover the air/water syringe handle and control buttons. A new tip is placed after each use, making sure that no plastic material is trapped over the orifice. The syringe is then purged by spraying water through the lines at the beginning of the day and end of the day for **two (2) minutes** to remove all potential microbial material that may have built up in the syringe lines.

Self-contained water systems attached to cart delivery systems allow for the use of treated/disinfected water to be used during treatment procedures. These special water lines are attached to the high speed handpiece lines, the ultrasonic scaler lines and the air/water syringe lines. Therefore, a protocol for setting up the water systems, purging the system and disengaging/cleaning the system must be established and reviewed.

Dental operatory cart/delivery systems may be connected to the municipal water supply or disconnected and attached to a self-contained water system. The ADA has established criteria stating that all dental offices shall deliver water into the patient's mouth using water with no more than 200 CFU (Colony Forming Units) of bacteria. In order to comply with this standard, dental offices often utilize water safety equipment.

Each bottle is especially made for the units, and must never be rinsed or cleaned using city water. Only distilled bottled water may be used for filling or cleaning of the bottles.

After each patient, air/water syringe and handpiece lines must be flushed for two (2) minutes. Place the air/water syringe or handpiece line into the HVE and turn on the HVE valve. Step on the rheostat to engage the handpiece line or depress the water button on the air/water syringe line. The suction system allows for the operator to purge without spraying water throughout the operatory area.

Note: Handpieces and air/water syringe tips must be removed prior to purging.

Following the completion of the day's work, the bottle system must be purged and the bottles removed from each cart. No water should remain in dental unit lines overnight or over the weekend. The sole purpose of using a bottled water system is to eliminate the possibility of **biofilm** developing in the lines where water is allowed to sit stagnant. This water encourages growth of microorganisms and, if not purged, develops into pathogenic microorganisms, capable of passing disease to the patient such as Legionella.

Purge all lines using water during the delivery of care (handpiece lines, ultrasonic scaler lines, air/water syringe) as before. When only air is flowing from the lines, the purge process is accurately completed. No water remains in the lines and the bottle is completely empty. This empty bottle remains on the cart to protect the unit and the tubing. Turn the "bottle water" toggle switch off and the main power button on the back of the unit. The unit is properly purged for the evening/weekend.

At the beginning of the next work day, follow the set-up procedure indicated earlier, making sure to hydrate the lines for a full two minutes.

The California RDA General Written and Law Examination Prep Book © 2017, 2018 • KB Dental Arts – Publisher

Between patients the air/water syringe must be purged 20 seconds. When the dental procedure is completed, all disposable and plastic barriers are disposed of properly and the handpiece tubing is **spray-wipe-sprayed** with an intermediate level disinfectant.

A disposable HVE or HVE tip is inserted into the respective hose for each patient. When the procedure is completed, the disposable tips must be thrown away. The evacuation housing is removed and prepared for autoclaving. All tubing is laid on top of the mobile cart and disinfected using the **spray-wipe-spray** technique. Replace handpieces in holders.

All vacuum systems must be cleaned by running a suction detergent agent after all invasive procedures and/or at the end of each day. The operator must wear appropriate personal protective equipment (PPE) including safety eyewear and utility gloves. After use, eyewear and utility gloves are cleaned and disinfected. All other PPE are disposed of properly.

DISCARDING OF CONTAMINATED MATERIALS

(22) Contaminated solid waste shall be disposed of according to applicable local, state, and federal environmental standards.

Disinfecting a barrier-protected operatory requires removal of all surface protective covers and disinfection of the area where the barrier joined the equipment. New barriers are applied. The used material must be discarded. If visible blood or excessive moisture is involved, California requires disposal of such items as a biohazard waste in red labeled bags and disposed of using an authorized waste management company.

LAB AREAS

(23) Splash shields and equipment guards shall be used on dental laboratory lathes. Fresh pumice and a sterilized or new ragwheel shall be used for each patient. Devices used to polish, trim, or adjust contaminated intraoral devices shall be disinfected or sterilized, properly packaged or wrapped and labeled with the date and the specific sterilizer used if more than one sterilizer is utilized in the facility. If packaging is compromised, the instruments shall be re-cleaned, packaged in new wrap, and sterilized again. Sterilized items will be stored in a manner so as to prevent contamination.

Routine procedures such as adjusting and polishing removable dental appliances require a laboratory area where infection control must be practiced. Regulations require all appliances be disinfected using an intermediate-level disinfectant prior to manipulation (adjustment) in a lab or other dental equipment.

Lathe manipulation of any prosthesis requires the use of a new rag wheel and fresh pumice. After use, the pumice will be discarded, the pumice tray cleaned and disinfected using an intermediate-level disinfectant, and a new rag wheel placed on the device. The splash guard will be disinfected with an intermediate-level disinfectant.

All lab burs and rotary devices must be cleaned and sterilized in accordance with the same procedures used for semi-critical instruments.

(24) All intraoral items such as impressions, bite registrations, prosthetic and orthodontic appliances shall be cleaned and disinfected with an intermediate-level disinfectant before manipulation in the laboratory and before placement in the patient's mouth. Such items shall be thoroughly rinsed prior to placement in the patient's mouth.

The California RDA General Written and Law Examination Prep Book © 2017, 2018 • KB Dental Arts – Publisher

IMPRESSIONS

Ideally, a dental impression should be rinsed with tap water after removal from the mouth and then disinfected. Several different disinfectants can be used. The rinsed impressions are placed in a closable container with an appropriate disinfecting solution. Zip-lock plastic bags work well in this application.

ASEPSIS IN RADIOLOGY

Infection control principles should also be observed when dental assistants take radiographs. Basic protocols include:

- Barriers are the best protect radiographic equipment as chemical disinfection is difficult to use on sensitive electronics.
- The exposure control switch should be protected with a disposable barrier.
- When using digital radiographic sensors, the sensor device is covered with an impervious barrier prior to placement intraorally.

The Dental Board of California's Infection Control Regulations

Effective 8/20/2011 by Order of Adoption issued by the Office of Administrative Law 7/21/2011

Section 1005 of Division 10 of Title 16 of the California Code of Regulations

§ 1005. Minimum Standards for Infection Control

(a) Definitions of terms used in this section:

(1) "Standard precautions" are a group of infection prevention practices that apply to all patients, regardless of suspected or confirmed infection status, in any setting in which healthcare is delivered. These include hand hygiene, use of gloves, gown, mask, eye protection, or face shield, depending on the anticipated exposure, and safe handling of sharps. Standard precautions shall be used for care of all patients regardless of their diagnoses or personal infectious status.

(2) "Critical items" confer a high risk for infection if they are contaminated with any microorganism. These include all instruments, devices, and other items used to penetrate soft tissue or bone.

(3) "Semi-critical items" are instruments, devices and other items that are not used to penetrate soft tissue or bone, but contact oral mucous membranes, non-intact skin or other potentially infectious materials (OPIM).

(4) "Non-critical items" are instruments, devices, equipment, and surfaces that come in contact with soil, debris, saliva, blood, OPIM and intact skin, but not oral mucous membranes.

(5) "Low-level disinfection" is the least effective disinfection process. It kills some bacteria, some viruses and fungi, but does not kill bacterial spores or mycobacterium tuberculosis var bovis, a laboratory test organism used to classify the strength of disinfectant chemicals.

(6) "Intermediate-level disinfection" kills mycobacterium tuberculosis var bovis indicating that many human pathogens are also killed. This process does not necessarily kill spores.

(7) "High-level disinfection" kills some, but not necessarily all, bacterial spores. This process kills mycobacterium tuberculosis var bovis, bacteria, fungi, and viruses.

(8) "Germicide" is a chemical agent that can be used to disinfect items and surfaces based on the level of contamination.

(9) "Sterilization" is a validated process used to render a product free of all forms of viable microorganisms.

(10) "Cleaning" is the removal of visible soil (e.g., organic and inorganic material) debris and OPIM from objects and surfaces and shall be accomplished manually or mechanically using water with detergents or enzymatic products.

(11) "Personal Protective Equipment" (PPE) is specialized clothing or equipment worn or used for protection against a hazard. PPE items may include, but are not limited to, gloves, masks, respiratory devices, protective eyewear and protective attire which are intended to prevent exposure to blood, body fluids and OPIM, and chemicals used for infection control. General work attire such as uniforms, scrubs, pants and shirts, are not considered to be PPE.

(12) "Other Potentially Infectious Materials" (OPIM) means any one of the following:

   (A) Human body fluids such as saliva in dental procedures and any body fluid that is visibly contaminated with blood, and all body fluids in situations where it is difficult or impossible to differentiate between body fluids;

   (B) Any unfixed tissue or organ (other than intact skin) from a human (living or dead);

   (C) Any of the following, if known or reasonably likely to contain or be infected with HIV, HBV, or HCV:

      (i) Cell, tissue, or organ cultures from humans or experimental animals;

      (ii) Blood, organs, or other tissues from experimental animals; or

      (iii) Culture medium or other solutions.

(13) "Dental Healthcare Personnel" (DHCP) are all paid and non-paid personnel in the dental health-care setting who might be occupationally exposed to infectious materials, including body substances and contaminated supplies, equipment, environmental surfaces, water, or air. DHCP includes dentists, dental hygienists, dental assistants, dental laboratory technicians (in-office and commercial), students and trainees, contractual personnel, and other persons not directly involved in patient care but potentially exposed to infectious agents (e.g., administrative, clerical, housekeeping, maintenance, or volunteer personnel).

(b) All DHCP shall comply with infection control precautions and enforce the following minimum precautions to minimize the transmission of pathogens in health care settings mandated by the California Division of Occupational Safety and Health (Cal/OSHA).

   (1) Standard precautions shall be practiced in the care of all patients.

   (2) A written protocol shall be developed, maintained, and periodically updated for proper instrument processing, operatory cleanliness, and management of injuries. The protocol shall be made available to all DHCP at the dental office.

   (3) A copy of this regulation shall be conspicuously posted in each dental office.

Personal Protective Equipment:

(4) All DHCP shall wear surgical facemasks in combination with either chin length plastic face shields or protective eyewear whenever there is potential for aerosol spray, splashing or spattering of the following: droplet nuclei, blood, chemical or germicidal agents or OPIM. Chemical-resistant utility gloves and appropriate, task specific PPE shall be worn when handling hazardous chemicals. After each patient treatment masks shall be changed and disposed. After each patient treatment, face shields and protective eyewear shall be cleaned, disinfected, or disposed.

(5) Protective attire shall be worn for disinfection, sterilization, and housekeeping procedures involving the use of germicides or handling contaminated items. All DHCP shall wear reusable or disposable protective attire whenever there is a potential for aerosol spray, splashing or spattering of blood, OPIM, or chemicals and germicidal agents. Protective attire must be changed daily or between patients if they should become moist or visibly soiled. All PPE used during patient care shall be removed when leaving laboratories or areas of patient care activities. Reusable gowns shall be laundered in accordance with Cal/OSHA Bloodborne Pathogens Standards (Title 8, Cal. Code Regs., section 5193).

Hand Hygiene:

(6) All DHCP shall thoroughly wash their hands with soap and water at the start and end of each workday. DHCP shall wash contaminated or visibly soiled hands with soap and water and put on new gloves before treating each patient. If hands are not visibly soiled or contaminated an alcohol based hand rub may be used as an alternative to soap and water. Hands shall be thoroughly dried before donning gloves in order to prevent promotion of bacterial growth and washed again immediately after glove removal. A DHCP shall refrain from direct patient care if conditions are present that may render the DHCP or patients more susceptible to opportunistic infection or exposure.

(7) All DHCP who have exudative lesions or weeping dermatitis of the hand shall refrain from all direct patient care and from handling patient care equipment until the condition resolves.

Gloves:

(8) Medical exam gloves shall be worn whenever there is contact with mucous membranes, blood, OPIM, and during all pre-clinical, clinical, post-clinical, and laboratory procedures. When processing contaminated sharp instruments, needles, and devices, DHCP shall wear heavy-duty utility gloves to prevent puncture wounds. Gloves must be discarded when torn or punctured, upon completion of treatment, and before leaving laboratories or areas of patient care activities. All DHCP shall perform hand hygiene procedures before donning gloves and after removing and discarding gloves. Gloves shall not be washed before or after use.

Needle and Sharps Safety:

(9) Needles shall be recapped only by using the scoop technique or a protective device. Needles shall not be bent or broken for the purpose of disposal. Disposable needles, syringes, scalpel blades, or other sharp items and instruments shall be placed into sharps containers for disposal as close as possible to the point of use according to all applicable local, state, and federal regulations.

Sterilization and Disinfection:

(10) All germicides must be used in accordance with intended use and label instructions.

(11) Cleaning must precede any disinfection or sterilization process. Products used to clean items or surfaces prior to disinfection procedures shall be used according to all label instructions.

(12) Critical instruments, items and devices shall be discarded or pre-cleaned, packaged or wrapped and sterilized after each use. Methods of sterilization shall include steam under pressure (autoclaving), chemical vapor, and dry heat. If a critical item is heat-sensitive, it shall, at minimum, be processed with high-level disinfection and packaged or wrapped upon completion of the disinfection process. These instruments, items, and devices, shall remain sealed and stored in a manner so as to prevent contamination, and shall be labeled with the date of sterilization and the specific sterilizer used if more than one (1) sterilizer is utilized in the facility.

(13) Semi-critical instruments, items, and devices shall be pre-cleaned, packaged or wrapped and sterilized after each use. Methods of sterilization include steam under pressure (autoclaving), chemical vapor and dry heat. If a semi-critical item is heat sensitive, it shall, at minimum, be processed with high level disinfection and packaged or

wrapped upon completion of the disinfection process. These packages or containers shall remain sealed and shall be stored in a manner so as to prevent contamination, and shall be labeled with the date of sterilization and the specific sterilizer used if more than one sterilizer is utilized in the facility.

(14) Non-critical surfaces and patient care items shall be cleaned and disinfected with a California Environmental Protection Agency (Cal/EPA)-registered hospital-grade disinfectant (low-level disinfectant) labeled effective against HBV and HIV. When the item is visibly contaminated with blood or OPIM, a Cal/EPA-registered hospital-grade intermediate-level disinfectant with a tuberculocidal claim shall be used.

(15) All high-speed dental hand pieces, low-speed hand pieces, rotary components and dental unit attachments such as reusable air/water syringe tips and ultrasonic scaler tips, shall be packaged, labeled and heat-sterilized in a manner consistent with the same sterilization practices as a semi-critical item.

(16) Single use disposable items such as prophylaxis angles, prophylaxis cups and brushes, tips for high-speed evacuators, saliva ejectors, air/water syringe tips, and gloves shall be used for one (1) patient only and discarded.

(17) Proper functioning of the sterilization cycle of all sterilization devices shall be verified at least weekly through the use of a biological indicator (such as a spore test). Test results shall be documented and maintained for 12 months.

Irrigation:

(18) Sterile coolants/irrigants shall be used for surgical procedures involving soft tissue or bone. Sterile coolants/irrigants must be delivered using a sterile delivery system.

Facilities:

(19) If non-critical items or surfaces likely to be contaminated are manufactured in a manner preventing cleaning and disinfection they shall be protected with disposable impervious barriers. Disposable barriers shall be changed when visibly soiled or damaged and between patients.

(20) Clean and disinfect all clinical contact surfaces that are not protected by impervious barriers using a California Environmental Protection Agency (Cal-EPA) registered, hospital-grade low- to intermediate-level disinfectant after each patient. The low-level disinfectants used shall be labeled effective against HBV and HIV. Use disinfectants in accordance with the manufacturer's instructions. Clean all housekeeping surfaces (e.g. floors, walls, sinks) with a detergent and water or a Cal-EPA registered, hospital-grade disinfectant. Products used to clean items or surfaces prior to disinfection procedures shall be clearly labeled and follow all material safety data sheet (SDS) handling and storage instructions.

(21) Dental unit water lines shall be anti-retractive. At the beginning of each workday, dental unit lines and devices shall be purged with air or flushed with water for at least two (2) minutes prior to attaching handpieces, scalers, air water syringe tips, or other devices. The dental unit lines and devices shall be flushed between each patient for a minimum of twenty (20) seconds.

(22) Contaminated solid waste shall be disposed of according to applicable local, state, and federal environmental standards.

Lab Areas:

(23) Splash shields and equipment guards shall be used on dental laboratory lathes. Fresh pumice and a sterilized or new ragwheel shall be used for each patient. Devices used to polish, trim, or adjust contaminated intraoral devices shall be disinfected or sterilized, properly packaged or wrapped and labeled with the date and the specific sterilizer used if more than one sterilizer is utilized in the facility. If packaging is compromised, the instruments shall be re-

– 163 –

cleaned, packaged in new wrap, and sterilized again. Sterilized items will be stored in a manner so as to prevent contamination.

(24) All intraoral items such as impressions, bite registrations, prosthetic and orthodontic appliances shall be cleaned and disinfected with an intermediate-level disinfectant before manipulation in the laboratory and before placement in the patient's mouth. Such items shall be thoroughly rinsed prior to placement in the patient's mouth.

(c) The Dental Board of California and Dental Hygiene Committee of California shall review this regulation annually and establish a consensus.

[1] Cal/EPA contacts: WEBSITE www.cdpr.ca.gov or Main Information Center (916) 324-0419.

Note: Authority cited: Section 1614, Business and Professions Code. Reference: Section 1680, Business and Professions Code.

CHAPTER REVIEW COMMENTS:

Infection control is a difficult discipline to teach. Although the concept of "sterilization" has been taught in dental schools and to dental assistants for several decades, the process of protecting the dental staff and the patients from cross-contamination with infectious materials has only been seriously focused on over the past 15 to 20 years. In fact, true dental infection control was just not a great concern in most dental practices until one dramatic event demonstrated to the profession the importance of the way dentistry looked at infectious diseases and the role we play in the prevention of such diseases in our work environment.

In 1999, the Dental Board of California adopted the first regulations for Infection Control governing all dental practices and practitioners. Although infection control protocols and procedures are performed by both licensed and unlicensed dental staff, the factors involved in the overall protection of the public is the rationale for making infection control one of the largest sections of the RDA examination. Regardless of the "training" you may have received in the workplace or in the classroom, the current examination statistics demonstrate that this section is the poorest performing section of the State examination – giving us strong reason to encourage all readers of this book to focus very carefully on the regulations and not what has been the common practices and principles used in the work environment.

END OF CHAPTER – CRITICAL THINKING QUESTIONS

1. Who on the dental team is responsible for maintaining proper Infection Control protocols?
2. What does the term "OPIM" stand for?
3. What is the difference between sterilization and disinfection?
4. What does asepsis mean?
5. What are the three classifications of instruments in preparation for reuse?
6. What is the most common method of sterilization utilized today?
7. What two articles of PPE **must** be changed after each patient?
8. What items are considered personal protective equipment?
9. What items should be placed into a sharps container?
10. Is it possible to sterilize a dental operatory and the equipment in it?
11. The use of a chemical germicide to disinfect a room must be preceded by what action in order for disinfection to occur?

12. The act of spraying a surface (or wetting it) with disinfectant chemical and wiping it dry is considered what type of action?

13. Regulations require the use of heavy-duty utility gloves when using disinfectants – what does this mean when you are cleaning and disinfecting a dental operatory?

14. What is the difference between reusable protective attire and disposal protective attire and how are they different when being handled?

15. Masks are required for all treatment procedures – does this include treatment procedures that do not involve a handpiece or rotary device?

CRITICAL THINKING QUESTION ANSWERS FOUND IN APPENDIX

Notes

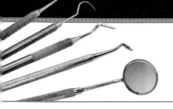

Unit 4 - Chapter 2

UNIT FOUR - SAFETY

CHAPTER TWO: RADIATION SAFETY PROCEDURES

EXAMINATION PLAN DATA:

Topic Area	Safety Procedures
Total Weight of Topic Area on Examination	30%
Subject Area	Radiation Safety
Percentage of Examination Questions in Radiation Safety Procedures	3%

RADIATION SAFETY PROCEDURES – TASKS AND KNOWLEDGE STATEMENTS

Tasks Associated with Topic Area	Knowledge Statements Associated with Topic Area
Implement measures to minimize radiation exposure to patient during radiographic procedures	Knowledge of legal and ethical requirements for RDAs and RDAEFs related to radiation safety
Implement measures to prevent and monitor scatter radiation exposure (e.g., lead shields, radiation dosimeter) to self and others during radiographic procedures	Knowledge of methods for the storage and disposal of radiographic film
Implement measures for the storage and disposal of radiographic film	

SCOPE OF PRACTICE – SPECIFIC TO RADIATION SAFETY PROCEDURES

According to the *Table of Allowable Duties*, the following may perform the stated functions:

An **unlicensed dental assistant** may perform radiographic duties under the *general supervision* of a supervising licensed dentist with successful completion of a course in Radiation Safety for California by a Board-approved provider.

Registered Dental Assistant (RDA):
A licensed dental assistant may perform all duties of an unlicensed assistant under either direct or general supervision as determined by the supervising/employer dentist.

The topic of Dental Radiology can be complex and vast. The RDA written examination will focus primarily on Radiation Safety for both the patient and the operator. Radiation safety is a crucial aspect of exposing radiographs. This chapter will focus only on the radiation safety aspect to make studying for the examination more manageable and relevant.

The California RDA General Written and Law Examination Prep Book © 2017, 2018 • KB Dental Arts – Publisher

KEY TERMS

Radiation	Forms of waves of energy emission through space or material
Lead Apron	A lead shield/drape used to protect the reproductive and blood-forming tissues from scatter radiation
Thyroid Collar	A flexible lead shield that can be easily wrapped around the patient's neck; often is part of the lead apron or may be separate
Ionizing Radiation	Radiation that produces ionization, resulting in harmful effects

DENTAL RADIATION

Each day, human beings are exposed to radiation while talking on their cell phones, watching TV, sitting in front of a computer or flying in an airplane. These daily activities expose us to some varying levels of radiation. Dental radiographs, or x-rays, also contain radiation. **Radiation** is defined as waves of energy emission through space and/or material. The amount of radiation used in dental imaging is small, but still causes biologic changes to occur. When exposing dental x-rays on patient, not all the x-rays pass through the patient to the dental film. The patient's body absorbs some x-rays as well. When the body tissues are exposed to x-rays some damage occurs to living cells. This can be referred to as ionizing radiation, or the harmful effect of x-rays in humans. The tissues can regenerate to a point, but will never fully return to their previous form.

Radiation has a cumulative effect on the human body. Each time the body is exposed to x-rays there is a small amount of damage done to the living tissues that cannot be fully reversed. Over time, the radiation "builds-up" within the tissues making the human body more susceptible to further damage. X-rays can damage reproductive cells passing along genetic defects to future generations. Body tissues are also affected, as discussed earlier, but the damages to these cells are not passed on to future generations. It is important to be aware of critical organs and tissues when exposing radiographs. The following are exposed to more radiation when taking dental x-rays:

1. *Skin:* the skin is in the direct beam of radiation; the skin will appear red, similar to a sunburn when high doses of radiation have been used; not typically seen in low dose dental x-rays.
2. *Lens of the eye:* many experts do not consider the lens of the eye to be at risk due to the low dose of radiation in dental x-rays; overexposure to radiation to can cause a cloudiness of the lens of the eye called cataracts.
3. *Thyroid gland:* located in the patient's neck; can be at risk if protective coverings are not used; use of a thyroid collar is recommended when taking dental x-rays; this gland is more sensitive in children than adults.
4. *Bone marrow:* there are bone marrow sites in the mandible and skull; changes in the bone marrow influenced by high amounts of radiation can result in leukemia.

USE OF THE LEAD APRON AND THYROID COLLAR

The amount of radiation a patient is exposed to while taking dental x-rays can be reduced by following some simple rules and guidelines. A lead apron is a wide, flexible covering placed over the patient once they are seated in the chair and prior to exposing dental radiographs.

The apron is a protective shield extending from the neck, covering the lap, to the patient's knees or mid-thigh. The length ensures that the reproductive organs (known as the gonadal area) of a patient is covered and protected from radiation exposure.

A thyroid collar is a flexible covering that surrounds only the neck of the patient. The lead-lined covering is intended to protect the thyroid gland from the effects of radiation exposure. It wraps around the patient's neck and is secured in place with Velcro. Today, the thyroid collar is frequently seen attached to the lead apron. The patient is fitted with both prior to any dental x-ray exposures.

The use of a lead apron with a thyroid collar is mandated in the state of California. Both are used solely for patient protection while taking dental x-rays. In California, the minimum thickness requirement of lead contained in the patient apron is .25 mm.

The lead apron and thyroid collar should be disinfected between patients. It is important to note that lead aprons and thyroid collars should never be folded when being stored. Folding will create cracks in the lead lessening its protective qualities. The lead apron and thyroid collar should be hung up or laid flat.

ADDITIONAL PATIENT PROTECTION METHODS

There are four additional patient protections the dental assistant should be knowledgeable about. These are:
1. Proper Technique
   - Using the proper technique when taking x-rays ensures the films will be quality films useful as diagnostic aides.
   - When a film is taken properly the first time, retakes are not necessary. This reduces the patient's exposure to radiation.
2. Film Speed (traditional film)/Image Receptor
   - The term film speed refers to the amount of radiation needed to create an image on the film.
   - Film speed is classified by letters; D, E and F speed films are the only speeds used for intraoral radiography.
   - Fast speed films are widely recommended as a form of patient protection.
   - Digital sensors have replaced traditional dental film and eliminate the need to select film speed.
3. Exposure Factors
   - Exposure factors refer to the settings on the dental x-ray unit.
   - Placing the kVP, mA and time setting to the correct level for the patient (Adult vs. pediatric) reduces their amount of radiation exposure.
   - Exposure settings are often adjusted for age of patient, area being radiographed and image receptor type.
4. Film/Sensor Holding Devices
   - May also be known as Image Receptor Holding Devices, if using digital vs. traditional radiology.
   - These devices hold the film or sensor in place for the operator while exposing the x-ray.
   - These keep the patients fingers and hands free of radiation exposure.
   - There is practically no difference in the holding devices used for digital sensors or for the traditional film technique; the devices are very similar in use and design.
   - Examples of image receptor holding devices are:
     - Snap-a-Rays
     - Disposable bite blocks (Styrofoam)
     - Paper bitewing tabs (disposable)
     - XCP RINN or XCP RINN-DS positioning device (aligns the beam)

[handwritten note: Fast speed film is better than lead apron.]

THE PROCESS OF COLLIMATION AND SCATTER RADIATION

Each x-ray machine is equipped with a **lead collimator**. The sole purpose of the collimator is to reduce the size of the radiation beam emitted from the lead-lined PID. The circular hole inside the collimator, also referred to as a **diaphragm**, is designed for the sole purpose of reducing the size of the x-ray beam to no more than 2.75" in diameter, approximately the size of a standard "size 2" x-ray film or image receptor. The reduction of the size of the useful beam emitted from the PID is referred to as the process of collimation; a process intended to protect the operator and patient from unused or scatter radiation.

OPERATOR PROTECTION FROM RADIATION EXPOSURE/SCATTER RADIATION

It is important to the health and well-being of any member of the dental team to follow safety guidelines when taking dental x-rays and to utilize radiation monitoring devices whenever possible. In California, the operator is required to wear a **dosimeter** to measure the amount of exposure to occupational radiation. It is worn while at work and never leaves the office.

The office may choose to monitor either for three (3) months out of every year, or one year out of every three (3). The only exception is in the event an employee becomes pregnant; the pregnant employee shall wear a dosimeter daily for the duration of her pregnancy.

Upon completion of any monitoring period, the office shall maintain records of the monitoring cycle in the OSHA manual in the event of state inspection.

Additional safety guidelines include standing at least six (6) feet away from the dental x-ray unit during exposure, standing behind lead-lined barrier or standard gypsum wall while exposing a dental x-ray and using the fastest exposure devices/techniques possible to maintain the ALARA (As Low As Reasonably Achievable) concept.

The filter stops the slow/weak waves

The colimator makes the waves into 2.75" tobe let out.

END OF CHAPTER – CRITICAL THINKING QUESTIONS

1. What is the definition of radiation?
2. What happens to body tissues when exposed to x-rays?
3. What is ionizing radiation?
4. What cells in the human body are damaged by the cumulative effect
5. What are patients draped with while x-rays are being exposed?
6. California law mandates the use of what?
7. What are the four patient protection techniques dental assistants should be knowledgeable in?
8. What device should a dental healthcare worker wear to monitor radiation levels?

CRITICAL THINKING QUESTION ANSWERS FOUND IN APPENDIX

A.L.A.R.A. – As low as Reasonably Achievable.

Unit 4 - Chapter 3

UNIT FOUR - SAFETY

CHAPTER THREE: OCCUPATIONAL SAFETY

EXAMINATION PLAN DATA:

Topic Area	Safety Procedures
Total Weight of Topic Area on Examination	30%
Subject Area	Infection Control
Percentage of Examination Questions in Occupational Safety	3%

OCCUPATIONAL SAFETY – TASKS AND KNOWLEDGE STATEMENTS

Tasks Associated with Topic Area	Knowledge Statements Associated with Topic Area
Implement protocols and procedures to protect operator from exposure during hazardous waste management	Knowledge of what constitutes hazardous waste and the protocols and procedures for its disposal
Package, prepare, and store hazardous waste for disposal	Knowledge of requirements for placing hazardous substances in secondary containers, (e.g., labeling, handling, applicable containers)
Store, label, and log chemicals used in a dental practice	

The US Occupational Safety and Health Administration (OSHA) is a federal agency dedicated to the safety and well-being of workers. OSHA sets and enforces protective standards and regulations that employers must follow to assure safe working conditions for their employees. OSHA provides training and education and requires employers to provide such training to all employees to make certain that the employers seek continual improvement in their safety standards.

All states are required to follow federally mandated OSHA safety guidelines; however, 26 states have their own OSHA programs by which the state requirements must meet or may exceed the federal mandate, in which case the state standards would supersede (take precedent). In California, we have Cal-OSHA.

In dentistry, the OSHA Bloodborne Pathogens Standard protects healthcare workers, including dental healthcare workers, from hazardous materials, harmful clinical procedures and other health-delivery job functions where the risk of occupational exposure is high. For our purposes, the focus of this section relates to hazardous materials handling, labeling, and communication to staff as to the hazards and health risks in materials handling.

The OSHA Hazard Communication Standard was developed specifically for the profession. Cal-OSHA has established standards in this area for which we will review in this chapter.

KEY TERMS

BBPS	OSHA's Bloodborne Pathogens Standard
Cal-DOSH	California Department of Occupational Safety and Health
CDC	Centers for Disease Control and Prevention
Contaminated Waste	Items such as gloves and cotton products that contain body fluids and other potentially infectious materials
DHS	Department of Health Services
EPA	Environmental Protection Agency; regulates the registration and use of hospital disinfectants
Exposure Controls	Materials and devices that prevent employee exposure to hazardous or infectious substances
Exposure Incident	Describes an injury involving either percutaneous or permucosal incident by an employee and must be reported on an incident report
FDA	Food and Drug Administration
GHS	Globally Harmonized System
OSHA	Occupational Safety and Health Administration
Parenteral	Transmission of bloodborne pathogens through the skin via a cut, human bite, abrasion or any break in the skin
Percutaneous	A sharps injury that penetrates through the skin
Permucosal	Coming in contact with mucous membranes such as eyes or the mouth
SDS	Safety Data Sheets *(formerly known as MSDS – Material Safety Data Sheets)*

Unit Four

ANNUAL OSHA TRAINING FOR THE WORKPLACE

The Cal-OSHA **Bloodborne Pathogens Standard** clearly states that all employees must receive training, at least annually, in the following areas:

- Bloodborne diseases
- Modes of transmission
- Fire and Emergency plan – protocols for the office
- Exposure Control Plan – protocols for the office
- Medical waste procedures
- Post-Exposure Plan – protocols for the office
- General Office Safety Plan – protocols for the office
- Hazard Communication Plan
- Injury and Illness Prevention Program – protocols for the office

HAZARD COMMUNICATION PROGRAM IN A DENTAL OFFICE

Every dental office is required by OSHA to have a written **Hazard Communication Program**. To comply with the Standard, the dental office must develop and implement a written compliance program consistent with the requirements specific to California.

Not all states are required to have certain elements of an OSHA Manual that California does – specifically, a written Injury and Illness Prevention Program (IIPP). The IIPP is unique to California and we will review this aspect of compliance later in the chapter.

Hazard Communication has a very specific purpose – to communicate the chemical hazards of each of the materials and solutions used by an employee in the commission of their specific duties and functions. For example, if an employee is required as part of their job description to clean the glass of the front office desk window, then the cleaner in which he/she uses to perform that task must have a communication protocol in place in the event the employee should spill, ingest or other harm themselves while using the product.

All dental healthcare personnel are required to obtain, at least, annual OSHA training to include proper handling, use and storage of dental materials. The Hazard Communication Officer must make certain that **Safety Data Sheets** (SDS) for each product are current and properly organized for easy access by employees in the event of a chemical exposure.

Dental offices are required to have SDS on file that contain the following product information:

1. Name, address, and emergency telephone number of the manufacturer who makes the chemical or material.
2. Hazardous ingredient data, such as permissible exposure limits.
3. Physical and chemical data that includes boiling and melting points, evaporation rate, vapor pressure, and water solubility.
4. Fire and explosion hazard data, such as flash point, flammable limits, and extinguishing media.
5. Reactivity data that includes stability and conditions to avoid, incompatibility, and any hazardous by-products.
6. Health hazard data, such as eye, skin, and respiratory protection, routes of entry, carcinogenicity, signs and symptoms of exposure, and emergency and first-aid procedures.
7. Precautions for safe handling and work practices such as handling and storing precautions, waste disposal method, normal clean up, and waste disposal methods.

Unit Four

The California RDA General Written and Law Examination Prep Book © 2017, 2018 • KB Dental Arts – Publisher

8. Control measures, such as respiratory protection, ventilation needs, protective clothing or equipment, and safe work practices.

Chemicals present a variety of hazards in the dental office because they may be flammable, toxic, caustic, corrosive, and carcinogenic (cancer causing). The Hazard Communications Officer must take on the role of Safety Officer when ensuring that a hazardous chemical inventory listing of all products used in the office is maintained. Ultimately, the employer is responsible for ensuring an SDS is available in the workplace for each hazardous material present.

When a product is dispensed or stored in a non-original container – also known as a secondary container – the item must be appropriately tagged and labeled in a manner which communicates the warnings for proper care, use, storage, PPE and emergency care. The warnings must correspond with the SDS for the specific product.

A container that is properly labeled when received from the supplier or manufacturer does not require an additional label. So long as a product remains in its **original container**, a SDS warning label is not required. The exception for labeling is single-use or "per-patient" dispensed items or products.

SDS LABEL COMPONENTS

Red Section: Flammability
Blue Section: Health
Yellow: Instability
White: Special Hazards/PPE

The dental office must also maintain a hazardous materials log, which is a list or binder of all hazardous materials used in the office, where is item is located, route of entry into the body and targeted organs.

The dentist is legally responsible to provide the training of staff in potentially hazardous materials and the Hazard Communication Program developed for the office for new employees within ten days of hire and whenever a new hazardous material is introduced into the office as well as at least annually thereafter.

Training must include:
- Availability of SDS materials
- Hazards of chemicals and proper handling
- An explanation of the labeling of hazardous chemicals in secondary containers
- Explanation of OSHA regulations
- How employees can obtain and use the appropriate hazard information for their safety

Employee training must be conducted during normal business hours using interactive resources – meaning that staff and the trainer need to be able to discuss and address questions about the content of the training. Staff training records must be kept for the duration of the staff member's employ plus three (3) years following separation of employment in the event the former employee requests copies of the training records.

Reducing hazards in the dental office can be accomplished by the following:
- Reading all product labels and following directions for use
- Keeping the number of hazardous chemicals to a minimum

- Storing chemicals and products in their original containers
- Avoid mixing two or more known hazardous chemicals together that may cause caustic cloud or explosion
- Washing and drying hands after handling all chemicals
- Wearing correct PPE whenever handling and storing chemicals
- Keeping the office and storage areas well ventilated
- Avoiding skin contact with chemicals
- Staying abreast of necessary handling instructions for all chemicals used in the practice
- Training on all new products introduced to the practice on a regular basis
- Disposing of all products and materials once a shelf-life has been reached
- Keeping a properly equipped and assembled emergency kit and chemical spill kit

THE OSHA HAZARD COMMUNICATION STANDARD – NEW GHS REQUIREMENTS EFFECTIVE 2016

In June, 2016, OSHA made improvements to the information available to employees for better protection against hazardous substances. Specifically, the United States Occupational Safety Administration joined with the United Nations to establish a method of identification and communication of chemical hazards known as the **Globally Harmonized System** or **GHS**.

First published in 2013, the GHS system created a standardized approach to identifying chemicals the same way regardless of what country they were sold in or used – for example, a chemical identified as toxic in one country was not necessarily identified as toxic in another.

The new GHS system addresses four (4) principal purposes:

- To establish a uniform process for determining chemical hazards
- To establish new and consistent use of hazard definitions and criteria
- To establish and require consistency among manufacturers with labeling
- To establish guidelines for standardizing the data on labels and Safety Data Sheets (SDS)

SDS LABEL CONTENT

Signal Word: Under the new labeling requirements, chemical manufacturers will be required to include a new "Signal Word" that gives you an idea of the severity of the hazard (Danger, Toxic, and Flammable)

Pictures or Pictograms: These symbols show the types of hazards and the areas affected by the chemical

Hazard Statements: Must be in English and identify the cautions you should use to protect yourself while using the chemical

Precautionary Statements: They are intended to form a set of standardized phrases giving advice about the correct handling of chemical substances and mixtures, which can be translated into different languages. Each precautionary statement is coded – under the new system the code begins with the letter "P"

Product Identifier: Label for substance should include the chemical identity of the substance

Supplier Identification: Name, address and telephone number of the manufacturer or supplier of the substance

These standardized labeling criteria, known as **harmonization**, will provide consistent labeling from different manufacturers, even of the same chemical, and will cut down on confusion of hazardous warnings and make it easier for workers to understand.

The California RDA General Written and Law Examination Prep Book © 2017, 2018 • KB Dental Arts – Publisher

The old Hazard Communication warning labels had to contain certain data but did not have to be organized on the label in any certain fashion. This allowed for one manufacturer's SDS to look totally different than another for the same product. This caused confusion and difficulty when trying to find hazard information.

NEW HAZARD CLASSIFICATIONS

The Hazard Classification is the system manufacturers use to determine the hazards of any given product. GHS has changed the classification used to provide users and manufacturers clearer criteria for classifying chemical hazards. These new specific criteria will help to ensure the evaluation of hazardous effects are consistent across manufacturers and that labels and SDS are more accurate as a result.

Once a hazard group and a hazard class have been identified, a hazard category must be assigned. Similar to the old SDS labeling system, a series of numbers is used to identify the severity of the category assigned; however, the new GHS system reverses the current numbering system, using (1) as the most severe and (4) as the least severe.

Old SDS Labeling – Hazard Categories	*New GHS Labeling – Hazard Categories*
4 = extremely severe level of hazard	1 = extremely severe level of hazard
3 = high level of hazard	2 = high level of hazard
2 = moderate level of hazard	3 = moderate level of hazard
1 = mild level of hazard	4 = mild level of hazard

EXPOSURE TO CHEMICALS

Chemicals can enter into the body one of three ways: inhalation of chemical vapors, ingestion of the chemical through eating or drinking, and absorption of the chemical through the skin.

Inhalation of gases and vapors from chemicals can cause direct damage to the respiratory system. Chemicals can also be absorbed through the skin upon direct contact or sometimes after repeated contact over a period of time. Ingestion through drinking or swallowing can occur when chemicals on the hands reach the mouth while eating or touching the mouth – handwashing is essential after handling chemicals in the dental office if gloves are not worn.

To avoid the routes of chemical exposure from occurring:
- Hand protection – wear gloves at all times when handling chemical agents
- Inhalation protection – wear a mask whenever handling chemical agents
- Eye protection – wear goggles or chin-length face shield when handling chemicals
- Protective clothing – wearing a lab coat or disposable gown during all chemical handling will avoid potential absorption of chemicals from splash or splatter onto clothes

EYEWASH STATIONS

OSHA requires that eyewash stations be installed in every workplace where chemicals are used. When in use, the eyewash unit will irrigate the eyes with a soft flow of water used to bathe the chemicals or irritants away from the eye.

Eyewash stations can be faucet-mounted, counter-mounted or wall-mounted and must be inspected monthly to ensure proper function and water flow. Employees must be trained in the proper use of the eyewash station as part of the Exposure Control training and reviewed at least annually.

Must be clearly
stated in Green!

WASTE MANAGEMENT

OSHA regulations as well as specific State regulations address best waste management practices in California when handling waste from the dental office for employee protection. When waste leaves the office, the EPA regulations apply to the disposal of the waste for environmental protection.

The classifications of waste are:
- **Regulated Waste** (Hazardous) – includes sharps, contaminated broken glass, burs, blades, endo files and suture needles (see Infectious Waste); blood, blood-soaked items, human tissues and biopsies; traps and filters that contain amalgam; requires special handling and special disposal by authorized providers.
- **Non-Regulated Waste** – includes contaminated waste without the presence of saturated blood such as saliva-soaked gauze, used patient bibs, and contaminated PPE.
- **Toxic Waste** (Hazardous) – includes waste that has a poisonous effect or that may result in pollutants; glutaraldehyde solutions; equipment cleaning solutions.
- **Infectious Waste** – is specific to sharps waste and must be contained and disposed of in closable, leak-proof, puncture-resistant containers with special labeling and regulated waste management services for destruction.
- **Photochemical Waste** – specific to radiographic lead foil and fixer; must be contained and managed by local and state approved disposal providers.
- **Pharmaceutical Waste** – includes medications, both prescription and over-the-counter, which have expired.
- **Universal/Recyclable Waste** – includes batteries, fluorescent lamps/lights.

Regular non-hazardous waste should be handled and recycled whenever possible; however, local waste management practices set by the dental office location may prescribe how even regular waste is handled. The dentist is responsible for proper packaging, labeling and transporting of waste generated in the dental office. Many dental offices choose to use a licensed transporter, a disposal service, or state authorized company to dispose of and treat regulated waste; either way, the dental office and the dentist is always responsible for the waste until it is rendered destroyed.

MANAGEMENT OF HAZARDOUS WASTE STREAMS

The following section addresses the proper management of materials commonly used in dental offices that are potentially hazardous or otherwise regulated materials. These materials include mercury and dental amalgam (elemental mercury, amalgam capsules, scrap amalgam, contact amalgam) x-ray processing wastes, lead foils or other heavy metals, disinfectants and medical waste.

DENTAL AMALGAM WASTES

Dental amalgam waste should never be discharged to the sewer or discarded with solid waste or medical waste. Dental amalgam is nearly 50% mercury, a metal that is classified as either a hazardous or universal waste when discarded, and also contains other heavy metals such as silver, zinc, copper and tin. If scrap dental amalgam is collected and sent away for recycling, then it is considered universal waste, as long as certain best management practices are followed (see asterisks below). If dental amalgam waste is discarded, then it must be removed offsite as hazardous waste.

BEST MANAGEMENT PRACTICES (BMPS)

- Do not rinse amalgam-containing traps, filters, or containers in the sink *
- Do not place amalgam, elemental mercury, broken or unusable amalgam capsules, extracted teeth with amalgam, or amalgam-containing traps and filters with medical "red-bag" waste or regular solid waste *

– 177 –

- Recycle, or manage as hazardous waste, amalgam, elemental mercury, broken or unusable amalgam capsules, extracted teeth with amalgam, amalgam-containing waste from traps and filters. Empty dental amalgam capsules containing no visible materials may be disposed of as a non-hazardous waste, except as required by local regulations *
- Collect and store **dry** dental amalgam waste in a designated, airtight container. Amalgam which is designated for recycling should be labeled "Scrap Dental Amalgam" with the name, address and phone number of your office and the date on which you first started collecting material in the container. In the past, dental amalgam scrap may have been kept under photographic fixer, water, or other liquid. If you should encounter amalgam stored in this manner, do not under any circumstances decant the liquid down the drain and discontinue this practice in the future. *
- Keep a log of your generation and disposal of scrap amalgam; inspectors may ask to see this to verify that your office is managing it correctly. A generation and disposal log is a record of what you placed in the amalgam container, when it was placed in the container, and when the container was picked up by or sent to a recycler or hazardous waste hauler.
- Check with your amalgam recycler for any additional requirements. Some recyclers do not accept contact amalgam (amalgam that has been in the patient's mouth); others may require disinfecting the amalgam waste. All recyclers have very specific packaging requirements.
- Separate excess contact dental amalgam from gauze that is retrieved during placement and place in an appropriate container.
- Use chair side traps to capture dental amalgam.
- Change, or clean, chair side traps frequently. Flush the vacuum system before changing the chair side trap.
- Change vacuum pump filters and screens at least monthly or as directed by the manufacturer.
- Check the p-trap under your sink for the presence of any amalgam-containing waste.
- Eliminate all use of bulk elemental mercury and use only encapsulated dental amalgam for amalgam restorations.
- Limit the amount of amalgam triturated to the closest amount necessary for the restoration, i.e. don't mix two spills when one spill would suffice. Keep a variety of amalgam capsule sizes on hand to ensure almost all triturated amalgam is used.
- Train staff that handle or may handle mercury-containing material in its proper use and disposal.
- By the year 2020, the use of amalgam sedimentation systems or amalgam separators shall be required by all dental offices in California.
- Do not use bleach to clean discharge systems as this may mobilize legacy mercury and amalgam in the system.

Mandatory per California Code of Regulations Title 22

AMALGAM TRAPS

Disposable amalgam traps are *preferable* to reusable traps because of the difficulty in effectively removing amalgam particles from the trap without discharging them to the sewer or garbage. Disposable traps should be changed weekly or more frequently if needed, or as recommended by the manufacturer of your equipment. It is recommended to use offsite recycling as a general practice.

Special handling and disposal of dental unit traps is required when used for dental procedures involving amalgam placement or removal. Unit traps used for all other procedures are carefully handled and may be disposed of in regular solid waste.

Amalgam Separators must be in traps now.

CONTACT AMALGAM (EXTRACTED TEETH CONTAINING AMALGAM)

Contact amalgam is amalgam that has been in contact with the patient. Examples are extracted teeth with amalgam restorations, carving scrap collected at chair-side, and amalgam captured by chair-side traps, filters, or screens as long as the sender certifies that they are not infectious wastes. Extracted teeth without attached tissue are considered non-medical wastes, unless the extracted teeth are deemed as biohazardous by the attending surgeon or dentist. Extracted teeth containing amalgam should be managed as hazardous waste in accordance with local and state requirements.

MEDICAL WASTE

The Department of Health Services (DHS) Environmental Management Branch regulates the storage, transportation, and disposal of regulated medical waste. In some counties, the management and enforcement of the Medical Waste Management Act has been delegated to the local health department. Regulated medical waste consists of sharps (anesthetic needles, blades, syringes) and bio-hazardous wastes (e.g. laboratory wastes, solid 'red-bag' wastes covered with blood or other potentially infectious materials, and pharmaceuticals). Medical wastes should be managed and disposed according to the requirements set by the Medical Waste Management Program of DHS or your local health department.

SHARPS WASTE

Disposable sharps should be placed in a proper sharps container. A sharps container should be located in each operatory and the sterilization lab per Cal/OSHA requirements. Full sharps containers should be disposed as medical waste; a registered hauler should transfer the sharps waste to a DHS-licensed treatment facility. Proper treatment by a permitted facility consists of either autoclave sterilization or incineration.

A sharps container shall meet all labeling requirements set forth by OSHA in the Bloodborne Pathogens Standard and shall be puncture resistant, leak-proof, and closeable.

BIO-HAZARDOUS WASTE

Solid 'red-bag' waste must be collected and disposed as regulated medical waste. You must contact a DHS-registered medical waste hauler for transfer to a DHS-licensed offsite treatment facility. Proper treatment by a permitted facility consists of either autoclave sterilization or incineration. Pharmaceutical waste, expired or partially-used, must be collected and transferred by a DHS-registered hauler to a DHS-licensed incinerator. Laboratory/surgical wastes must be collected and transferred by a DHS-registered hauler to a DHS-licensed incinerator. An example of this type of waste would be biopsy tissue.

UNIVERSAL WASTES

In 2001, the State of California adopted the Universal Waste Rule to regulate the generation, storage and disposal for a special category of wastes. The category of "universal wastes" includes certain hazardous wastes that are commonly generated by businesses. Because they pose a lower risk to people and the environment than other hazardous wastes, "universal wastes" are regulated based on a relaxed set of standards.

The requirements direct small quantity generators, such as dental offices, to ship their waste to a qualified universal waste handler, a universal waste transfer station, a recycling facility, or a hazardous waste disposal facility. The materials may also be accepted at some community hazardous waste collection events. They may not be disposed of in the regular trash.

The California RDA General Written and Law Examination Prep Book © 2017, 2018 • KB Dental Arts – Publisher
This book and the individual contributions contained within are protected under Copyright by the Publisher

Managing these wastes is not complicated, but you do need to follow these rules:

- Do not accumulate for longer than one year.
- Document the length of time you began accumulation.
- Label or mark packages to identify the type.
- Never try to treat or alter the wastes in a way which may alter their characteristics.
- Clean up any releases of universal wastes and repackage cleanup debris.

Below is a list of wastes which are included in the "universal waste" category that may be present in a dental office:

- *Aerosol cans* – Not considered a hazardous waste when completely empty, however, non-empty containers may be a universal waste if the remaining *propellant* is ignitable, or toxic or the *product* itself is ignitable, corrosive, or toxic. An aerosol containing pesticides, for example, would be considered a universal waste.
- *Batteries* – Included in the regulation are rechargeable, alkaline, button and small, sealed, lead-acid batteries. Batteries are a unique product comprised of heavy metals and other elements. Some of these toxic heavy metals include nickel, cadmium, mercury, nickel metal hydride and lead. It is these elements that can threaten our environment if not properly discarded.
- *Light tubes and lamps* – Fluorescent light tubes, high intensity discharge, and sodium vapor lamps contain mercury and other hazardous elements. They become a hazardous waste when the bulb or lamp no longer functions. Businesses may accumulate fluorescent tubes and lamps for up to one year prior to disposal. If you have a property management company that changes your light tubes and lamps for you, it is advised that you check with them to ensure they are being managed properly. These items must be recycled, or they must be managed as a hazardous waste.
- *Mercury-containing items* – Mercury-containing thermometers, thermostats, blood-pressure gauges and switches are considered universal wastes. (Note: Amalgam has been regulated as a universal waste for several years and was never exempted for small businesses like the other items listed).
- *Computer monitors, televisions, and other electronic devices* – Many of these devices can contain lead and other toxic metals that cannot be disposed of in the regular trash. Cathode ray tubes (TV's and computer monitors) must be recycled or they must be managed as a hazardous waste.

EXPOSURE CONTROL PLAN

In addition to the physical and chemical hazards of the dental office, dental assistants must be aware of the biological hazards to avoid occupational exposure to illness and disease.

OSHA's Bloodborne Pathogens Standard (BBPS) contains specific regulations to protect dental office employees by limiting occupational exposure to blood, saliva and OPIM. The dental office must have a written Exposure Control Plan designed to identify tasks, procedures and job classifications where occupational exposure takes place. Access to the Exposure Control Plan by employees is the responsibility of the employer.

The exposure control plan must include the following:

- Engineering and work practice controls used in the office setting such as handwashing protocols and available facilities, sharps management protocols, and eyewash station information
- Measures used to involve the use of standard (universal) precautions while treating patients and the personal protection devices available in the office

The California RDA General Written and Law Examination Prep Book © 2017, 2018 • KB Dental Arts – Publisher
This book and the individual contributions contained within are protected under Copyright by the Publisher

- Housekeeping schedule for cleaning; protocols and engineering controls to be used by employees when handling contaminated laundry, handling barriers, sharps containers, and oversight of regulated and non-regulated waste
- Information on the Hepatitis B vaccine and all vaccinations being offered by the employer
- Information regarding the reporting of exposure incidents such as needle stick incidents

The procedures specified in the plan are intended as goals, as standards to which everyone will work. As staff develops new, better procedures, these should be incorporated into the plan. Periodic evaluation and modification of the exposure control procedures will be completed. The Bloodborne Pathogens Standard states the exposure control must updated at least annually. Monitoring of the procedures and changes must be documented.

CARE PROCEDURE IN THE EVENT OF AN ACCIDENTAL EXPOSURE INCIDENT

In the event of an accidental exposure incident, the dental assistant should immediately stop what he/she is doing and report the incident to the office manager, doctor or safety officer. If the incident involves the hands, gloves must be removed, if worn, and treatment of the injury begins using the following protocols:

1. If the affected area is bleeding, squeeze it gently until a small amount of blood is released.
2. Wash hands thoroughly using antimicrobial soap and luke-warm water. Do not expose the injury to harsh chemicals like bleach or alcohol.
3. After drying hands, apply a small amount of antiseptic such as Neosporin cream to the affected area and cover with bandage or gauze and tape.
4. Immediately ask for an Exposure Reporting package from the Safety Officer or doctor and complete the following documents:
   a. Exposure Report Form – name, date, report of actions leading up to and including the exposure incident, what caused the incident to occur, and what action will be taken to ensure the incident does not occur again.
   b. Sharps Injury Log – complete log data including name, date and action which led to incident.
   c. Permission for Blood Testing – provide signature to accept or decline post-exposure medical care and blood testing for communicable disease testing.
   d. Seek medical attention – go to doctor or local medical care facility to receive follow-up care and blood testing; post exposure prophylaxis may be ordered.

FOLLOW-UP PROCEDURES

In the event of an exposure incident, the employer will follow the recommendations of the US Public Health Service and the Centers for Disease Control & Prevention (CDC) recommended protocols for testing, medical examination, prophylaxis, and counseling procedures. These procedures include:

1. Provide immediate care to the wounded employee.
2. Employees who have an exposure are required to report the exposure and must be given instruction in follow-up procedures.
3. Identify the source individual (if possible and if permitted by law) and, with the source individual's consent, test the source individual for HIV and HBV carrier status. Do not test source of known HBV and HIV status.
4. The employee is informed of the source's test results.
5. After obtaining employee's consent, collect the exposed employee's blood for immediate testing or store the collected blood for 90 days to allow for a delayed decision to test.

The California RDA General Written and Law Examination Prep Book © 2017, 2018 • KB Dental Arts – Publisher

6. The exposed employee is advised to report and seek medical evaluation of any disease or illness that occurs within 12 weeks after exposure.
7. The exposed employee may refuse any medical evaluation, test, or follow-up recommendation. This should be documented.

OCCUPATIONAL RISK CLASSIFICATIONS

The OSHA BBPS requires employers to document and train each employee based on categories of exposure or potential exposure. Categories of classifications may be 1, 2 and 3 or A, B, and C and are determined by the staff level and tasks performed *(see chart below)*.

The Standard defines an occupational exposure as a reasonably anticipated skin, eye, or mucous membrane exposure or any percutaneous injury involving blood or OPIM. Percutaneous and Permucosal exposures pose the greatest risk for transmission for HIV, HBV and HCV.

Occupational Risk Classifications		
Category	**Definition**	**Employee Type**
I or A	Routinely exposed to blood, saliva, OPIM, chemical germicides	Dentist, assistant, hygienist, sterilization assistant, clinical support staff
II or B	Occasional exposure to blood, saliva, OPIM; periodically don PPE to help clinical staff	Business office or front office staff who occasionally assist with clinical procedures or sterilization tasks
III or C	Never exposed to body fluids or chemicals	Financial staff, business office, office manager, insurance clerk

EMPLOYEE TRAINING

The BBP Standard requires the dentist/employer to provide, at least annually, training in infection control procedures and safety issues to all personnel who are classified as Category 1 and 2 (or Category A and B). Category 3 employees, those who never have the potential for exposure, are not required to obtain disease transmission or exposure incident training as they are employees who should never have the potential for such exposure.

All training must be recorded, and records retained for the duration of an employee's tenure as an employee plus three (3) years.

CHAPTER REVIEW COMMENTS:

There is a critical difference between infection control and occupational safety and health guidelines (OSHA). Do you know the difference?

In principal, many dental assistants do not know the difference and this is a basic concept that often causes confusion. Simply put:
- Infection control is for patient safety
- OSHA is for employee safety

When protocols for each safety category merge, we have a combination of employee and patient safety guidelines that work in concert for the overall protection of both the worker and the patient during dental procedures. Often, one basic principal falls short making the other principal less effective and meaningful for everyone's safety in the dental office.

END OF CHAPTER – CRITICAL THINKING QUESTIONS

1. What does the term OSHA stand for?

2. What is the best way for dental healthcare workers to prevent disease transmission?

3. What document is every dental office required to have per OSHA?

4. What are SDS and why are they important?

5. Who is legally responsible for providing OSHA training to employees in a dental office?

6. How many days after initial employment should a new employee receive OSHA training?

7. How is regulated waste disposed of in dental offices?

8. Is scrap amalgam considered hazardous or regulated waste?

9. Are dental offices considered small or large quantity generators of specific types of waste?

10. What are the rules to follow when managing waste in the dental office setting?

CRITICAL THINKING QUESTION ANSWERS FOUND IN APPENDIX

Notes

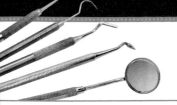

Bonus Chapter 1

BONUS CHAPTER I - DENTAL INSTRUMENT REVIEW

Dental Instruments are utilized in dentistry to complete dental procedures, such as general restorative procedures, preventive and specialized procedures. Each instrument is designed for a specific purpose. Instruments should not be referred to as "tools" as this terminology can be disconcerting to the patient. It is important to understand and recognize the most common instruments in dentistry. Each dentist will have preferences as to their dental instruments and will rely on the chairside assistant to prepare, organize, sterilize and hand off the correct instrument for each part of the procedure.

INSTRUMENT IDENTIFICATION AND SEQUENCE

It is important for the assistant to know the instruments to properly prepare the treatment room for a procedure. It is also important to understand the procedure, so the instruments can be placed in the proper sequence of use for ease during the procedure. Instruments usually have names but can also have numbers that designate the type of instrument. Specialty instruments often have numbers that universally identify its purpose and design. General restorative instruments usually have names that identify its purpose and design, while some have both names and numbers. The chairside assistant should learn both the names and numbers of the instruments where applicable.

An instrument tray or cassette is arranged from left to right. The arrangement is based on the steps in the procedure. Every tray or cassette will start with the basic setup: *mouth mirror, explorer, and cotton forceps* (some dentists may also include the periodontal probe). The additional instruments needed to complete the necessary procedure are added to the right of the basic instruments. Therefore, it is critical for the chairside assistant to be knowledgeable in both instrument identification and steps in the procedures performed in that particular office.

INSTRUMENT CLASSIFICATION

Instruments are referred to as hand or rotary instruments. Hand instruments are used by the operator, grasping the instruments in a specific manner. The action of the instrument is performed by the operator's hand. This chapter will focus primarily on hand instruments. Rotary instruments are used by utilizing a motor built into the instrument, such as a dental handpiece. The action of rotary instrument is performed by use of the motor.

Hand instruments have three parts:
A. **the handle**: this is the portion of the instrument held by the operator
B. **the shank**: this is the portion of the instrument that attaches the handle and the working end of the instrument.
C. **the working end**: this is the portion of the instrument that performs the work and will have a point, a blade or a nib which can be either smooth or serrated.

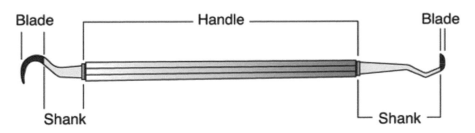

Hand instruments can be single or double ended depending on the operator's preference. Double-ended instruments have working ends at both ends of the instrument for ease in switching from the right to the left of a patient's mouth.

Below is a listing of generalized dental instruments utilized in restorative procedures along with their use and purpose in dentistry. The instruments are divided into the four categories of restorative dental procedures:
- examination,
- hand cutting,
- restorative and
- accessory.

EXAMINATION:

Mouth Mirror:	used for light reflection, indirect vision, tissue protection, and retraction.
Explorer:	many different kinds; double/single ended; helps to locate decay and check existing restorations.
Cotton Pliers/Forceps:	used to place and retrieve small objects, such as cotton rolls.
Periodontal Probe:	checks, locates, and measures pockets around teeth.

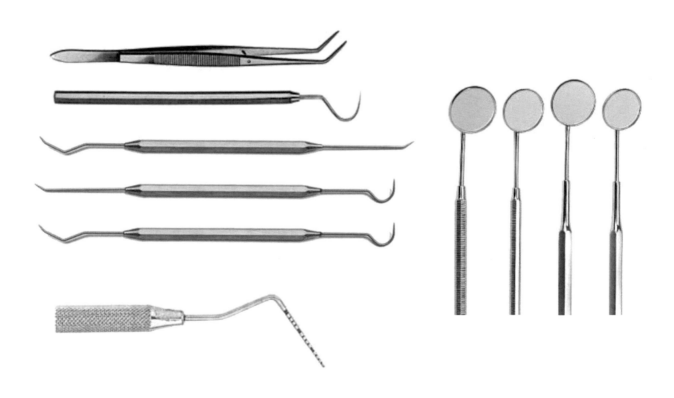

The California RDA General Written and Law Examination Prep Book © 2017, 2018 • KB Dental Arts – Publisher

HAND CUTTING:

The following is an illustrated listing of basic operative instruments used for cavity preparation. Candidates are encouraged to review other publications for a more detailed listing and illustrations of the various instruments used in clinical dentistry.

Hoe:

Hatchet: Used to refine and smooth the walls and floor of a tooth preparation.

Chisel:

Gingival Margin Trimmer (GMT):   similar to a hatchet, except the blade is curved and not flat and the cutting end is angled and not straight like a hatchet.

Spoon Excavators: large and small ends; removes caries manually; removes temporary fillings and materials and can be used to remove cement from restorations.

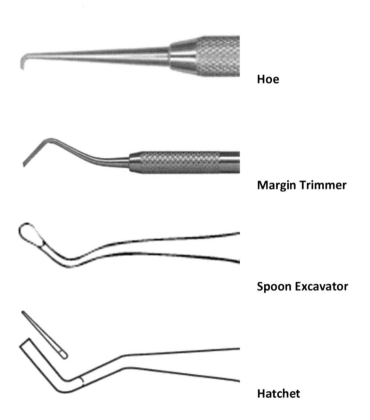

Hoe

Margin Trimmer

Spoon Excavator

Hatchet

The California RDA General Written and Law Examination Prep Book © 2017, 2018 • KB Dental Arts – Publisher

RESTORATIVE:

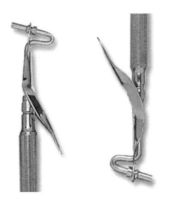

Amalgam Carrier: double ended; small end/large end; used to carry amalgam to the tooth prep

Amalgam Condenser: large and small ends; double or single ended; used to pack amalgam into the tooth prep

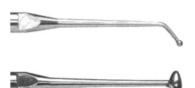

Burnishers: refines and makes smooth freshly placed amalgam; can be used to invert a rubber dam; types and shapes of burnishers: Football, Beavertail, Ball and Acorn

Discoid-Cleoid Carver: ideal for carving occlusal amalgams

Half-Hollenback Carver: ideal for carving interproximally

Woodson Plastic Instrument: used to place and shape dental material such as composite

ACCESSORY ITEMS: Candidates are encouraged to review other publications for a more detailed listing and illustrations of the various accessory items described below.

Amalgam Well:	freshly mixed amalgam is placed into the well; picked up by the amalgam carrier for transfer to the operator
Articulating Paper:	blue or red carbon paper used to check occlusion or bite
Articulating Paper Holder:	holds articulating paper
Crown & Bridge Scissors:	used to trim preformed temps or retraction cord
Bite Block:	props mouth open
Bur Block:	holds burs during a procedure
Color Code Rings:	used to organize instruments by procedure or use and location
Wax Spatula:	places wax on models in the lab setting
Cement Spatula:	mixes dental materials such as liners, bases and cements
Scalpel:	blade used to make incisions (Bard Parker)

SPECIALTY INSTRUMENTATION

The following section provides a listing of basic orthodontic instrumentation utilized for the limited RDA procedures listed under each.

ORTHODONTIC INSTRUMENTS:

Some illustrations have been provided in the Orthodontic Chapter of this book. Candidates are encouraged to review all the various sizes, shapes and styles of these orthodontic instruments using the internet and other textbook resources.

Orthodontic Scaler:	used to place and remove elastic ties; removes separators.
Elastic Separating Pliers:	pliers that have notches at the tips where the elastic separator is placed; the operator squeezes the handles of the pliers together causing the elastic to stretch thin allowing the separator to slide in to the contact area of the adjacent teeth.
Bird Beak Pliers:	used to aid in placement of steel separating springs.
Ligature Director:	used to assist in placing the elastic or wire ligature tie around the bracket.
Pin and Ligature Cutter:	snips the wire ligature tie once it has been tied around the bracket or during removal.
Ligature Tying Pliers:	aid in tying of ligature wires around brackets; have narrow serrated beaks similar to those of a hemostat.

The California RDA General Written and Law Examination Prep Book © 2017, 2018 • KB Dental Arts – Publisher

Posterior Band Remover Pliers: assists operator in removing bands without placing stress on the teeth or causing patient discomfort.

Howe Plier: can be used to check for loose parts (bands, brackets, etc.) of the fixed appliance.

END OF CHAPTER – CRITICAL THINKING QUESTIONS

1. What term should *not* be used to describe instruments?

2. What instruments make up the basic set-up?

3. Why is it important for dental assistants to be knowledgeable about dental instruments?

4. How are instruments arranged on a tray or in a cassette?

5. What are the two classifications of instruments?

6. Name and describe the three parts of a hand instrument.

CRITICAL THINKING QUESTION ANSWERS FOUND IN APPENDIX

The California RDA General Written and Law Examination Prep Book © 2017, 2018 • KB Dental Arts – Publisher
This book and the individual contributions contained within are protected under Copyright by the Publisher

Bonus Chapter 2

BONUS CHAPTER II – LEGAL DUTIES, SETTINGS AND LICENSURE

KEY TERMS

Core courses	CE courses providing education in basic principles and practices of dentistry
Dental Practice Act (DPA)	Defines the legal requirements necessary to practice dentistry and the scope of dental practice
Mandatory courses	CE courses required by the Dental Board of California for license renewal
Supplemental courses	CE courses not dealing with direct sciences

The dental healthcare team is the primary care unit within the profession of dentistry. The team consists of the Dentist, the dental assistant, Registered Dental Assistant or Registered Dental Assistant in Extended Functions, the Registered Dental Hygienist or Registered Dental Hygienist in Alternative Practice and the business office staff.

The definition of dentistry in California is stated in the law as:

§ 1625. _Dentistry_ is the diagnosis or treatment, by surgery or other method, of diseases and lesions and the correction of malposition's of the human teeth, alveolar process, gums, jaws, or associated structures; and such diagnosis or treatment may include all necessary related procedures as well as the use of drugs, anesthetic agents, and physical evaluation.

Every day, dental professionals are faced with issues involving the legal requirements and voluntary standards in the delivery of dental treatment. The **Dental Practice Act (DPA)** in California defines the legal requirements necessary to practice dentistry and the scope of dental practice. The legal standards for dental care are derived from both common law and statutory law, such as the DPA which is enacted by the state's legislative body.

The dental professional is governed not only by the DPA but also by voluntary standards, such as the principles of ethics that were developed and implemented by the dental profession itself. Both legal requirements and voluntary standards are implemented for the protection of the dental consumer – the patient.

THE STEPS TO ETHICAL DECISION MAKING:

1. Is the task I am about to perform legally delegable to me?
2. Do I possess the necessary license, permit or certificate to perform the function?
3. Am I physically, mentally and educationally competent to perform this function?
4. Am I performing this function in a safe working environment that meets the standards of Cal-DOSH (Division of Occupational Safety and Health)?
5. Has the patient been properly informed about his/her treatment?
6. Am I respecting the patient's right to privacy and confidentiality?

7. Am I maintaining complete and accurate patient records, and preserving those records and all patient data within the guidelines of HIPAA laws to preserve their confidentiality?
8. Am I willing to compromise my standards for the lack of ethics or legal responsibility on the part of an employer or fellow employees?
9. Do I maintain current knowledge of changes in dental practice act requirements, the laws pertaining to the practice of dentistry and dental assisting, occupational safety and health and infection control regulations?
10. Do I place my patient first and foremost and protect my patient's privacy and rights at all times without compromise?

THE DENTAL ASSISTANT – DEFINED

Although the term "dental assistant" is used in a general way in most workplace environments, the reality of the term is very different now in California and should be recognized for what it truly means based on the legal definition.

The Dental Practice Act states:

> *1750. (a) A dental assistant is an individual who, without a license, may perform basic supportive dental procedures, as authorized by Section 1750.1 and by regulations adopted by the Board, under the supervision of a licensed dentist. "Basic supportive dental procedures" are those procedures that have technically elementary characteristics, are completely reversible, and are unlikely to precipitate potentially hazardous conditions for the patient being treated.*

While "dental assistant" is a general term, the meaning is very different when describing the legal and ethical functions of the dental assistant as a member of the dental team; specifically, the duties and functions of a dental assistant are the duties and functions of an UNLICENSED dental assistant. The DPA is very clear as to the difference between a dental assistant (unlicensed), a Registered Dental Assistant (licensed) and a Registered Dental Assistant in Extended Functions (licensed).

KNOWING YOUR LEGAL DUTIES AND FUNCTIONS

UNLICENSED DENTAL ASSISTANTS (DA):

(a) A **dental assistant** may perform the following duties under the *general supervision* of a supervising licensed dentist:

> (1) Extra-oral duties or procedures specified by the supervising licensed dentist provided that these duties or procedures meet the definition of a basic supportive.
> (2) Operate dental radiography equipment for the purpose of oral radiography if the dental assistant has complied with certification requirements.
> (3) Perform intraoral and extraoral photography.

(b) A **dental assistant** may perform the following duties under the *direct supervision* of a supervising licensed dentist:

> (1) Apply non-aerosol and non-caustic topical agents.
> (2) Apply topical fluoride.
> (3) Take intraoral impressions for all non-prosthodontic appliances.
> (4) Take facebow transfers and bite registrations.

The California RDA General Written and Law Examination Prep Book © 2017, 2018 • KB Dental Arts – Publisher
This book and the individual contributions contained within are protected under Copyright by the Publisher

Bonus Chapters

(5) Place and remove rubber dams or other isolation devices.

(6) Place, wedge, and remove matrices for restorative procedures.

(7) Remove post-extraction dressings after inspection of the surgical site by the supervising licensed dentist.

(8) Perform measurements for the purposes of orthodontic treatment.

(9) Cure restorative or orthodontic materials in operative site with a light-curing device.

(10) Examine orthodontic appliances.

(11) Place and remove orthodontic separators.

(12) Remove ligature ties and archwires.

(13) After adjustment by the dentist, examine and seat removable orthodontic appliances and deliver care instructions to the patient.

(14) Remove periodontal dressings.

(15) Remove sutures after inspection of the site by the dentist.

(16) Place patient monitoring sensors.

(17) Monitor patient sedation, limited to reading and transmitting information from the monitor display during the intraoperative phase of surgery for electrocardiogram waveform, carbon dioxide and end tidal carbon dioxide concentrations, respiratory cycle data, continuous noninvasive blood pressure data, or pulse arterial oxygen saturation measurements, for the purpose of interpretation and evaluation by a supervising licensed dentist who shall be at the patient's chairside during this procedure.

(18) Assist in the administration of nitrous oxide when used for analgesia or sedation. A dental assistant shall not start the administration of the gases and shall not adjust the flow of the gases unless instructed to do so by the supervising licensed dentist who shall be present at the patient's chairside during the implementation of these instructions. This paragraph shall not be construed to prevent any person from taking appropriate action in the event of a medical emergency.

(c) Under the supervision of a registered dental hygienist in alternative practice, a dental assistant may perform intraoral retraction and suctioning.

LICENSED REGISTERED DENTAL ASSISTANTS (RDA):

(a) A **registered dental assistant** may perform all of the following duties:

(1) All duties that a dental assistant is allowed to perform.

(2) Mouth-mirror inspections of the oral cavity, to include charting of obvious lesions, existing restorations, and missing teeth.

(3) Apply and activate bleaching agents using a non-laser light-curing device.

(4) Use of automated caries detection devices and materials to gather information for diagnosis by the dentist.

(5) Obtain intraoral images for computer-aided design (CAD), milled restorations.

(6) Pulp vitality testing and recording of findings.

(7) Place bases, liners, and bonding agents.

(8) Chemically prepare teeth for bonding.

(9) Place, adjust, and finish direct provisional restorations.

(10) Fabricate, adjust, cement, and remove indirect provisional restorations, including stainless steel crowns when used as a provisional restoration.

(11) Place post-extraction dressings after inspection of the surgical site by the supervising licensed dentist.

Bonus Chapters

(12) Place periodontal dressings.

(13) Dry endodontically treated canals using absorbent paper points.

(14) Adjust dentures extra-orally.

(15) Remove excess cement from surfaces of teeth with a hand instrument.

(16) Polish coronal surfaces of the teeth.

(17) Place ligature ties and archwires.

(18) Remove orthodontic bands.

(b) A registered dental assistant may only perform the following additional duties if he or she has completed a board-approved registered dental assistant educational program in those duties, or if he or she has provided evidence, satisfactory to the board, of having completed a board-approved course in those duties.

(1) Remove excess cement with an ultrasonic scaler from supragingival surfaces of teeth undergoing orthodontic treatment.

(2) The allowable duties of an orthodontic assistant permit holder.

(3) The allowable duties of a dental sedation assistant permit holder.

(4) The application of pit and fissure sealants.

A registered dental assistant licensed on and after January 1, 2010, shall provide evidence of successful completion of a Board-approved course in the application of pit and fissure sealants prior to the first expiration of his or her license that requires the completion of continuing education as a condition of renewal. The license of a registered dental assistant who does not provide evidence of successful completion of that course shall not be renewed until evidence of course completion is provided.

LICENSED REGISTERED DENTAL ASSISTANTS IN EXTENDED FUNCTIONS (RDAEF):

(a) A registered dental assistant in extended functions licensed on or after January 1, 2010, is authorized to perform all duties and procedures that a registered dental assistant is authorized to perform and those duties that the board may prescribe by regulation.

(b) A registered dental assistant in extended functions licensed on or after January 1, 2010, is authorized to perform the following additional procedures under _direct supervision_ and pursuant to the order, control, and _full professional responsibility of a licensed dentist_:

(1) Conduct preliminary evaluation of the patient's oral health, including, but not limited to, charting, intraoral and extra-oral evaluation of soft tissue, classifying occlusion, and myofunctional evaluation.

(2) Perform oral health assessments in school-based, community health project settings under the direction of a dentist, registered dental hygienist, or registered dental hygienist in alternative practice.

(3) Cord retraction of gingivae for impression procedures.

(4) Size and fit endodontic master points and accessory points.

(5) Cement endodontic master points and accessory points.

(6) Take final impressions for permanent indirect restorations.

(7) Take final impressions for tooth-borne removable prosthesis.

(8) Polish and contour existing amalgam restorations.

(9) Place, contour, finish, and adjust all direct restorations.

(10) Adjust and cement permanent indirect restorations.

(11) Other procedures authorized by regulations adopted by the board.

(c) All procedures required to be performed under direct supervision shall be checked and approved by the supervising licensed dentist prior to the patient's dismissal from the office.

ALLOWABLE DUTIES OF SPECIAL PERMIT HOLDER IN DENTAL ASSISTING

ORTHODONTIC ASSISTANT PERMIT HOLDER (OAP):

A person holding an orthodontic assistant permit may perform the following duties under the *direct supervision* of a licensed dentist:

(a) All duties that a dental assistant is allowed to perform.

(b) Prepare teeth for bonding, and select, preposition, and cure orthodontic brackets after their position has been approved by the supervising licensed dentist.

(c) Remove only orthodontic brackets and attachments with removal of the bonding material by the supervising licensed dentist.

(d) Size, fit, and cement orthodontic bands.

(e) Remove orthodontic bands and remove excess cement from supragingival surfaces of teeth with a hand instrument.

(f) Place and ligate archwires.

(g) Remove excess cement with an ultrasonic scaler from supragingival surfaces of teeth undergoing orthodontic treatment.

DENTAL SEDATION ASSISTANT PERMIT HOLDER (DSAP):

A person holding a dental sedation assistant permit may perform the following duties under the *direct supervision* of a licensed dentist or other licensed health care professional authorized to administer conscious sedation or general anesthesia in the dental office:

(a) All duties that a dental assistant is allowed to perform.

(b) Monitor patients undergoing conscious sedation or general anesthesia utilizing data from noninvasive instrumentation such as pulse oximeters, electrocardiograms, capnography, blood pressure, pulse, and respiration rate monitoring devices. Evaluation of the condition of a sedated patient shall remain the responsibility of the dentist or other licensed health care professional authorized to administer conscious sedation or general anesthesia, who shall be at the patient's chairside while conscious sedation or general anesthesia is being administered.

(c) Drug identification and draw, limited to identification of appropriate medications, ampule and vial preparation, and withdrawing drugs of correct amount as verified by the supervising licensed dentist.

(d) Add drugs, medications, and fluids to intravenous lines using a syringe, provided that a supervising licensed dentist is present at the patient's chairside, limited to determining patency of intravenous line, selection of injection port, syringe insertion into injection port, occlusion of intravenous line and blood aspiration, line release and injection of drugs for appropriate time interval. The exception to this duty is that the supervising licensed dentist shall administer the initial dose of a drug or medication.

(e) Removal of intravenous lines.

(f) Any additional duties that the board may prescribe by regulation.

(g) The duties listed in subdivisions (b) to (e), inclusive, may not be performed in any setting other than a dental office or dental clinic.

MANDATORY EDUCATION REQUIREMENTS FOR UNLICENSED DENTAL ASSISTANTS

The employer of a dental assistant shall be responsible for ensuring that the dental assistant who has been in continuous employment for 120 days or more, has already successfully completed, or successfully completes, all of the following within a year of the date of employment:

    (1) A Board-approved two-hour course in the Dental Practice Act.

    (2) A Board-approved eight-hour course in infection control.

    (3) A course in basic life support offered by an instructor approved by the American Red Cross or the American Heart Association, or any other course approved by the Board as equivalent and that provides the student the opportunity to engage in hands-on simulated clinical scenarios.

The employer of a dental assistant shall be responsible for ensuring that the dental assistant maintains certification in basic life support.

CONTINUING EDUCATION REQUIREMENTS FOR LICENSED DENTAL ASSISTANTS AND DENTAL ASSISTANTS WITH SPECIAL PERMITS

There are three (3) types of continuing education courses available for licensed and permitted dental assistants in California.

- Mandatory
- Core
- Supplemental

Mandatory coursework includes infection control, OSHA, BLS certification and Dental Practice Act education every two (2) years.

Core coursework is considered those courses that provide education in the basic principles and practices of dentistry such as courses in dental materials, dental sciences, preventive services, esthetic and corrective dental procedures, nutrition, and subjects addressing dental disease.

Supplemental coursework is considered areas of dentistry not dealing with direct sciences and are, therefore, limited to a maximum of only 20% of the total required units for license or permit renewal. For example, a Registered Dental Assistant is required to complete 25 units of continuing education every two (2) years from the time of licensure and consistent with the date of license expiration when first issued a license. This means that only 20% of the 25 required units may be obtained in subjects considered to be supplemental. The topics are defined in regulations in the following way:

(1) **Mandatory courses** required by the Board for license renewal to include a Board-approved course in Infection Control, a Board-approved course in the California Dental Practice Act and completion of certification in Basic Life Support.

    (A) At a minimum, course content for a Board-approved course in Infection Control shall include all content of Section 1005 and the application of the regulations in the dental environment.

    (B) At a minimum, course content for the Dental Practice Act shall instruct on acts in violation of the Dental Practice Act and attending regulations, and other statutory mandates relating to the dental practice. This includes utilization and scope of practice for auxiliaries and dentists; laws governing the prescribing of drugs;

The California RDA General Written and Law Examination Prep Book © 2017, 2018 • KB Dental Arts – Publisher
This book and the individual contributions contained within are protected under Copyright by the Publisher

citations, fines, revocation, and suspension, license renewal, and the mandatory reporter obligations set forth in the Child Abuse and Neglect Reporting Act and the Elder Abuse and Dependent Adult Civil Protection Act and the clinical signs to look for in identifying abuse.

(C) The mandatory requirement for certification in Basic Life Support shall be met by completion of either:

(i) An American Heart Association (AHA) or American Red Cross (ARC) course in Basic Life Support (BLS) or,
(ii) A BLS course taught by a provider approved by the American Dental Association's Continuing Education Recognition Program (CERP) or the Academy of General Dentistry's Program Approval for Continuing Education (PACE).

A Basic Life Support course shall include all of the following:
1. Instruction in both adult and pediatric CPR, including two-rescuer scenarios;
2. Instruction in foreign-body airway obstruction
3. Instruction in relief of choking for adults, child and infant
4. Instruction in the use of automated external defibrillation with CPR; and
5. A live, in-person skills practice session, a skills test and a written examination.

(2) **Core courses** in the actual delivery of dental services to the patient or the community, such as:

(A) Courses in preventive services, diagnostic protocols and procedures (including physical evaluation, radiography, dental photography) comprehensive treatment planning, charting of the oral conditions, informed consent protocols and recordkeeping.
(B) Courses dealing primarily with nutrition and nutrition counseling of the patient.
(C) Courses in esthetic, corrective and restorative oral health diagnosis and treatment.
(D) Courses in dentistry's role in individual and community health emergencies and, disasters and disaster recovery.
(E) Courses that pertain to the legal requirement governing the licensee in the areas of auxiliary employment and delegation of responsibilities; the Health Insurance Portability and Accountability Act (HIPAA) and actual delivery of care.
(F) Courses pertaining to federal, state and local regulations, guidelines or statute regarding workplace safety, fire and emergency, environmental safety, waste disposal and management, general office safety, and all training requirements set forth by the California Division of Occupational Safety and Health (Cal-DOSH) including the Bloodborne Pathogens Standard.
(G) Courses pertaining to the administration of general anesthesia, conscious sedation, oral conscious sedation or medical emergencies.
(H) Courses pertaining to the evaluation, selection, use and care of dental instruments, sterilization equipment, operatory equipment, and personal protective attire.
(I) Courses in dependency issues and substance abuse such as alcohol and drug use as it relates to patient safety, professional misconduct, ethical considerations or malpractice.
(J) Courses in behavioral sciences, behavior guidance, and patient management in the delivery of care to all populations including special needs, pediatric and sedation patients when oriented specifically to the clinical care of the patient.
(K) Courses in the selection, incorporation, and use of current and emerging technologies.

(L) Courses in cultural competencies such as bilingual dental terminology, cross-cultural communication, provision of public health dentistry, and the dental professional's role in provision of care in non-traditional settings when oriented specifically to the needs of the dental patient and will serve to enhance the patient experience.

(M) Courses in dentistry's role in individual and community health programs.

(N) Courses pertaining to the legal and ethical aspects of the insurance industry, to include management of third party payer issues, dental billing practices, patient and provider appeals of payment disputes and patient management of billing matters.

(3) **Supplemental:** Courses in the following areas are considered to be primarily of benefit to the licensee and shall be limited to a maximum of 20% of a licensee's total required course unit credits for each license or permit renewal period:

(A) Courses to improve recall and scheduling systems, production flow, communication systems and data management.

(B) Courses in organization and management of the dental practice including office computerization and design, ergonomics, and the improvement of practice administration and office operations.

(C) Courses in leadership development and team development.

(D) Coursework in teaching methodology and curricula development.

(E) Coursework in peer evaluation and case studies that include reviewing clinical evaluation procedures, reviewing diagnostic methods, studying radiographic data, study models and treatment planning procedures.

(F) Courses in human resource management and employee benefits.

(4) Courses considered to be of direct benefit to the licensee or outside the scope of dental practice in California include the following, and ***shall not be recognized for continuing education credit are***:

(A) Courses in money management, the licensee's personal finances or personal business matters such as financial planning, estate planning, and personal investments.

(B) Courses in general physical fitness, weight management or the licensee's personal health.

(C) Presentations by political or public figures or other persons that do not deal primarily with dental practice or issues impacting the dental profession;

(D) Courses designed to make the licensee a better business person or designed to improve licensee personal profitability, including motivation and marketing.

(E) Courses pertaining to the purchase or sale of a dental practice, business or office; courses in transfer of practice ownership, acquisition of partners and associates, practice valuation, practice transitions, or retirement.

(F) Courses pertaining to the provision of elective facial cosmetic surgery as defined by the Dental Practice Act in Section 1638.1, unless the licensee has a special permit obtained from the Board to perform such procedures pursuant to Section 1638.1 of the Code.

(5) Completion of a course does not constitute authorization for the attendee to perform any services that he or she is not legally authorized to perform based on his or her license or permit type.

CHAPTER COMMENTS:

Although the Dental Practice Act does not specifically refer to the three (3) categories of continuing education (CE) for license renewal as Mandatory, Core and Supplemental, the dental community has utilized these definitions to best describe the requirements for professional development to be accomplished by all licensees and permit holders.

Licensees and permit holders are required to renew and complete CE that meets the three (3) categories as described herein:

- Mandatory
- Core
- Supplement

The Board's regulations contained in this chapter clearly identify the types of courses licensees and permit holders need to complete each renewal period. As newly licensed Registered Dental Assistants (RDAs), it is important that you remember the three categories of acceptable CE and select the courses you attend or take on-line very carefully. Using the DPA and the Continuing Education regulations as your guide, the courses you select for license or permit renewal will be successfully accepted if your license or permit should be audited for compliance.

END OF CHAPTER – CRITICAL THINKING QUESTIONS

1. What is the California DPA?
2. What two things govern the dental profession?
3. Under California law, does the dental assistant need to be licensed to place and remove rubber dams or other isolation devices?
4. Under California law, does the dental assistant need to be licensed to place bases, liners, and bonding agents?
5. Under California law, does the dental assistant need to be licensed to perform mouth mirror inspections of the oral cavity, to include charting of obvious lesions, existing restorations and missing teeth?
6. Under California law, does the dental assistant need to be licensed to use the automated caries detection device and materials to gather information for caries diagnosis by the dentist?
7. What does "OAP" stand for?
8. What are the mandatory education requirements for unlicensed dental assistants?
9. Name three mandatory courses needed for continuing education requirements for licensed dental assistants and special permit holders.
10. What are the core courses defined as for continuing education requirements for licensed dental assistants and special permit holders?

CRITICAL THINKING QUESTION ANSWERS FOUND IN APPENDIX

Bonus Chapters

Notes

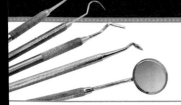
Glossary of Key Terms

Unit One, Chapter One – Patient Treatment and Care – Dental Fundamentals

Blacks Cavity Classifications	System by which a carious lesion is classified by its size and location on a tooth
Buccal/Facial	Surface of the tooth closest to the cheeks or face
Contact	An area where the mesial or distal surface of one tooth touches the adjacent tooth
Contour	A curved surface
Cuspids	Considered anterior teeth (aka: canine teeth); considered the cornerstone of the dental arch
Dental Caries	Tooth disease caused by bacteria (aka: Dental Decay, Cavity, Carious Lesion)
Dentition	A set of natural teeth in the dental arch
Distal	Surface of the tooth the farthest distance away from the midline
Embrasure	The triangular space toward the gingiva between the proximal surfaces of two teeth
Incisors	Central and lateral; located in the anterior of the mouth; defined as anterior teeth
Lingual	Surface of the tooth closest to the tongue
Malocclusion	The abnormal or unnatural contact of the maxillary and mandibular teeth when closed together
Mesial	Surface of the tooth closest to the midline
Midline	Imaginary vertical line that divides the mouth in half
Molars	Largest teeth in the mouth; considered posterior teeth
Occlusal/Incisal	Biting or tearing surface of the tooth
Occlusion	The natural contact of the maxillary and mandibular teeth when closed together
Premolars	Cross between molars and cuspids; located in posterior of the mouth
Quadrant	Division of a whole into four equal parts
Third Molars	"Wisdom" teeth; last teeth to erupt into the mouth

The California RDA General Written and Law Examination Prep Book © 2017, 2018 • KB Dental Arts – Publisher
This book and the individual contributions contained within are protected under Copyright by the Publisher

Unit One, Chapter Two – Review of Basic Chairside Skills

Clock Concept	Indicates operating zones for DHCW's
Four-Handed dentistry	One dentist and one assistant practicing at the chair
HVE	High Volume Evacuation
Instrument Grasp	How the instrument is held by the operator
Position of Use	Transferring of the instrument positioned towards the area where it will be used
Six-Handed Dentistry	One dentist and two assistants practicing at the chair
Subsupine	Patient's head is lower than their feet
Supine	Patient is lying flat on their back and the chair is parallel to the floor
Transfer Zone	Area where instruments are exchanged between the dentist and the assistant
Upright	90-degree position of the chair; used when patient enters or exits chair

Unit One, Chapter Three – Patient Screening & Education

Allergic Reaction	A hypersensitivity to a material, product, food or animal that produces an immune response that can be life threatening
Bleach	Tooth whitening agent that produces whiter, brighter teeth
Bitewing	Type of image used for interproximal examination and shows the crowns of both arches on one film
Charting	A documentation process of previous and needed dental work using symbols and colors
Control Panel	Portion of the x-ray unit that contains the master switch, the indicator light, selector and exposure buttons
Digital Image	Electronic signals captured by sensors and displayed on a computer monitor
Drug Addiction	A physical dependency on a drug
Endogenous Stains	Occur within the tooth structure during development and occur due to systemic disturbances
Exogenous Stains	Occur outside the tooth and are caused by environmental factors

Extrinsic Stains	Occur on the external surfaces of the tooth and can be removed by means of coronal polishing
Hemostasis	The process of arresting bleeding using vasoconstrictors to encourage coagulation
Intrinsic Stains	Occur within the tooth surfaces caused by environmental sources and cannot be removed by means of coronal polishing
Panoramic Film/image	Extraoral image captured either on film or digitally; provides a wide view of both the upper and lower jaws
Periapical	Radiographic view that shows the crown, root tip and surrounding structures
Plaque	Colorless, soft deposit found on teeth that contains bacteria
Positioning Device	Intraoral device used to position and hold the film or sensor
Post-Op Instructions	Directions given to a patient following treatment that will aid in healing or encourage patient comfort
Premedication	Taking of pre-treatment medication (antibiotics) to prevent disease
Pulse oximetry	Measurement of the level of oxygen in the blood
Radiograph	Image produced on photosensitive film by exposing the film to radiation and processing with chemistry
Sensitivity	A heightened response to a substance but not as strong as an allergic reaction
Sensor	A solid image receptor that contains a silicon chip with an electric current
Standard of Care	Level of knowledge and care comparable with that of other dentists who are treating similar patients under similar conditions
Treatment Plan	A map or plan of action created for the patient based upon the findings recorded during the charting portion of new patient appointment or recall visit
Tubehead	Part of the x-ray machine that contains the x-ray tube and the high voltage and low voltage transformers
Vasoconstrictors	A medicament that shrinks the capillaries in tissues thereby decreasing the blood flow temporarily to an area

Glossary

Unit One, Chapter Four – Medical Emergency Preparedness

Allergy	A hypersensitivity to a substance
Anaphylaxis	A life threatening allergic reaction affecting the patients breathing
Antigen	Substance that causes an immune response
EpiPen	Portable device that delivers a dose of epinephrine to the patient exposed to a known allergen
Localized Allergic Reaction	A slow-moving reaction contained to one area of the body
Medical Emergency	An unforeseen set of circumstances which call for immediate action regarding a person who has become suddenly ill or injured while being treated in a dental office
Nitrous Oxide	Tasteless, colorless, sweet smelling gas used with oxygen to relax patients during dental treatment
Sign	Something someone can observe happening with the patient
Symptom	Something the patient is feeling and needs to describe
Syncope	Fainting

Unit One, Chapter Five – Legal Requirements & Ethical Principles

Abandonment	Discontinuation of a patient/provider relationship once it has been established; discontinuing treatment once begun without cause or notification to the patient
Autonomous	Independent; not controlled by others or outside forces; self-directed; independent in mind and judgment
Beneficence	The state or quality of being kind, charitable and promoting good will
Character	A description of a person's attributes, traits and abilities; the qualities that define a person or group; could be used to define moral or ethical strength
Code of Ethics	A collection of rules or guidelines addressing the ethical standards of a profession or professional entity
Confidentiality	That which is held in confidence; done or communicated in secret; the state of trust placed in a dental assistant by a patient so as not to communicate those items which are privileged

Discrimination	Treatment or consideration placed on class or category rather than individual merit; treating persons differently based on their physical, mental or emotional state, race or gender
Ethics	A set of principles of right conduct; the general nature of morals and of the specific moral choices made by a person
Fiduciary Responsibility	Holding of something of trust to another; a relationship based on the trusted responsibility between patient and health care provider
Implied	A term used when data or knowledge is not specifically stated verbally or in writing; an inferred statement
Implied Consent	By nature of being present in the treatment facility, it is implied that the patient is seeking treatment; a dentist may not communicate the full details of the treatment plan – therefore treatment may begin with implied consent without agreeing in writing or verbally
Informed Consent	The act of providing information, verbally or in writing, to and ensuring the understanding of the patient, as to the nature of proposed treatment, financial responsibilities, potential risks, options for treatment, potential outcomes, and impact on the patients physical and oral health
Negligence	Failure to exercise the degree of care considered reasonable under the circumstances resulting in an unintended injury to a patient; lack of reasonable and prudent care of a patient in a healthcare setting
Nonmaleficence	The principle of "doing no harm"; a state of non-injury to a patient during the provision of dental care services
Professionalism	A quality set in standards and methods of performance demonstrating skill, knowledge and professional ability demonstrated consistently
Scope of Practice	The range of duties and functions legally allowable under the defined areas of providership such as type of license, permit or certificate held; set forth by the state Dental Practice Act and the laws of the state
Direct Supervision	A licensed dentist must be physically present in the treatment facility during the performance of the function; the function must be checked and approved by the supervising dentist prior to dismissal of the patient from the office
General Supervision	Does not require the physical presence of the dentist during the performance of certain procedures based on instructions given by the supervising dentist

Glossary

Unit Two, Chapter One – Direct & Indirect Restorations

Base	Placed as a measure of protection for the pulp; protects, insulates and soothes when decay or trauma have disturbed the pulp
Calcium Hydroxide	Main medicament found in a dental liner that is soothing to the pulp
Digital Impression	Picture of the prepped tooth used to design and fabricate a permanent crown
Direct Restorations	Materials placed directly on or in the tooth surfaces
Embrasure	Triangular space, towards the gingiva, between two adjacent teeth
Etchant	An acidic tooth conditioner that aids in roughening-up either enamel or dentin in preparation for bonding
Exothermic	A chemical reaction that releases energy or heat
Festooning	Trimming or to trim
Indirect Restorations	Permanent or temporary restorations designed outside the patient's mouth
Liner	A medicament which acts as a barrier against pulpal irritation caused by decay and other stimuli
Polymerization	The process of setting, curing, hardening a dental material
Provisional Coverage	A temporary restoration or temporary crown
Self-Etching Adhesive	A bonding adhesive containing etchant; eliminates the etch step in the bonding procedure
Smear Layer	Secretion created by the layers of the tooth in response to being prepared for a restoration
Temporary Sedative Dressing	A temporary filling; also known as Direct Provisional Restoration

Unit Two, Chapter Two – Preventive Dental Procedures

Calculus	Mineralized, or hardened, plaque
Clinical Crowns	Portion of the tooth visible when the patient opens their mouth
Coronal Polishing	A technique used to remove plaque and stains from the coronal portions of the teeth

Dental Sealants	Preventive procedure where the occlusal pit and fissures are sealed with a form of resin to prevent caries on the surfaces of posterior teeth
Disclosing Agents	Coloring agents that make visible when applied to the teeth
Filled Resin	Contains fillers making it more resistant to wear
Fulcrum	A finger rest or stabilizing point for the operator
Grit	The texture of a material; refers to polishing agents in this context
Plaque	Colorless, soft deposit found on teeth that contains bacteria
Polishing Agent	An abrasive or dentifrice used in the rubber polishing cup to polish the teeth
Prophy Paste	A mixture of different ingredients that are packaged into round plastic, disposable containers; a type of polishing agent
Sealant Retention	Length of time in which the sealant remains in place and prevents decay
Selective Polishing	Only teeth or surfaces with stain are polished
Supragingival	Above the gum line
Unfilled Resin	No fillers are added

Unit Three, Chapter One – Endodontic & Periodontal Procedures

Endodontic Terms:

Abscess	An infection within the bone commonly found at the tip of the root; referred to as the apical abscess
Apex	The clinical tip of the root
Apicoectomy	Surgical endodontic procedure involving the removal of the tip of the root
Dental Dam	Rubber sheet (6x6) used to isolate a tooth or series of teeth; prevents materials from entering the oral cavity; prevents salivary contamination of the working area
Endodontist	A dentist with advanced education specializing in endodontic therapy
Gutta Percha	Plastic-like final canal filling material used to replace the removed pulp from the root canal space(s)
Necrotic	Dead tissue; term used to describe a dead pulp
Obturate	Fill the canal with gutta percha

Glossary

The California RDA General Written and Law Examination Prep Book © 2017, 2018 • KB Dental Arts – Publisher

Paper Points	Used to dry canal(s) of the tooth after final filing, shaping and irrigating; used prior to the placement and cementation of the gutta percha
Pulp/Pulpal	The nerve of the tooth; pulpal refers to the area of the tooth that is the pulp
Pulpectomy	Complete removal of the tooth pulp
Pulpitis	Inflammation of the tooth pulp (nerve)
Pulpotomy	Partial removal of the tooth pulp
Radiographic Apex	The visual tip of the root; used to visually measure the length of the canals before, during and after endodontic treatment
RCT	Root Canal Therapy or Root Canal Treatment
Sodium Hypochloride	Bleach solution used to irrigate and disinfect canal spaces during the filing and shaping process
Vital	Live tissue; a positive response to stimuli indicates that the tooth is still alive

Periodontal Terms:

Periodontal Dressing	A pliable material placed directly over the surgical site while the area heals
Periodontics	Specialty of dentistry focused on the health of the periodontium
Periodontist	Dental specialist with an advanced education in periodontics
Periodontium	Consists of the alveolar bone, periodontal ligaments and gingiva

Unit Three, Chapter Two – Orthodontic Procedures

Malocclusion	Improper contact of the teeth when they contact
Occlusion	Contact between teeth when they bite closed
Orthodontics	Dental specialty interested in the prevention, diagnosis, interception and treatment of malocclusion
Archwire	A wire shaped to conform to the dental arch that can be used with dental braces as a source of force in correcting irregularities in the position of the teeth; archwires can also be used to maintain existing dental positions

Glossary

Bracket	Small metal or ceramic attachments used to fasten or secure an archwire. These attachments are soldered or welded to an orthodontic band or cemented directly onto the teeth
Orthodontic Bands	Pre-formed stainless-steel bands fitted around the teeth and cemented into place; used to anchor an appliance to the teeth or secure an archwire to the molars
Separator	Elastomeric or spring devices that assist in creating 1 mm of separation between contacts, so the orthodontic band can be properly seated.
Ligature Tie	An elastomeric tie or wire tie that encircles the bracket around the tie wings securing the arch wire to the fixed appliance

Unit Three, Chapter Three – Implants, Oral Surgery & Extractions

Alveolitis	Inflammation of the alveolar bone; aka, "dry socket"
Blood Clot	Body's natural way of stopping bleeding from the socket
Needle Holder	Surgical Instrument used to hold the suture needle
Oral Surgeon	Dental surgical specialist with advanced education in oral surgery
Suture Scissors	A surgical scissor designed with shorter, very sharp blades, with a half-moon shape in the blade to ensure grasp of the suture material prior to cutting

Unit Three, Chapter Four – Prosthetic Appliances

Edentulous	A mouth without teeth
Full Denture	Removable prosthesis that replaces all of the teeth in one arch
Partial Denture	Removable prosthesis that replaces a certain number of teeth in one arch
Pressure Points	Specific areas on a partial or full denture that may apply pressure or rub against the underlying soft tissue
Sore Spot	A pressure point(s) on the soft tissue caused by the partial or full denture that has progressed into causing discomfort on the underlying soft tissue

Glossary

Unit Four, Chapter One – Safety: Infection Control

ADA	American Dental Association
Aseptic Technique	Employing all forms of washing, sanitizing, disinfecting, and sterilization of items that come in contact with patients
CDC	Centers for Disease Control and Prevention
DHCP	Dental Healthcare Personnel
EPA	Environmental Protection Agency
HCV	Hepatitis-C Virus
HIV	Human Immunodeficiency Virus
Microorganisms	Those living things too small to be seen by the naked eye
Mycobacterium Tuberculosis var Bovis	Tuberculosis (TB)
OPIM	Other Potentially Infectious Materials
OSHA	Occupational Safety and Health Administration
Pathogens	Harmful disease-causing microorganisms
PPE	Personal Protective Equipment
Spores	Bacteria with an outer covering that protects them from chemical disinfectants

Unit Four, Chapter Two – Safety: Radiation Safety

Radiation	Forms of waves of energy emission through space or material
Lead Apron	A lead shield/drape used to protect the reproductive and blood-forming tissues from scatter radiation
Thyroid Collar	A flexible lead shield that can be easily wrapped around the patient's neck; may be attached to lead apron or used as a separate device
Ionizing Radiation	Radiation that produces ionization, resulting in harmful effects

The California RDA General Written and Law Examination Prep Book © 2017, 2018 • KB Dental Arts – Publisher
This book and the individual contributions contained within are protected under Copyright by the Publisher

BBPS	OSHA's Bloodborne Pathogens Standard
Cal-DOSH	California Department of Occupational Safety and Health
CDC	Centers for Disease Control and Prevention
Contaminated Waste	Items such as gloves and cotton products that contain body fluids and other potentially infectious materials
DHS	Department of Health Services
Don	To put on or place on
EPA	Environmental Protection Agency; regulates the registration and use of hospital disinfectants
Exposure Controls	Materials and devices that prevent employee exposure to hazardous or infectious substances
Exposure Incident	Describes an injury involving either percutaneous or permucosal incident by an employee and must be reported on an incident report
FDA	Food and Drug Administration
GHS	Globally Harmonized System
OSHA	Occupational Safety and Health Administration
Parenteral	Transmission of bloodborne pathogens through the skin via a cut, human bite, abrasion or any break in the skin
Percutaneous	A sharps injury that penetrates through the skin
Permucosal	Coming in contact with mucous membranes such as eyes or the mouth
SDS	Safety Data Sheets *(formerly known as MSDS – Material Safety Data Sheets)*

Glossary

Notes

The California RDA General Written and Law Examination Prep Book © 2017, 2018 • KB Dental Arts – Publisher
This book and the individual contributions contained within are protected under Copyright by the Publisher

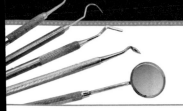

Addendum

Below are three dental charting examples to use as a reference. The first Charting example is a computerized version of common conditions that would be charted for the record. The second is a charting example of using a red/blue pencil and paper to chart the dental conditions. The final example is a screen shot from the Dentrix Dental computer software of how a dental chart appears within a dental software system. Quick charting reminder: the color red means "work to be done" or "needs to be done" while the color blue means "existing" or "has been done".

Example #1: Computerized version of common dental charting symbols

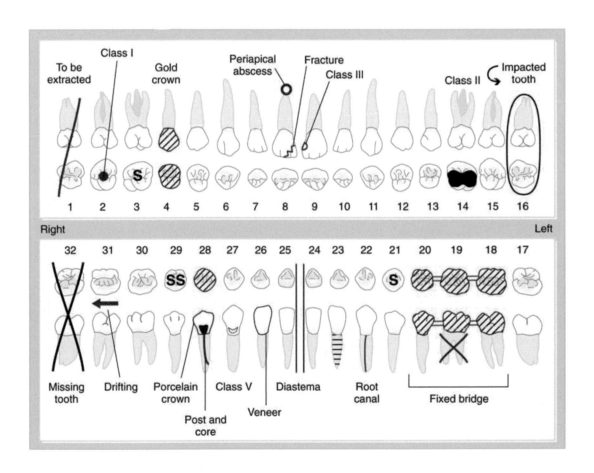

Example #2: Red/Blue Pencil and Paper Charting

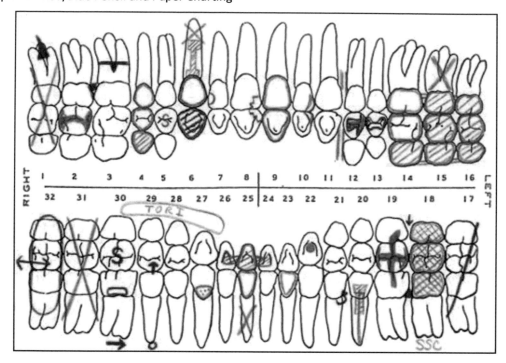

Key:

#1 = missing tooth; root fragment left behind that needs to be removed

#2 = mesio-occlusal-distal (MOD) restoration present

#3 = distal (D) decay and class II furcation

#4 = PFM crown present

#5 = dental sealant present

#6 = missing tooth; dental implant present; PFM crown needed

#7 = distal (D) restoration present

#8 = mesial-incisal-lingual (MIL) restoration needed

#9 = porcelain crown present

#10 = distal-lingual (DL) restoration present

#11 - #12 = diastema present

#12 = distal-occlusal (DO) recurrent decay

#13 = mesial-occlusal-distal (MOD) restoration needed

#14 - #16 = three-unit gold bridge present

#15 = missing tooth; replaced by pontic in three-unit bridge

#17 = tooth to be extracted

#18 = stainless steel crown present; supereruption

#19 = mesial-occlusal-distal-buccal-lingual (MODBL) restoration present

#20 = root canal treatment (RCT) and build-up (post & core) present

#21 = rotated tooth

#22 = lingual (L) restoration present

#23 = veneer present

#24 - #26 = Maryland or Cantilever bridge

(continued)

#25 = missing tooth

#27 = facial (Class V) composite restoration present

#29 = supereruption and periapical abscess

#30 = sealant needed; buccal (Class V) restoration needed; mesial drifting occurring

#31 = tooth missing

#32 = horizontally impacted tooth

#27 - 30 = lingual torus mandibularis present

Example #3: Chart from Dentrix Dental Software

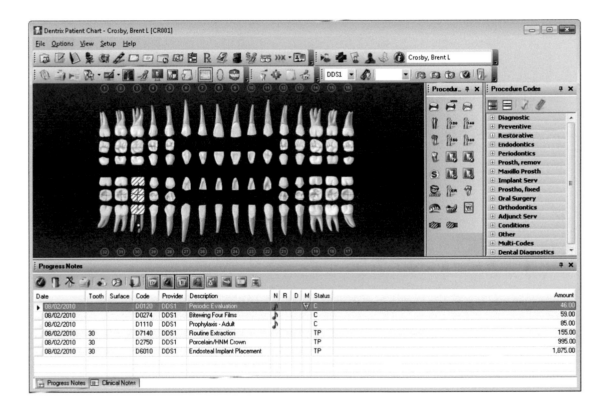

Notes

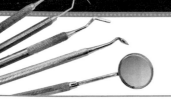

Answer Key to CTQ's

Answer Key to Critical Thinking Questions (CTQ's)

Unit One, Chapter One – None for This Chapter

Unit One, Chapter Two – Review of Basic Chairside Skills

1. Describe the various roles dental assistants assume in the dental office.

   Business or administrative assistant, dental office manager and chairside or clinical assistant.

2. Who is responsible for knowing what duties dental assistants are allowed to perform under California Law?

   It is the responsibility of the employee to know what duties they are legally allowed to perform under California law.

3. What is the rheostat and where is it located in the dental office?

   The rheostat is a foot pedal that controls the dental handpieces attached to the dental unit. It is located on the floor near the back of the dental chair towards the operator's side.

4. Name and describe the patient positions in the dental chair.

   - Upright: position the chair should be in when patient is entering or exiting the chair; 90-degree angle.
   - Supine: patient is lying flat on their back and the chair is parallel to the floor; most common position for the completion of dental work.
   - Sub-supine: places the patient's head lower than their feet.

5. The assistants stool should be how many inches higher than the operator?

   The assistants stool should be positioned four (4) to six (6) inches higher than the operator.

6. Why should the assistants stool be higher than the operators?

   It helps the assistant gain access and visualization into the patient's mouth.

7. What information does the clock concept provide?

   The clock concept designates working areas for each member of the dental team providing direct patient care.

8. Draw a clock and label each zone for both a right and left-handed operator.

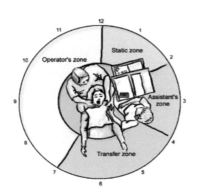
Right

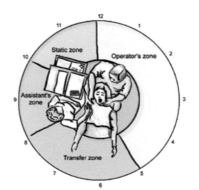
Left

The California RDA General Written and Law Examination Prep Book © 2017, 2018 • KB Dental Arts – Publisher

CTQ Answers

9. What is four handed dentistry?

   Four handed dentistry is a team approach to delivering dental care. One dentist and one assistant perform dental care on a patient in ergonomically pleasing, seated positions around the dental chair. One dentist and one assistant = four hands.

10. Why is light positioning important?

   Light positioning is important, so both the dentist and the assistant can see into the oral cavity. The placement, adjustment and care of the overhead patient light are the responsibility of the chairside assistant.

11. What does "position of use" mean and when is it important?

   The term "position of use" refers to the instrument being transferred with the working end pointing toward the arch (maxillary or mandibular) being worked on.

12. Which hand is used for instrument exchange?

   The left hand is used for instrument exchange.

Unit One, Chapter Three – Patient Screening & Education

1. Do you know the difference between an allergy and sensitivity?

   An allergy is a hypersensitivity to a material, substance, food or animal. It creates an immune response from the body's systems causing symptoms for the patient that can range from mild to severe. Some allergies may be severe resulting in anaphylactic shock and is life threatening. Sensitivity is a small or mild reaction to a material, substance, food or animal. There are generally no symptoms for the patient to deal with and no life-threatening responses occur.

2. When a patient indicates an "allergy to Novocain", what does this really mean?

   This means the patient has had a past reaction to an ingredient in the anesthetic called Epinephrine. Epinephrine is added to prolong the working effect of the anesthetic. Epinephrine works very similar to Adrenaline found in the human body. Therefore, the patient may feel an increased heart rate, rapid breathing, and sweating. Novocain is a type of anesthetic that has not been used in dentistry for many years. The anesthetic used today is Lidocaine or Xylocaine, each containing Epinephrine. There are anesthetics without Epinephrine for patients who are sensitive or allergic to it.

3. Do you know the common medical conditions that may require a patient to take pretreatment oral prophylaxis (premedication)?

   Patients may be required by their medical doctor to take premedication prior to dental work if they have a heart condition or have had joint replacement surgeries. The dentist should consult with the patient's doctor to ensure proper protocol is being followed for the patient's conditions.

4. If a patient indicates they are required to take premedication prior to dental treatment and they did not do so for the current appointment, what is the next step the assistant should take?

   Let the dentist know that the patient forgot to take to their premedication. Some dentists will keep antibiotics in the office for just such an occurrence and will administer the antibiotics on site. Some dentists may reappoint the patient if they do not have antibiotics on site.

The California RDA General Written and Law Examination Prep Book © 2017, 2018 • KB Dental Arts – Publisher

5. Where fear and anxiety about being at the dental office is present, what steps should an assistant take during the health history and dental review to help alleviate those fears?

Let the patient know that it is okay to ask as many questions as they need to. Be approachable and stay with the patient until the dentist comes into the operatory. Tell the patient they are in control of the procedure and can stop at any time for a break. Using a calm reassuring tone of voice when speaking is effective and use the patients name frequently. Explain the procedure and what they can expect during treatment. During more stressful parts of the procedure, such as the injection of anesthetic, physically touch the patient's arm or hand. This will help calm them and provides a distraction from their anxiety about the injection.

6. What is a vasoconstrictor?

A vasoconstrictor is a medicament that shrinks the capillaries thereby decreasing the blood flow temporarily to an area.

7. What common drug used in dentistry is used to act as a vasoconstrictor?

Epinephrine. Hemostatic agents frequently contain epinephrine.

8. What common body fluid is arrested by complete hemostasis?

Blood

9. What drug or drugs can a patient take to prevent a vasoconstrictor from working effectively?

Coumadin or any other type of blood thinners will make it more difficult for a vasoconstrictor to work properly.

10. What are the various methods of charting?

Electronic charting via computer software or charting by hand with a paper chart and a red/blue pencil can complete charting. There are symbols used to denote various treatments needed or previously completed. The chart is an important part of the patient's treatment plan.

11. Why is it important to create a treatment plan for each patient?

It is critical to know what teeth the patient has present, previous dental work that has been completed and what dental work the patient needs to have completed. A treatment plan creates a plan of action, or a map, indicating how the dental team will proceed with dental treatments for the patient.

12. Why is it important to provide patients with post-operative instructions?

It is important to provide patients with post op care instructions, so they will understand how to care for their dental health and take care of themselves following a dental appointment. Some dental procedures can be invasive, and the patient may need to take extra care for a few days following the treatment. Post op instructions encourage patient comfort. These instructions should be presented in writing as well as verbally.

13. How are caries diagnosed?

Caries are diagnosed by means of intraoral examination using an explorer, during an intraoral examination where the teeth are visually inspected, via radiographs, by caries indicator dyes and by caries automated detector devices (caries detectors).

The California RDA General Written and Law Examination Prep Book © 2017, 2018 • KB Dental Arts – Publisher
This book and the individual contributions contained within are protected under Copyright by the Publisher

14. What is the difference between endogenous and exogenous staining?

Endogenous stains occur within the tooth during development and occur due to systemic disturbances. Exogenous stains occur outside the tooth and are caused by environmental factors.

15. What do vital signs measure?

Vital signs measure and monitor a patient's overall health level and status.

16. There are four (4) vital sign measurements. What are they?

The four (4) vital sign measurements are:

1. Temperature
2. Pulse
3. Respiration
4. Blood Pressure (BP)

17. What is pulse oximetry and why is it important in dentistry?

Pulse oximetry is how the concentration of oxygen in the blood is measured or a measurement of the blood-oxygen level. Pulse oximetry is important in dentistry because some offices have their patients use general anesthesia or utilize "sleep" dentistry. Patients that are asleep need to have the oxygen level monitored in their brains to make sure enough oxygenated blood is present. Brain damage can occur if the oxygen saturation level falls too low. A pulse oximeter monitors oxygen saturation levels and will set off an alarm if levels start to fall.

Unit One, Chapter Four – Medical Emergency Preparedness

1. What is a medical emergency?

A medical emergency is an unforeseen set of circumstances that call for immediate action regarding a person who has become suddenly ill or injured while being treated in the dental office.

2. What is the difference between a sign and a symptom?

- Sign = something that can be observed or seen; examples: paleness, sweating, shivering.

- Symptom = something the patient is feeling and experiencing but is not visible; examples: patient states they are experiencing nausea, dizziness, nervousness.

3. Does a dental professional need to be certified in Basic Life Support (BLS) and CPR?

Yes, the dental professional is required to obtain and maintain certification in BLS/CPR for the Healthcare Provider.

4. Is it mandatory for every dental office to have a medical emergency kit?

It is not mandatory but is recommended for offices to carry basic medical emergency items.

5. What is the number one drug utilized in a dental office during a medical emergency?

The number one drug utilized in the dental office during a medical emergency is oxygen.

CTQ Answers

The California RDA General Written and Law Examination Prep Book © 2017, 2018 • KB Dental Arts – Publisher

6. What are an allergy and an antigen? How are they connected?

An allergy is a hypersensitivity to an antigen. An antigen is a substance that causes an immune response. This antigen triggers an allergic state called an allergen.

7. What are the two (2) factors to consider when evaluating an allergic reaction?

Two (2) important factors to consider when evaluating an allergic reaction are:

1. *Speed* with which the symptoms occurred (i.e., rash, blotchy skin, itchy eyes)

2. *Severity* of the reaction (how bad are the above signs and symptoms)

8. What state does nitrous oxide usage produce in a patient undergoing treatment?

Nitrous oxide produces a Stage I anesthesia/analgesia state for the patient which allows the patient to relax while still being able to communicate fully with the dental team.

9. What effects of nitrous oxide should be explained to the patient prior to use?

The assistant should next explain the sensations the patient may experience while on nitrous. Some examples may include:

- Feelings of well-being

- Giddiness

- A floaty, detached sensation

- A slight level of lightheadedness

- An enhanced level of relaxation

- Sensations of warmth in their limbs

- A slight tingling feeling

10. What medical emergency occurs most often in the dental setting?

Syncope (fainting) is the most common emergency in a dental office.

11. What is a CVA?

Cerebrovascular Accident or a Stroke

12. If a medical emergency occurs, what should be recorded in the patient record?

If a patient experiences a medical emergency, documentation of the event is of the utmost importance. The event must be recorded in detail; nothing is too small to include in the documentation. The following should be recorded:

- Full explanation of exactly what type of event occurred

- Describe the treatment provided to the patient

- Describe the condition the patient was in when they left the office

- A follow up phone call should be placed to the patient and/or their family that evening or the next day to inquire about the patient's condition

- Both the dentist and the assistant should review each other's documentation and sign the chart.

Unit One, Chapter Five – Legal Requirements & Ethical Principles

1. What does the term autonomous mean?

   Autonomous means independent in mind and judgement.

2. Nonmaleficence means _____. Why is this important?

   Nonmaleficence means "do no harm". The principle of "do no harm" is an important safety measure to maintain a state of non-injury to the patient during the provision of dental care services.

3. What are the responsibilites of a mandated reporter?

   Licensed dental professionals are designated by law and are required to report suspected cases of abuse and neglect while in their professional capabilities.

4. What is a Code of Ethics? Does dentistry have a Code of Ethics?

   A Code of Ethics is a collection of rules or guidelines addressing the ethical standards of a profession or professional entity. Yes, dentistry does have a Code of Ethics. Each licensure category (DDS, RDH and RDA) has a Code of Ethics and the Dental Practice Act (DPA) contains a Code of Ethics.

5. Professionalism is _____.

   A quality set in standards and methods of performance demonstrating skill, knowledge and professional ability demonstrated consistently.

6. Why is informed consent important?

   Informed consent is important so the patient can make the correct decision for their dental care and treatment. Informed consent provides information to the patient so they fully understand the nature of the proposed treatment plan, financial responsibilities, potential risks, options for treatment, potential outcomes, and impact on their physical and oral health.

7. What are ethics?

   Ethics are a set of principles of right conduct; the general nature of morals and of the specific moral choices made by a person.

8. What is the difference between general and direct supervision?

   General Supervision does not require the physical presence of the dentist during the performance of certain procedures based on instructions given by the supervising dentist. Direct Supervision requires the physical presence of the supervising dentist in the treatment facility during the performance of certain procedures. The dentist must check the function prior to the dismissal of the patient from the treatment area.

9. What does the term Scope of Practice mean? Why is it important to understand this concept?

   Scope of Practice means the range and duties legally allowable under the defined areas of providership such as license type, permit or certificate held. The Scope of Practice is set forth by the state Dental Practice Act and the laws of the state. It is important to understand this concept since Scope of Practice dictates what procedures and duties an unlicensed DA, a RDA and a RDAEF are legally allowed to perform in the State of California. This understanding will be tested on the RDA Written Examination and the practicing assistant should be aware of what they are legally allowed to perform in the practice.

CTQ Answers

The California RDA General Written and Law Examination Prep Book © 2017, 2018 • KB Dental Arts – Publisher

10. What does negligence mean?

   Negligence means the failure to exercise the degree of care considered reasonable under the circumstances resulting in an unintended injury to a patient.

Unit Two, Chapter One – Direct & Indirect Restorations

1. The term provisional is a technical term used to describe what type of restoration?

   A temporary crown.

2. What is the principal purpose of using a base during a restorative procedure?

   The purpose of using a base during a restorative procedure is protect, insulate and soothe a pulp that has experienced trauma or the presence of decay very close to or partially into it. A base is used as a measure of protection for the pulp.

3. Is there a difference between a temporary sedative dressing and a temporary filling?

   No, there is no difference between a temporary sedative dressing and a temporary filling. They are two different names for the same procedure.

4. What does the term exothermic mean when mixing certain types of dental cement?

   Exothermic means that the material gives off heat when setting after the mixing phase.

5. Zinc Oxide Eugenol (ZOE) is considered to be the least irritating of all dental cements – why?

   ZOE is considered the least irritating of all the dental cements because it contains eugenol. Eugenol contains oil of cloves, which is known for its soothing, healing qualities.

6. What is a direct restoration?

   Direct restorations are materials placed directly on or in the tooth surfaces during treatment. The types of direct restorations include: amalgam, composite, glass ionomers and temporary restorative materials.

7. What is an indirect restoration?

   Indirect restorations are permanent restorations designed outside the patient's mouth and then bonded or cemented to the tooth upon completion. The types of indirect restorations are: gold crowns, ceramic crowns, bridges, inlays or onlays.

8. What type of matrix is used for anterior composite resin or glass ionomer restorations?

   The matrix used for anterior composite resin types restorations is a mylar strip. The mylar strip is also known as a clear or celluloid strip.

9. A matrix must be used to create a temporary proximal wall for which classifications of tooth preps?

   Class II, III, and IV

10. On the tofflemire retainer, the diagonal slots of the head are always placed towards what surface?

   The diagonal slots always face the gingiva whether the tooth is on the maxillary or the mandibular.

11. A seated band extends no further than _____ above the occlusal surface of the tooth.

   1 – 2 mm

The California RDA General Written and Law Examination Prep Book © 2017, 2018 • KB Dental Arts – Publisher

12. What is the purpose for using a wedge?

A wedge is placed to provide anatomic contour and hold the matrix band firmly against the gingival margin of the tooth preparation.

13. What is the consequence of a poorly placed wedge?

An overhang

14. The wedge is placed from the _____ surface when restoring posterior teeth.

Lingual

Unit Two, Chapter Two – Preventive Dental Procedures

1. What is a preventive procedure?

A preventive procedure is a measure taken by the dental team in an effort to avoid the development of caries, or dental tooth decay.

2. What are the two (2) common preventive procedures performed by RDA's?

1. Coronal Polishing

2. Dental Sealants

3. When may a dental assistant perform the function of Coronal Polishing?

A dental assistant may perform the function of coronal polishing when a certification course on the subject has been successfully completed and the dental assistant has also obtained their RDA license.

4. Why is a fulcrum important when Coronal Polishing?

A fulcrum prevents slipping and causing injury to the patient while polishing. The fulcrum stabilizes the operator's hand and is used as a safety measure for the patient.

5. Who may legally place a dental sealant?

The RDA may place dental sealants after the successful completion of a certification course and have obtained RDA licensure. A dentist and a hygienist may place dental sealants. An unlicensed DA is not allowed to place dental sealants.

6. What is the difference between a filled and an unfilled sealant material?

Filled sealant = has fillers added to the resin material making it more resistant to wear.

Unfilled sealant = does not have fillers added to the resin material.

Although the materials are different, there is no difference in the quality of the sealant being placed, whether using a filled or an unfilled sealant material.

7. What does polymerization mean?

Polymerization means to set, cure or harden a material.

8. What is the life expectancy of a properly placed sealant?

Ten (10) years is the life expectancy of a properly placed sealant.

The California RDA General Written and Law Examination Prep Book © 2017, 2018 • KB Dental Arts – Publisher

1. What is the definition of endodontics?

   Endodontics is a specialty of dentistry focused on the prevention, diagnosis and treatment of the dental pulp.

2. What are the two (2) main causes of pulpal damage?

   1. Dental decay

   2. Trauma

3. What is the difference between a subjective exam and an objective exam?

   Subjective exam: Patient reports chief complaint to the assistant and describes what they have been feeling.

   Objective exam: information gathered by the dentist and the assistant through examination, x-rays, and various forms of endodontic testing.

4. Give an example of a question a dental assistant could ask during the subjective exam.

   "How long has the upper right tooth been bothering you?" or "Does the tooth wake you up in the middle of the night?"

5. What is a control tooth? Why is a control tooth important?

   A control tooth is a healthy tooth, similar in size to the suspect tooth from the opposite quadrant on the same arch. A control tooth is important as it allows the dental team to gather information for comparison from the same tooth in the opposite quadrant.

6. Name and describe the four pulp vitality tests utilized for endodontic testing.

   1. Palpation: application of pressure onto the apical portion of the suspect tooth.

   2. Percussion: tapping the suspect tooth with the end of the mouth mirror.

   3. Thermal testing: the use of hot and cold temperatures against the suspect tooth to determine the health status of the tooth.

   4. Electric pulp testing: the use of a handheld device called pulp tester to determine if the pulp is in the process necrosis.

7. Why are radiographs important while performing an endodontic procedure?

   Radiographs show the dentist how far they have instrumented a canal and how close they are to the apex. The radiographs show the dentist where they are at each step of the procedure.

8. How does the dentist determine canal length?

   The dentist, through the use of the working length x-ray taken during the endo series determines canal length.

9. What is the purpose of paper points? Why are they an important step?

   The purpose of paper points is to dry the canal prior to filling with gutta percha. If the canal is wet, then the gutta percha cannot flow into the canal properly resulting in an incompletely filled canal.

10. Name the conditions a dentist is searching for relating to the health of the tooth during the objective exam.

The Endodontist is looking for the following:

- Swelling of the face or gingival tissues around the questionable tooth

- Present decay and its extent around the questionable tooth

- Tooth mobility

- Periodontal issues with the questionable tooth

- A recently placed large restoration in the questionable tooth

- Pulpal exposure of the questionable tooth

11. The specialty of periodontics is concerned with what?

Periodontics is focused on the health of the periodontium.

12. What structures of the oral cavity make up the periodontium?

The periodontium consists of the alveolar bone, periodontal ligaments and the gingiva.

13. What is Perio Pak? What purpose does it serve?

Perio Pak is a periodontal dressing material that is mixed and placed over a periodontal surgical site to protect the area while it heals. Perio Pak or a periodontal dressing acts as a bandage over the surgical site.

14. Name and describe each type of periodontal dressing.

1. ZOE dressing: mixed by hand and rolled into long "worm like" shapes.

2. Non-Eugenol dressing: mixed by hand or supplied in an automix gun technique; placed directly onto the surgical site immediately after mixing.

Unit Three, Chapter Two – Orthodontic Procedures

1. Describe Angle's classifications of malocclusion.

- Class I: normal molar relationship; the anterior teeth may be crowded or rotated.
- Class II: molars are not in proper alignment giving the maxillary teeth the appearance of protruding over the mandibular teeth; referred to as the "Buck tooth" appearance.
- Class III: molars are not in proper alignment, giving the mandibular teeth the appearance of protruding out over the maxillary teeth; referred to as the "Bulldog appearance".

2. Per California law, who is allowed to place orthodontic bands? Who is allowed to remove orthodontic bands?

Sizing, fitting and cementation of orthodontic bands are completed by either the Orthodontist or the assistant who has obtained the OAP (Orthodontic Assistant Permit). The Orthodontist or the RDA or RDAEF may accomplish the removal of the orthodontic bands, at treatment completion or for re-cementation during treatment.

3. What is a fixed appliance?

The fixed appliance = full set of braces (bands, brackets, archwire, ligatures)

The California RDA General Written and Law Examination Prep Book © 2017, 2018 · KB Dental Arts – Publisher
This book and the individual contributions contained within are protected under Copyright by the Publisher

4. What is called the "cornerstone" of the fixed appliance?

    The orthodontic bands are considered the cornerstone of the fixed appliance.

5. What is placed into the wire by the orthodontist?

    A pattern is placed into the archwire by the Orthodontist. The pattern is a design created by the Orthodontist (based on the patient's treatment plan) that twists and bends the arch wire in various directions.

6. Name and describe the instruments that assist in arch wire placement.

    The ortho specialty instruments that assist in arch wire placement are:

    - Wire cutter: trims the arch wire extraorally
    - Distal end cutter: trims the arch wire intraorally
    - Howe Pliers or Weingart Utility Pliers: used to place and/or remove the arch wire into the brackets and tubing; assists in sliding the wire into place and positions the archwire into the brackets.

7. What does ligating, or ligation, mean?

    Ligation means to tie down or secure the arch wire at each bracket.

8. What items can be used to accomplish ligation?

    Brackets can be ligated with either wire ligature ties or elastomeric ligature ties.

Unit Three, Chapter Three – Implants, Oral Surgery & Extractions

1. What is a post extraction dressing?

    A post extraction dressing is better known as "packing the socket". Oral surgeons generally prefer not to place post extraction dressing, so the area can heal without any coverings. However, if the blood clot is disturbed or never forms then a post extraction is placed into the socket to prevent an infection of the alveolar bone.

2. What is alveolitis?

    Alveolitis, also known as "dry socket", is an inflammation of the alveolar bone due to a blood clot dislodging or never forming after a tooth is extracted. The blood clot acts like a barrier between the environment in the oral cavity and the alveolar bone. If the blood clot is not present, then the bone is exposed to many levels of bacteria and an infection or inflammation will occur.

3. What is done if a patient is experiencing alveolitis?

    If a patient is experiencing alveolitis, they will be asked to come to the dental office where the following will occur:

    - Clean and irrigate the socket to remove any debris that may have entered the socket.

    - Place a medicated gauze pack, or post extraction dressing, into the socket area to promote healing.

    - Instruct the patient to return to the office within 24 to 48 hours to have a fresh post extraction dressing placed. The patient may return several times for fresh dressings until the area begins to heal or feels better.

- Instruct the patient to rinse the socket (using a disposable syringe) at least three times per day with a warm salt water rinse to encourage healing and remove food debris from the socket.

Placement of post extraction dressing is also known as "packing the socket." The medicated gauze pack acts as the blood clot while the surgical area has time to heal appropriately. The medication in the pack soothes the inflammation in the area relieving the intense discomfort the patient experiences. This technique, coupled with prescribing pain medications, will help the patient heal and feel better rapidly.

4. What are the two types of suture materials?

The two types of suture materials are Absorbable and Non-absorbable.

5. What should never be cut when removing sutures from a patient's mouth?
Never cut the knot of the suture. The knot should be held by cotton forceps and suture scissors should gently cut just under the knot tied in the suture material. Cutting the knot itself can make it harder to remove the suture without causing additional trauma to the healing gingival tissue.

6. Once the suture material is removed, what should the assistant do as a safety precaution?
The assistant should check the patient's treatment record to see how many sutures were originally placed. The assistant should count the number of sutures present in the patients mouth to ensure the suture numbers match. Sometimes a suture can fall out or become dislodged. As the assistant removes the sutures, the sutures should be placed on a 2 x 2 gauze to account for all sutures removed.

Unit Three, Chapter Four – Prosthetic Appliances

1. What is a full denture?

A full denture is a removable prosthesis that replaces all of the teeth in one arch.

2. What is a partial denture?

A partial denture is a removable prosthesis that replaces a certain number of teeth in one arch.

3. What is a sore spot?

A sore spot is a pressure point (or several) on the soft tissue caused by the partial or full denture that has progressed into causing discomfort on the underlying soft tissue.

4. Why does a sore spot need to be adjusted?

The patient will not want to wear the denture if it is uncomfortable. Additionally, it is unhealthy for the soft tissue to have a continual sore spot present. It can become infected or increase in size causing more issues in the future.

5. What are the two materials used to indicate sore spots on the base of the denture?

   1. PIP – Pressure Indicating Paste

   2. Disclosing wax

6. What equipment is utilized to adjust sore spots?

An acrylic lab bur and a straight handpiece are used with PIP to adjust sore spots extraorally.

CTQ Answers

The California RDA General Written and Law Examination Prep Book © 2017, 2018 • KB Dental Arts – Publisher

7. How should the denture be adjusted?

The denture should be adjusted little by little with no big "chunks" removed from the denture extraorally. The denture should always be adjusted extraorally.

8. Who is legally allowed to adjust a denture?

The dentist, the RDA and/or the RDAEF are legally allowed to adjust a denture extraorally.

Unit Four, Chapter One – Safety: Infection Control

1. Who on the dental team is responsible for maintaining proper Infection Control protocols?
All members of the clinical dental team are responsible for maintaining proper infection control techniques.

2. What does the term "OPIM" stand for?

OPIM = Other Potentially Infectious Materials

3. What is the difference between sterilization and disinfection?

Sterilization = the destruction of all microorganisms including spores

Disinfection = kills some microorganisms, but not spores

4. What does asepsis mean?

Asepsis = free from disease

5. What are the three (3) classifications of Instruments in preparation for reuse?

Three (3) classifications of instruments =

1. Critical

2. Semi-Critical

3. Non-Critical

6. What is the most common method of sterilization utilized today?

The most common method of sterilization used today is heat sterilization.

7. What two articles of PPE <u>must</u> be changed after each patient?

The two articles of PPE that must be changed after each patient are gloves and masks.

8. What items are considered personal protective equipment?

PPE = gloves, masks, protective eyewear, protective attire – gowns and lab coats.

9. What items should be place into a sharps container?
Items placed into a biohazardous sharps container are: anesthetic needles, used carpules containing blood or residual anesthetic solution, burs, scalpel blades, orthodontic wire, used abrasive strips; any item that could puncture through garbage bags and cause injury to another.

CTQ Answers

The California RDA General Written and Law Examination Prep Book © 2017, 2018 • KB Dental Arts – Publisher
This book and the individual contributions contained within are protected under Copyright by the Publisher

10. Is it possible to sterilize a dental operatory and the equipment in it?

    No, it is not possible to sterilize the dental operatory and the equipment in it. However, it can be disinfected by properly following disinfection protocol and guidelines.

11. The use of a chemical germicide to disinfect a room must be preceded by what action in order for disinfection to occur?

    The surfaces in the operatory must be pre-cleaned first.

12. The act of spraying a surface (or wetting it) with disinfectant chemical and wiping it dry is considered what type of action?

    "Spray-Wipe" which is to clean only. This must be followed by "Spray and Wait" in order to disinfect.

13. Regulations require the use of heavy-duty utility gloves when using disinfectants – what does this mean when you are cleaning and disinfecting a dental operatory?

    This means the DHCW must wear utility gloves when using the chemical disinfectants in the operatory.

14. What is the difference between reusable protective attire and disposal protective attire and how are they different when being handled?

    Reusable protective attire can be laundered or cleaned and then used again by the DHCW. Disposable protective attire is used once and discarded. New protective attire is then worn by the DHCW. Disposable protective attire is discarded in the trash. Reusable protective attire is to be laundered on site and not removed from the office by the employee.

15. Masks are required for all treatment procedures – does this include treatment procedures that do not involve a handpiece or rotary device?

    Yes, a mask is required for _ALL_ dental procedures even those not involving a handpiece or rotary device.

Unit Four, Chapter Two – Safety: Radiation Safety

1. What is the definition of radiation?

    Radiation is defined as waves of energy emission through space and/or material.

2. What happens to body tissues when exposed to x-rays?

    When the body tissues are exposed to x-rays some damage occurs to living cells.

3. What is ionizing radiation?

    Ionizing radiation is the harmful effect of x-rays in humans.

4. What cells in the human body are damaged by the cumulative effect of x-rays?

    Reproductive cells are damaged by the cumulative effect of x-rays in the human body passing along genetic defects to future generations.

5. What are patients draped with while x-rays are being exposed?

    Patients are draped with a lead apron with a thyroid collar attached.

The California RDA General Written and Law Examination Prep Book © 2017, 2018 • KB Dental Arts – Publisher

6. California law mandates the use of what?

   California law mandates the use of a lead apron with a thyroid collar.

7. What are the four (4) patient protection techniques dental assistants should be knowledgeable in?

   1. Proper technique
   2. Film speed
   3. Exposure factors
   4. Film holding devices

8. What device should a dental healthcare worker (DHCW) wear to monitor radiation levels?

   DHCW's should wear dosimeter badges to monitor exposure levels to radiation.

Unit Four, Chapter Three – Safety: Occupational Safety

1. What does the term OSHA stand for?

   OSHA stands for Occupational Safety and Health Administration. OSHA is concerned for the safety of the employee in the workplace.

2. What is the best way for dental healthcare workers to prevent disease transmission?

   The best way for DHCW's to prevent disease transmission is through simple hand washing. This is a critical step in reducing the transmission of microbes in a healthcare setting. Routine hand washing removes most of the transient microbes and some of the resident microbes found on the hands.

3. What document is every dental office required to have per OSHA?

   Every dental office is required by OSHA to have a written Hazard Communication Plan. The office must develop and implement a written compliance program consistent with the requirement specific to California.

4. What are SDS and why are they important?

   SDS = Safety Data Sheets

   SDS are important because they communicate any chemicals that may be present in the product being used. Chemicals present a variety of hazards in the dental office because they may be flammable, toxic, caustic, corrosive, and carcinogenic (cancer causing).

5. Who is legally responsible for providing OSHA training to employees in a dental office?

   The Dentist is legally responsible to provide the training of staff.

6. How many days after initial employment should a new employee receive OSHA training?

   Within 10 days of being hired.

7. How is regulated waste disposed of in dental offices?

   Regulated waste is also known as hazardous waste and should be disposed of in sharps containers when appropriate or into appropriate containers for special removal from the dental office by a waste company.

8. Is amalgam, or amalgam scraps, considered hazardous or regulated waste?

   Yes, amalgam and amalgam scraps are considered regulated waste (aka hazardous waste).

CTQ Answers

The California RDA General Written and Law Examination Prep Book © 2017, 2018 • KB Dental Arts – Publisher

9. Are dental offices considered small or large quantity generators of specific types of waste?

Dental offices are considered small quantity generators.

10. What are the rules to follow when managing waste in the dental office setting?

  1. Do not accumulate for longer than one year.

  2. Document the length of time you began accumulation.

  3. Label or mark packages to identify the type.

  4. Never try to treat or alter the wastes in a way that may alter their characteristics.

  5. Clean up any releases of universal wastes and repackage cleanup debris.

Bonus Chapter - Dental Instrument Review

1. What term should *not* be used to describe instruments?

   Instruments should not be referred to as "tools" as this terminology can be disconcerting to the patient.

2. What instruments make up the basic set-up?

   Mouth Mirror, Explorer, Cotton Forceps (some dentists may also include the periodontal probe)

3. Why is it important for dental assistants to be knowledgeable about dental instruments?

   It is important for dental assistants to be knowledgeable about instruments as they are responsible for instrument tray setups and procedure set ups.

4. How are instruments arranged on a tray or in a cassette?

   Instruments are arranged from left to right on an instrument tray or in a cassette. The arrangement is based on the steps in the procedure.

5. What are the two classifications of instruments?

   1. Hand instruments – action of the instrument is done by the operator's hand.
   2. Rotary instruments – utilized by a motor built into the instrument, such as a dental handpiece.

6. Name and describe the three parts of a hand instrument.

   1. Handle – portion of the instrument held by the operator.
   2. Shank – portion of the instrument that attaches the handle and the working end of the instrument.
   3. Working end – portion of the instrument that performs the work and will have appoint, a blade or a nib that can be either smooth or serrated.

Bonus Chapter - Legal Duties, Settings and Licensure

1. What is the California DPA?

   The California Dental Practice Act defines the legal requirements necessary to practice dentistry and the scope of dental practice.

The California RDA General Written and Law Examination Prep Book © 2017, 2018 • KB Dental Arts – Publisher
This book and the individual contributions contained within are protected under Copyright by the Publisher

2. What two things govern the dental profession?

    The two things that govern the dental profession are the DPA and voluntary standards, such as the principles of ethics that were developed and implemented by the dental profession itself.

3. Under California law, does the dental assistant need to be licensed to place and remove rubber dams or other isolation devices?

    No, the assistant does not need to be licensed.

4. Under California law, does the dental assistant need to be licensed to place bases, liners, and bonding agents?

    Yes, as a Registered Dental Assistant (RDA) or Registered Dental Assistant in Extended Functions (RDAEF).

5. Under California law, does the dental assistant need to be licensed to perform mouth mirror inspections of the oral cavity, to include charting of obvious lesions, existing restorations and missing teeth?

    Yes, as a Registered Dental Assistant (RDA) or Registered Dental Assistant in Extended Functions (RDAEF).

6. Under California law, does the dental assistant need to be licensed to use the automated caries detection device and materials to gather information for caries diagnosis by the dentist?

    Yes, as a Registered Dental Assistant (RDA) or Registered Dental Assistant in Extended Functions (RDAEF).

7. What does "OAP" stand for?

    Orthodontic Assistant Permit.

8. What are the mandatory education requirements for unlicensed dental assistants?

    1. A Board-approved two-hour course in the Dental Practice Act.
    2. A Board-approved eight-hour course in infection control.

    A course in basic life support offered by an instructor approved by the American Red Cross or the American Heart Association, or any other course approved by the Board as equivalent and that provides the student the opportunity to engage in hands-on simulated clinical scenarios.

    3. The employer of a dental assistant shall be responsible for ensuring that the dental assistant maintains certification in basic life support.

9. Name three (3) mandatory courses needed for continuing education requirements for licensed dental assistants and special permit holders.

    1. Infection Control
    2. CPR
    3. California Dental Practice Act (DPA)

10. What are the core courses defined as for continuing education requirements for licensed dental assistants and special permit holders?

    Core courses are defined as instruction in the actual delivery of dental services to the patient or the community; for example, a course in diagnostic protocols and preventive services.

Notes

CTQ Answers

CALIFORNIA RDA WRITTEN AND LAW EXAM PREP BOOK - TEST BANK

The following test bank is not sectioned out by subject or chapter in order to better resemble the RDA Written and Law Combined Examination. An answer key has been provided. It is this comprehensive collection of questions that, if successfully studied, will effectively prepare you for the RDA written examination. Good luck!

1. What charting symbol best indicates a tooth that is not visible in the mouth?
    a. Circle around the tooth
    b. Outline with diagonal lines
    c. X through the tooth
    d. Diagonal lines

2. A base is placed _____ :
    a. as a measure of protection for the pulp.
    b. when decay or damage is too close to the pulp.
    c. on the floor of the tooth preparation.
    d. A, B and C are all correct.

3. According to the Dental Board regulations, how long should sterilization monitoring records be stored?
    a. Three years from the date the load was originally processed
    b. One week after the load was originally processed
    c. One year
    d. One year after each sterilizer involved was first monitored

4. Which of the following is an example of an OSHA-required sharp with engineered injury protection?
    a. A cardboard needle guard added to a dental anesthetic needle
    b. A butterfly needle used to administer IV sedation
    c. A self-sheathing needle attached to a dental anesthetic syringe
    d. A needle cap holder built into an instrument cassette

5. The air/water syringe is primarily used during the coronal polishing procedure to _____ :
    a. irrigate the oral cavity.
    b. dry the tooth surfaces.
    c. encourage drying of the mucosa.
    d. remove the remaining paste.

6. Which of the following should be performed FIRST if an adult patient does not have a pulse?
    a. Call for emergency assistance
    b. Administer oxygen
    c. Call the patient's medical doctor
    d. Administer CPR

The California RDA General Written and Law Examination Prep Book © 2017, 2018 • KB Dental Arts – Publisher

7. Oral surgical procedures require the use of _____:
   a. chemical agents to disinfect the water and water lines.
   b. sterile irrigating solutions using a sterile delivery system.
   c. water that meets the Food and Drug Administration (FDA) surface water standards.
   d. water that meets Environmental Protection Agency (EPA) drinking water standards.

8. When setting up an instrument tray or cassette, the instruments should be set up _____:
   a. from right to left.
   b. from left to right.
   c. from top to bottom.
   d. from bottom to top.

9. Who legally owns a patient's dental radiographs?
   a. The patient
   b. The radiologist
   c. The dentist
   d. The physician

10. Calcium hydroxide is used in dentistry as a _____.
    a. base.
    b. liner.
    c. matrix.
    d. All of the above answers are correct.

11. Prior to sterilization, loose contaminated instruments are processed in an ultrasonic cleaner to _____:
    a. clean then disinfect.
    b. remove all microorganisms.
    c. remove debris and bioburden.
    d. disinfect then clean.

12. A critical step for healthcare workers in preventing the spread of disease is proper hygiene of one's _____:
    a. hair.
    b. eyes.
    c. face.
    d. hands.

13. The purpose of dental sealants is _____:
    a. to prevent decay from spreading.
    b. to prevent decay in the pits and fissures of teeth.
    c. to promote good oral health.
    d. to prevent decay from interproximal spaces.

14. Elevating the patient's feet above the head to increase blood flow to the brain is the response to what medical condition?
    a. Heart problems
    b. Syncope
    c. Allergic reaction
    d. Diabetes

15. Angle's classifications are used to classify and describe _____:
    a. natural teeth in the dentition.
    b. types of dental caries.
    c. malocclusion.
    d. hand instruments.

16. The portion of a dental instrument held by the operator is called the _____:
    a. shank.
    b. working end.
    c. tip.
    d. handle.

17. Which of the following describes the best way to remain approachable to an anxious patient?
    a. Work slowly
    b. Encourage questions
    c. Encourage quiet
    d. Work quickly

18. The patient chart is a permanent record in the dental office and is the property of whom?
    a. The dentist
    b. A court of law
    c. The patient
    d. The dental practice

19. The dental history portion of a patient record provides the dental team with what information?
    a. Future dental care and treatment
    b. Previous dental care and treatment
    c. Dental procedures that are legal for the dental assistant to complete
    d. Data about the previous dentist

20. Which of the following products contains calcium hydroxide?
    a. Dycal
    b. ZPC
    c. ZOE
    d. Polycarboxylate

Test Bank

21. What type of mechanical device is used to clean contaminated instruments prior to sterilization?
    a. Hypersonic
    b. Ultrasonic
    c. Supersonic
    d. Subsonic

22. While cleaning contaminated instruments, an assistant receives a percutaneous injury to the finger. The assistant should FIRST _____:
    a. notify the dentist/employer.
    b. wash hands with soap and water.
    c. wipe puncture site with glutaraldehyde.
    d. be evaluated by a physician.

23. Why are pits and fissures susceptible to caries?
    a. Saliva pools in these areas
    b. Fluoride is less effective in these areas
    c. These areas are hard to evaluate on a radiograph
    d. These areas are difficult to clean
    e. Both B and D are correct

24. Clinical considerations for patients with bronchial asthma should include _____:
    a. paying attention to vinyl use.
    b. shorter appointments to reduce stress.
    c. having ammonia inhalant available.
    d. avoiding the use of sedatives.

25. Spreaders and pluggers are used in the
    a. placement of a gold foil.
    b. obturation of a root canal.
    c. seating of a Maryland bridge.
    d. placement of an amalgam restoration.

26. Which instrument is ideal for carving occlusal amalgams?
    a. Burnisher
    b. Half-Hollenback carver
    c. Discoid-cleoid carver
    d. Beavertail burnisher

27. According to State law, who is legally allowed to place a base during a restorative procedure?
    a. Dentist
    b. RDA
    c. DA
    d. Both A and B are correct

28. According to the Dental Board regulations, what is the proper method for decontaminating impressions before sending them to the laboratory?
    a. Clean and disinfect using an intermediate level disinfectant
    b. Clean with soap and water
    c. Spray with mouth wash
    d. Disinfect, package and sterilize

29. A single-use item reduces the risk of disease transmission because it is _____.
    a. cleaned and not reused.
    b. sterilized and reused.
    c. disinfected and reused.
    d. discarded and not reused.

30. Are sealants the only preventive measure used in Dentistry?
    a. Yes
    b. No

31. During a sealant procedure, the process of polymerization occurs using which of the following methods?
    a. Using a damp cotton pellet over the placed material
    b. Using a curing light of sufficient strength to penetrate the sealant material
    c. Using a self-cure material which does not require the use of a curing light
    d. Both B and C are correct

32. A patient with which of the following medical conditions may benefit from prophylactic sublingual nitroglycerin?
    a. Neuromuscular disorders
    b. Endocrine disorders
    c. Cardiovascular disorders
    d. Pulmonary disorders

33. Which of the following is one sign of anaphylactic shock?
    a. Erythema
    b. Respiratory distress
    c. Itching
    d. Rise in blood pressure

34. To prevent alveolitis after a tooth extraction, the patient should be instructed to
    a. rinse vigorously the first 24 hours.
    b. take aspirin for the first 24 hours.
    c. place ice packs on the face.
    d. avoid drinking through a straw.

35. The dental specialty that deals with the diagnosis and treatment of disease of supporting tissues is
_____:
   a. endodontics.
   b. pediatrics.
   c. orthodontics.
   d. periodontics.

36. The dental unit provides necessary electricity and hoses with air and water to the patient chair and the _____ delivery system is positioned behind the patient's head.
   a. front
   b. rear
   c. side
   d. top

37. Which instrument is used to place and remove elastic ties and remove orthodontic separators?
   a. Elastic separating pliers
   b. Wax spatula
   c. Scalpel
   d. Orthodontic scaler

38. What is a temporary sedative dressing or a direct provisional restoration?
   a. A temporary crown
   b. A permanent restoration
   c. A temporary filling
   d. None of the above

39. According to State law, who is legally allowed to place a liner during a restorative procedure?
   a. Dentist
   b. RDA
   c. DA
   d. Both A and B are correct

40. Which set of precautions is intended to prevent exposure to all body fluids?
   a. Generic
   b. Universal
   c. Standard
   d. Direct

41. _____ is defined as being primarily large-particles of water, saliva, blood, microorganisms, and other debris found in the spray from dental handpieces.
   a. Blood
   b. OPIM
   c. Spatter
   d. Bioburden

The California RDA General Written and Law Examination Prep Book © 2017, 2018 • KB Dental Arts – Publisher

42. According to OSHA, which infection control measure is considered the most critical for reducing the transmission of microbes in the healthcare setting?
    a. Immunization
    b. Disinfection
    c. Hand washing
    d. Sterilization

43. A used dental anesthetic needle is an example of _____:
    a. non-disposable waste.
    b. household waste.
    c. general waste.
    d. regulated waste.

44. Why is clear sealant material less desirable?
    a. It is less attractive
    b. It is more difficult to evaluate
    c. It does not match tooth color
    d. It is contraindicated with dental restorations

45. What is the difference between filled and unfilled sealants regarding retention rates?
    a. No difference
    b. Filled is much stronger
    c. Unfilled will last longer
    d. The filler is weaker

46. If a blood pressure reading of 142/96 is obtained on an adult, it is classified as _____:
    a. hypotension.
    b. normal.
    c. hypertension.
    d. pre-hypertension

47. What is the ratio of breaths to compressions for an adult victim when CPR is performed?
    a. 1 breath/5 compressions
    b. 2 breaths/7 compressions
    c. 2 breaths/30 compressions
    d. 3 breaths/20 compressions

48. A surgical dressing that is applied to the surgical site for protection is called a _____:
    a. osteoplasty.
    b. periodontal pocket.
    c. periodontal dressing.
    d. ostectomy.

49. When, in centric occlusion, the mandibular anterior teeth cannot be seen, the diagnosis is _____.
    a. overjet.
    b. crossbite.
    c. open bite.
    d. overbite.

50. What type of radiograph is most commonly exposed during endodontic procedures?
    a. Periapical
    b. Cephalometric
    c. Panoramic
    d. Bitewing

51. All <u>but</u> which instrument listed is part of a basic instrument set-up?
    a. Mouth mirror
    b. Cotton forceps
    c. College pliers
    d. Explorer

52. When working with a left-handed dentist, the instrument transfer zone is located where?
    a. Between 2 and 4 o'clock
    b. Between 4 and 6 o'clock
    c. Between 5 and 8 o'clock
    d. Between 6 and 8 o'clock

53. The _____ provides removal of large amounts of fluid and debris from the patient's mouth.
    a. high volume evacuator
    b. saliva ejector
    c. high speed handpiece
    d. air/water syringe

54. Which two materials are best used as a temporary sedative dressing?
    a. Zinc oxide eugenol and composite
    b. Calcium hydroxide and polycarboxylate
    c. Intermediate restorative material and Zinc oxide eugenol
    d. Polycarboxylate and zinc phosphate

55. When using etchant, how long is it left on the tooth structure?
    a. 10 seconds
    b. 1 minute (60 seconds)
    c. 15-20 seconds
    d. 20-25 seconds

56. Routine hand washing removes _____:
- a. all of the transient microbes and all of the resident microbes.
- b. most of the transient microbes and some of the resident microbes.
- c. none of the transient microbes but all of the resident microbes.
- d. some of the resident microbes but none of the transient microbes.

57. The primary reason a surgical face mask must be used during a dental procedure is to _____:
- a. avoid the odors of various dental materials.
- b. protect the DHCP from respiratory infection.
- c. avoid the need for high-volume evacuation.
- d. protect the DHCP from exposure to spatter, spray or splash

58. Employees must receive training regarding hazardous chemicals at what interval(s)?
- a. Upon hire and monthly thereafter.
- b. Upon hire and during all safety training sessions.
- c. Upon hire and annually thereafter.
- d. Upon hire, whenever a new hazard is introduced, and at least annually.

59. The OSHA Hazard Communication Standard is based on the premise that an employee has the right to know about the _____:
- a. sterilization in the office.
- b. instruments in the office
- c. patients in the office.
- d. chemicals in the office.

60. Which of the following viral infections can be prevented through immunization?
- a. Recurrent herpes
- b. Human immunodeficiency virus
- c. Hepatitis B
- d. Hepatitis C

61. Sealants are placed _____:
- a. in pits and fissures.
- b. on cingulums.
- c. in grooves.
- d. on marginal ridges.

62. What is the range of shelf life of sealants materials?
- a. 3 to 6 months
- b. 6 to 12 months
- c. 18 to 36 months
- d. Indefinitely

Test Bank

63. Which of the below is most commonly used in a medical emergency?
    a. Ammonia capsules
    b. Nitroglycerin
    c. Epinephrine
    d. Oxygen

64. In emergency care, the acronym AED represents
    a. Automated external defibrillator
    b. Auxiliary examination device
    c. Acute emergency drill
    d. Airway that is externally directed

65. To ease the placement of orthodontic bands, what procedure is completed to open the contact between teeth?
    a. Wearing of a positioner
    b. Placement of a ligature tie
    c. Bonding of a bracket
    d. Placement of a separator

66. How are brackets adhered to a tooth?
    a. Cement
    b. Sealant
    c. Bonding agent
    d. Wax

67. What endodontic procedure would be performed to partially remove the pulp?
    a. Apicoectomy
    b. Pulpectomy
    c. Pulpotomy
    d. Retrograde

68. What portion of a dental instrument has a blade, point or nib?
    a. Handle
    b. Shank
    c. Working end
    d. None of the above

69. Which device is used to assist in keeping a patient's mouth open during a restorative procedure?
    a. Rubber dam
    b. Bite block
    c. Cotton pellets
    d. Cotton rolls

70. Which orthodontic instrument is used to snip off wire ligatures once they have been tied around a bracket?
    a. Bird beak pliers
    b. Howe plier
    c. Ligature director
    d. Pin and ligature cutter

71. The smear layer is _____:
    a. oil left behind during the placement of the restoration.
    b. a protective secretion produced by the layers of the teeth.
    c. not able to be removed.
    d. Both B and C are correct statements.

72. Etchant material is _____:
    a. typically, electric blue in color.
    b. 37-39% phosphoric acid.
    c. very bitter tasting.
    d. All of the above are correct statements.

73. Instrument cassettes should be wrapped _____:
    a. immediately after sterilization.
    b. after cleaning and before sterilization.
    c. immediately before storing.
    d. after instruments cool from sterilization.

74. When using the air/water syringe during dental treatment, which of the following personal protective equipment items is required by the Dental Board regulations?
    a. Gloves, mask, and gown
    b. Gloves, mask, gown, and eye protection
    c. Gloves and mask
    d. Gloves, mask, gown, eye protection, and shoe covers

75. According to the Board regulations, instruments, items or devices that penetrate soft tissue or bone are categorized as _____:
    a. multi-critical.
    b. semi-critical.
    c. non-critical.
    d. critical.

76. According to the Occupational Safety and Health Administration (OSHA), annual bloodborne pathogens training program should include _____:
    a. the trainer's background and relevant credentials.
    b. how the training program was created and by whom.
    c. relevant research documents.
    d. the modes of disease transmission.

77. Which of the following modes of disease transmission best describes a human bite?
   a. Parenteral
   b. Bloodborne
   c. Indirect
   d. Airborne

78. Used radiograph fixer solution is usually considered _____:
   a. hazardous waste.
   b. household waste.
   c. contaminated waste.
   d. general waste.

79. What patient safety precaution(s) should be considered when one is placing sealants?
   a. Keep the etchant off the soft tissue
   b. Use only after the patient has been anesthetized
   c. Have the patient wear eyewear
   d. Both A and C are correct statements.

80. What is the main cause of sealant failures?
   a. Polymerization
   b. Moisture contamination
   c. Deep pits and fissures
   d. Occlusion interference

81. What is the purpose of coronal polishing?
   a. To remove calculus
   b. To remove stains and plaque
   c. To prepare teeth for a restoration
   d. To remove inflamed gingiva

82. What does the AED provide to the heart?
   a. Oxygen
   b. Jolt of an electrical current
   c. Blood
   d. Heat

83. _____ is a term used to describe what a patient is feeling and is unobservable to the dental assistant or dentist.
   a. Diagnosis
   b. Sign
   c. Explanation
   d. Symptom

84. What is the medical term for fainting?
    a. Stroke
    b. Seizure
    c. Syncope
    d. Senile

85. The medical term for chest pain is _____:
    a. Angioplasty.
    b. Angina.
    c. Angiogram.
    d. Anemia.

86. _____ is a mandated section within an office OSHA manual that is used to communicate the chemical hazards of each of the materials and solutions used by an employee.
    a. Fire and emergency plan
    b. Work place safety plan
    c. Hazard communication plan
    d. Injury and illness prevention plan

87. _____ is the main medicament found in a dental liner and stimulates secondary dentin.
    a. Zinc phosphate
    b. Calcium hydroxide
    c. Composite resin
    d. Etchant

88. _____ is a surgical periodontal treatment.
    a. Scaling
    b. Root planning
    c. Gingivectomy
    d. Gingival curettage

89. Motions are categorized into _____ categories dependent upon the extent of the motion and the nature of the movement.
    a. 3
    b. 4
    c. 5

90. Which classification of movement is defined as movement of fingers only such as picking up a single item from a flat surface?
    a. Class I
    b. Class II
    c. Class III
    d. Class IV

Test Bank

91. Dental instruments used in general dentistry are divided into _____ categories of restorative procedures.
    a. 2
    b. 3
    c. 4
    d. 5

92. What benefit does etchant provide during the bonding process?
    a. roughens up the enamel and/or dentinal layers in preparation for bonding
    b. desiccates the tooth
    c. eliminates a step from the bonding process
    d. all of the above

93. A self-etching adhesive eliminates the need to _____.
    a. rinse etchant from the tooth
    b. dry the tooth structure after placement
    c. adjust the restoration after placement

94. According to State law, who is legally allowed to place etchant on tooth structure for purposes of a restoration or dental sealants?
    a. Dentist
    b. RDA
    c. DA
    d. Both A and B are correct

95. Which item of personal protective equipment must be removed before leaving operatories or areas of patient activities?
    a. Mask
    b. Gloves
    c. Protective eyewear
    d. Protective clothing

96. What agency regulates the registration of disinfectants and chemical sterilant used in dentistry?
    a. FDA
    b. CDC
    c. EPA
    d. OSHA

97. Which of the following is the best infection control practice for clinical contact surfaces that are difficult or impossible to clean?
    a. Disinfecting with low-level disinfectant.
    b. Disinfecting with high-level disinfectant.
    c. Covering gloves with an impervious barrier.
    d. Covering surfaces with an impervious barrier.

98. Which party is responsible for ensuring a Safety Data Sheet is available in the work place for each hazardous material?
    a. Manufacturer
    b. Employer
    c. Distributor
    d. Employee

99. Which of the following statements most accurately defines engineering controls?
    a. Human behavior or practices that prevent employee exposure to hazardous or infectious substances.
    b. Evaluation of employee job performance.
    c. Documentation of sterilization and biological monitoring.
    d. Materials and devices that prevent employee exposure to hazardous or infectious substances.

100. Safety Data Sheets (SDS) are required by OSHA's _____:
    a. Community Health Standard.
    b. Hazard Communication Standard.
    c. Dental Procedures Standard.
    d. Bloodborne Pathogens Standard.

101. A coronal polishing procedure is _____:
    a. a fluoride treatment.
    b. the removal of stain following scaling.
    c. the removal of calculus.
    d. the removal of decay.

102. What is the purpose of selective polishing?
    a. To polish only teeth that are visible
    b. To polish the occlusal surfaces of teeth
    c. To polish only teeth with stain
    d. To polish the facial surfaces of teeth

103. Stains that may be removed from the surfaces of the teeth are _____:
    a. extrinsic stains.
    b. natural stains.
    c. intrinsic stains.
    d. infected stains.

104. The medication a patient with asthma would most likely carry at all times is _____:
    a. nitroglycerin.
    b. insulin.
    c. bronchodilator.
    d. analgesia.

Test Bank

105. What kind of allergic response could be life threatening?
    a.   Grand mal seizure
    b.   Anaphylaxis
    c.   Myocardial infarction
    d.   Airway obstruction

106. An abnormal decrease of glucose in the blood can cause _____:
    a.   Angina
    b.   Hypoglycemia
    c.   Seizure
    d.   Hyperglycemia

107. When the dentist taps on a tooth, what diagnostic test is being performed?
    a.   Mobility
    b.   Heat
    c.   Palpation
    d.   Percussion

108. The diagnosis of inflamed pulp tissue is _____:
    a.   Pulpitis.
    b.   Pulpotomy.
    c.   Pulpectomy.

109. Another term for necrotic is _____:
    a.   living.
    b.   dead.
    c.   non-vital.
    d.   Both B and C are correct.

110. What portion of the pulp would the dentist remove in a pulpotomy?
    a.   Coronal portion
    b.   Root portion
    c.   Complete pulp
    d.   Only the infected portion

111. During the instrument exchange process, the assistant hands off an instrument to the dentist so that the working end of the instrument is pointed toward the arch (maxillary or mandibular) being worked on. The term used to describe this exchange method is called:
    a.   Palm grasp
    b.   Pencil grasp
    c.   Position of use
    d.   Position of exchange

The California RDA General Written and Law Examination Prep Book © 2017, 2018 • *KB Dental Arts – Publisher*

112. Which non-mechanical dental hand instrument is best used to remove dental caries?

    a.   Explorer

    b.   Scaler

    c.   Chisel

    d.   Spoon excavator

113. Which of the listed instruments is categorized as a restorative instrument?

    a.   Woodson plastic instrument

    b.   Amalgam well

    c.   Explorer

    d.   Hatchet

114. Which of the listed instruments is categorized as an examination instrument?

    a.   Gingival margin trimmer

    b.   Cement spatula

    c.   Articulating paper holder

    d.   Cotton forceps

115. The term polymerization means to _____.

    a.   cure.

    b.   set.

    c.   harden.

    d.   all of the above are correct.

116. If a material notes that it is "dual cure" that means _____.

    a.   the material needs a curing light to harden

    b.   the material will harden during its own setting time

    c.   the material will enter the initial setting phase on its own but needs the curing light to complete the setting process.

    d.   the material requires using a curing light two times to harden

117. A provisional coverage also could be called _____.

    a.   a temporary restoration or an indirect provisional restoration.

    b.   a temporary filling.

    c.   a permanent crown.

    d.   a direct restoration.

118. The two types of temporary crowns are _____ or _____.

    a.   polymerized or cured

    b.   custom or preformed

    c.   alginate or polyvinylsiloxane

    d.   gold or alloy

119. Routine hand washing for dental healthcare personnel includes the use of _____:
    a.   water and alcohol-based hand rub.
    b.   an alcohol-based hand rub followed by a iodine rinse.
    c.   water and plain liquid soap.
    d.   water and plain liquid soap followed by an alcohol-based hand rub.

120. A surgical mask must be changed _____:
    a.   after every thirty minutes of wear.
    b.   after every patient.
    c.   only if visibly wet.
    d.   only if visibly soiled.

121. All disinfectants should be used _____:
    a.   on environmental surfaces.
    b.   for hand hygiene.
    c.   according to the manufacturer's directions.
    d.   on metal instruments before heat sterilization.

122. The accessibility of the exposure control plan for employees is the responsibility of the _____:
    a.   designated trainer.
    b.   employer.
    c.   employee.
    d.   department manager.

123. According to the OSHA Bloodborne Pathogens Standard, each dental office must have an exposure control plan that is _____:
    a.   written and reviewed at least once every year.
    b.   verbal and reviewed at least once every five years.
    c.   verbal and reviewed at least once every year.
    d.   written and reviewed at least once every five years.

124. Stains that cannot be removed from the surfaces of the teeth are _____:
    a.   extrinsic stains.
    b.   natural stains.
    c.   intrinsic stains.
    d.   infected stains.

125. Which is the most common technique for stain removal?
    a.   Scaler
    b.   Toothbrush
    c.   Floss
    d.   Rubber cup polishing

126. Toward which direction should the polishing stroke be directed?
    a.   Toward the incisal
    b.   Toward the gingiva
    c.   Toward the occlusal
    d.   Both A and C are correct

127. If a medication were placed sublingually, where would it be placed?
    a.   Ancillary
    b.   Rectally
    c.   Under the tongue
    d.   Topically

128. _____ is the act of providing information, verbally or in writing, ensuring the understanding by the patient as to the nature of the proposed dental treatment.
    a.   Nonmaleficence
    b.   Confidentiality
    c.   Implied consent
    d.   Informed consent

129. When the body reacts negatively to a drug, what is occurring?
    a.   Adverse effect
    b.   Response
    c.   Symptom
    d.   Sign

130. An analgesic would be prescribed for _____:
    a.   hives.
    b.   fever.
    c.   pain relief.
    d.   fainting.

131. Which would be an example of an antibiotic?
    a.   Aspirin
    b.   Codeine
    c.   Erythromycin
    d.   Meperidine

132. A drug that is prescribed to slow the clotting of blood is _____:
    a.   aspirin.
    b.   valium.
    c.   coumadin.
    d.   monistat.

Test Bank

133. The term "obturate" means to _____:
    a. open a pulpal canal.
    b. examine a pulpal canal.
    c. fill a pulpal canal.
    d. surgically remove a pulpal canal.

134. The irrigation solution most commonly used during root canal therapy is _____:
    a. water from the air-water syringe.
    b. sodium hypochlorite.
    c. concentrated sodium hypochlorite.
    d. phosphoric acid.

135. The material commonly used for filling an endodontically treated canal is _____:
    a. amalgam.
    b. composite.
    c. gutta percha.
    d. IRM.

136. Similar to a hatchet, the _____ instrument has a curved blade, is not flat and the cutting end is angled.
    a. spoon excavator
    b. hoe
    c. chisel
    d. gingival margin trimmer

137. A _____ controls dental handpieces and is attached to the dental unit via hoses.
    a. tubing
    b. overhead light
    c. dental cart
    d. rheostat

138. The assistant's stool should be positioned _____:
    a. 4 to 6 inches below the operator.
    b. 4 to 6 inches above the operator.
    c. 4 to 6 inches away from the patient.
    d. 4 to 6 inches above the patient.

139. The _____ position places the patient's head lower than their feet.
    a. sub-supine
    b. supine
    c. upright
    d. parallel

140. A custom temporary is made out of _____ material.
   a.   metal
   b.   alginate
   c.   acrylic
   d.   cement

141. According to State law, who is legally allowed to fabricate and cement a provisional restoration?
   a.   Dentist
   b.   RDA
   c.   DA
   d.   Both A and B are correct

142. Which of the following can be used as both a provisional coverage for adult patients and a permanent restoration for pediatric patients?
   a.   Custom temporary
   b.   Preformed temporary
   c.   Stainless steel crown
   d.   Any of the above can be correct

143. The term festooning means to _____.
   a.   trim
   b.   polish
   c.   contour and shape
   d.   none of the above

144. When putting on personal protective equipment, which item should be put on last, just before patient care begins?
   a.   Protective clothing
   b.   Protective eyewear
   c.   Gloves
   d.   Mask

145. In accordance with Dental Board regulations, the high-speed hand piece line and air/water syringe should be flushed with water _____.
   a.   at the time of sterilization.
   b.   after each patient.
   c.   once a week.
   d.   once a day.

146. _____ is a slow-moving reaction contained to one area of the body.
   a.   Antigen
   b.   Localized allergic reaction
   c.   Allergy
   d.   Syncope

The California RDA General Written and Law Examination Prep Book © 2017, 2018 • KB Dental Arts – Publisher

Test Bank

147. According to OSHA requirements, a sharps container must be _____:
    a.   leak-proof on the bottom only.
    b.   puncture resistant and see through.
    c.   leak-proof, puncture resistant and closeable.
    d.   leak-proof on the sides only.

148. Which of the following would be regulated under OSHA's Hazard Communication Standard?
    a.   Bonding brushes
    b.   Sterile gauze
    c.   Bonding etchant
    d.   Non-sterile gauze

149. When should chairside environmental barriers be changed?
    a.   After every patient
    b.   At the middle of and at the end of each day
    c.   At the end of each day
    d.   Immediately after they are touched

150. The primary active agent in the solution used for unsaturated chemical vapor sterilization is _____:
    a.   water.
    b.   xylene.
    c.   alcohol.
    d.   formaldehyde.

151. What damage can result from using the prophy angle at high speed?
    a.   It can cause frictional heat
    b.   It can remove dentin
    c.   It can cool the tooth
    d.   It can etch enamel

152. What oral conditions contraindicate the use of an ultrasonic scaler?
    a.   Patients with demineralization
    b.   Narrow periodontal pockets
    c.   Exposed dentin
    d.   All of the above

153. What is the more common term for a dental prophylaxis?
    a.   Prophy
    b.   Sealants
    c.   Scaling
    d.   Root Plaining

154. Who can perform a dental prophylaxis?
    a. Dentist
    b. Dental assistant
    c. Dental hygienist
    d. Both A and C are correct

155. A scavenger unit is used for respiratory protection during the use of _____:
    a. nitrous oxide.
    b. ultrasonic cleaners.
    c. aerosol sprays.
    d. cavitron units.

156. The use of nitrous oxide and oxygen gases together is known as what?
    a. Oral sedation
    b. Localized anesthesia
    c. General anesthesia
    d. Inhalation sedation

157. The chairside assistant should routinely scan the patient during treatment from their head to their feet. If there is a problem with the patient that the assistant can observe, it is said to be _____:
    a. a symptom.
    b. a sign.
    c. a condition.
    d. an emergency condition.

158. If epinephrine is found in the office emergency kit, it is commonly used for what purpose?
    a. Syncope
    b. Angina pectoris
    c. Allergic reaction
    d. Hyperventilation

159. _____ is a specific area on a partial or denture that may press or rub against the underlying soft tissue.
    a. Blister
    b. Hyperocclusion
    c. Sore spot
    d. Pressure point

160. What type of moisture control is recommended for root canal therapy?
    a. Cotton pellets
    b. Cotton rolls
    c. Dry angles
    d. Dental dam

Test Bank

161. What surface of the posterior tooth would the dentist enter with a rotary bur when opening a canal for root canal therapy?
    a.   Occlusal
    b.   Facial
    c.   Mesial
    d.   Incisal

162. _____ must precede any disinfection or sterilization process.
    a.   Rinsing
    b.   Cleaning
    c.   Soaking
    d.   Packaging

163. _____ is a removable prosthesis that replaces one or several teeth.
    a.   Bridge
    b.   Denture
    c.   Partial
    d.   Custom tray

164. Fixed prosthodontics is commonly referred to as _____:
    a.   Operative
    b.   Crown and bridge
    c.   Dentures
    d.   Prosthetics

165. What could be a contraindication to a patient receiving fixed prosthodontics?
    a.   Overweight
    b.   Over the age of 60
    c.   Poor oral hygiene
    d.   Poor personal hygiene

166. The required hand protection when processing instruments in preparation of sterilization is _____:
    a.   Latex-free medical examination gloves
    b.   Chemical-resistant utility gloves
    c.   Puncture-resistant utility gloves
    d.   Synthetic medical examination gloves

167. What piece of lab equipment is used to grind away plaster or stone?
    a.   Model trimmer
    b.   Lathe
    c.   Bunsen burner
    d.   Laboratory handpiece

The California RDA General Written and Law Examination Prep Book © 2017, 2018 • KB Dental Arts – Publisher

168. Which technique is used by the operator to prevent injury to the patient if the operator's hand or the instrument slips while in use during treatment?
    a. Injury and illness prevention program
    b. Work practice control
    c. Palm grasp
    d. Fulcrum

169. For a right-handed dentist, where is the static zone located?
    a. 12 – 2 o'clock
    b. 2 – 4 o'clock
    c. 4 – 7 o'clock
    d. 7 – 12 o'clock

170. For a left-handed dentist, the assistant's zone is located
    a. between 12 and 5 o'clock.
    b. between 5 and 8 o'clock.
    c. between 2 and 4 o'clock.
    d. between 8 and 10 o'clock

171. The _____ grasp is when the instrument is held in the palm of the operator's hand.
    a. palm-thumb grasp
    b. palm grasp
    c. pen grasp
    d. none of the above

172. The _____ are used to trim around the margin of a stainless-steel crown.
    a. surgical scissors
    b. crown and bridge scissors
    c. iris scissors
    d. suture scissors

173. What is a luting agent?
    a. an adhesive, like a cement, that holds two structures together
    b. etchant
    c. primer
    d. any of the above

174. Once a permanent restoration is cemented in place with permanent cement the only way to remove it is with _____.
    a. a spoon excavator.
    b. a chisel and mallet.
    c. a handpiece and bur.
    d. any of the above would work.

Test Bank

175. Zinc Oxide Eugenol (ZOE) is what type of cement?
    a. permanent
    b. temporary
    c. intermediate
    d. permanent and temporary

176. When should impervious barriers used in the dental operatory be changed?
    a. After every patient
    b. At the middle of and at the end of each day
    c. At the end of each day
    d. Immediately after they are touched

177. According to Dental Board regulations, biological monitors for assessing the effectiveness of a sterilizer are to be used _____ for each sterilizer used I the dental office.
    a. weekly
    b. daily
    c. yearly
    d. monthly

178. _____ gloves are to be used when the dental operatory is broken down, striped of its barriers and surface disinfected using a germicidal agent.
    a. Sterile surgeon's gloves
    b. Chemical-resistant utility gloves
    c. Medical examination gloves
    d. Poly-vinyl over gloves

179. The correct steps to take when a glove rips or tears during a procedure are _____:
    a. wash the glove, dry the glove, and continue with procedure.
    b. disinfect glove, dry glove, and continue with procedure.
    c. remove the glove and immediately place fresh gloves.
    d. remove the glove, wash and dry hands, and don new gloves.

180. The purpose of dating packages of sterilized instruments is to _____:
    a. retrieve and sterilize packs after six months.
    b. document the number of sterilizer runs.
    c. identify the sterilization date
    d. retrieve packs in the event of a sterilization failure.

181. According to regulations, protective eyewear, surgical masks, gloves, and gowns or lab coats are _____:
    a. personal protective equipment.
    b. infection protection gear.
    c. office protective supplies.
    d. positive protection material.

182. According to OSHA, safety measures that should be taken when using dental materials with potentially hazardous chemicals must be found in a _____:

    a.   Chemical Safety Data Sheet.

    b.   Safety Data Sheet.

    c.   Material First Aid Manual.

    d.   Chemical First Aid Manual.

183. Which of the following is an example of regulated medical waste?

    a.   Patient bibs

    b.   Biopsy tissue

    c.   Used gloves

    d.   Damp cotton rolls

184. The first step in addressing (treating) an accidental exposure injury should be _____:

    a.   complete the procedure.

    b.   wash the exposed skin with soap and water.

    c.   complete an exposure incident report.

    d.   go the nearest hospital emergency room.

185. _____ is the benchmark microorganism that classifies a disinfectant as intermediate.

    a.   Human immunodeficiency virus

    b.   Hepatitis B virus

    c.   Herpes simplex 1 virus

    d.   M. tuberculosis var bovis

186. Hazard communication labeling (SDS) is required when using secondary containers for products/materials used in the dental office. The purpose of the labeling is to _____:

    a.   communicate the hazardous chemical(s) in the product.

    b.   communicate the location of the safety data sheet in the SDS binder.

    c.   communicate the level of risk of flammability, health reaction and PPE to be used around the product.

    d.   All of the above.

187. Photochemical waste is defined as _____:

    a.   glutaraldehydes and x-ray cleaning solutions.

    b.   sharps and broken glass.

    c.   medications and prescriptions.

    d.   radiographic lead foil and fixer.

188. Universal/Recyclable waste is defined as _____:

    a.   glutaraldehydes and x-ray cleaning solutions.

    b.   batteries and fluorescent lamps.

    c.   medications and prescriptions.

    d.   radiographic lead foil and fixer.

189. A percutaneous sharps injury refers to a _____:
   a.   sharps injury that does not penetrate the skin.
   b.   sharps injury that does penetrate the skin but requires no reporting.
   c.   sharps injury that does penetrate the skin and requires reporting.
   d.   sharps injury that only remains in the body for a short time.

190. Another term used to describe a systemic allergic reaction is _____ and is a life- threatening condition.
   a.   anaphylaxis
   b.   localized
   c.   symptom
   d.   asthma

191. Of the common medical emergencies in a dental setting, the emergency where a patient experiences nausea, pounding heartbeat and feeling warm is _____:
   a.   postural hypotension.
   b.   angina pectoris.
   c.   asthma attack.
   d.   syncope.

192. Of the common medical emergencies in a dental setting, the emergency where a patient experiences a bad mood, anxiety and appears sweaty is _____:
   a.   hypoglycemia.
   b.   hyperglycemia.
   c.   hyperemia.
   d.   epileptic seizure.

193. If the patient experiences an asthma attack while being treated, the dental team should _____:
   a.   remove all materials from the patient's mouth.
   b.   place the patient in an upright seated position.
   c.   hand the patient their bronchodilator.
   d.   perform all of the above procedures.

194. In performing cardiovascular resuscitation on an adult patient, the first important step to perform is _____.
   a.   checking the patient for responsiveness.
   b.   grabbing the oxygen tank and ambo bag.
   c.   calling 911.
   d.   beginning compressions.

195. _____ is a measurement of how hard the heart must work to pump blood through the body.
   a.   Respiration rate
   b.   Pulse
   c.   Temperature
   d.   Blood pressure

196. _____ is another type of vital sign that measures the concentration of oxygen in the blood.
    a. Systolic reading
    b. Diastolic reading
    c. Pulse oximetry
    d. Electrocardiogram

197. A/An _____ is a substance that causes an immune response.
    a. Antigen
    b. Antibody
    c. Allergy
    d. None of the above

198. An effective product from the office emergency kit when needing to treat a patient experiencing a fainting episode is:
    a. aspirin.
    b. oxygen.
    c. valium.
    d. ammonia inhalant.

199. The "A" in the CAB of basic life support stands for _____:
    a. access.
    b. automatic.
    c. airway.
    d. assess.

200. What is a contraindication for a patient when a procedure calls for gingival retraction cord impregnated with epinephrine?
    a. Diabetes
    b. Epilepsy
    c. Hypothyroidism
    d. Cardiovascular disease

201. The dental assistant's responsibility in an emergency situation is to _____:
    a. recognize the symptoms and signs of a significant medical complaint.
    b. provide appropriate support in implementing emergency procedures.
    c. diagnose a specific condition or emergency situation.
    d. Both A and B are correct.

202. An automated external defibrillator (AED) is used for all *except* to _____:
    a. re-establish the proper heart rhythm by defibrillation.
    b. automatically perform CPR for 15 minutes.
    c. monitor the patient's heart rhythm.
    d. shock the heart.

Test Bank

203. According to State law, who is legally allowed to remove excess cement with a hand instrument?

    a.   RDH

    b.   RDA

    c.   DA

    d.   None of the above

204. _____ is a surgical procedure involving the removal of the tip of the root.

    a.   Apicoectomy

    b.   Pulpitis

    c.   Pulpectomy

    d.   Extraction

205. The material placed in a denture that will pinpoint sore spots is called _____

    a.   impression paste.

    b.   PIP paste.

    c.   polishing paste.

    d.   pigment paste.

206. What is the main effective ingredient in tooth whitening material?

    a.   Hydrogen peroxide

    b.   Sodium hypochlorite

    c.   Carbamide peroxide

    d.   Chlorhexidine

207. Using traditional radiographic procedures, which of the following is considered a clinical contact surface?

    a.   Bitewing tab

    b.   X-ray film

    c.   Panoramic cassette

    d.   X-ray control panel

208. What is the proper management for work surfaces that become contaminated with blood?

    a.   Disinfect with alcohol wipes

    b.   Wipe with a dry cloth

    c.   Clean and then disinfect

    d.   Spray with water and soak

209. Instruments with the greatest risk of transmitting infection are _____:

    a.   semi-critical instruments.

    b.   noncritical instruments.

    c.   secondary instruments.

    d.   critical instruments

The California RDA General Written and Law Examination Prep Book © 2017, 2018 • KB Dental Arts – Publisher

This book and the individual contributions contained within are protected under Copyright by the Publisher

210. Torn gloves should be replaced _____:
    a. as soon as possible.
    b. before entering the lab.
    c. after the patient leaves.
    d. at the end of the day.

211. To reduce the risk of disease transmission in the dental office, it is recommended to _____:
    a. use non-disposable items whenever possible.
    b. reuse disposable items whenever possible.
    c. use disposable items whenever possible.
    d. use items that can only be disinfected whenever possible.

212. Which of the following best describes the appropriate container for a biopsy specimen?
    a. Reusable container that is heat-sterilized after use
    b. Reusable container that is disinfected after use
    c. Single-use leak proof container with a biohazard symbol
    d. Single-use sharps container with a biohazard symbol

213. Which of the following is recommended for managing contamination of digital radiographic sensors that cannot be heat sterilized?
    a. The use of impervious barriers followed by cleaning and disinfection
    b. The use of impervious barriers followed by chemical sterilization
    c. Cleaning and disinfection alone
    d. The use of impervious barriers alone

214. Solutions used for cooling and irrigating during oral surgical procedures must be delivered through _____:
    a. a sterile delivery device.
    b. a dental unit with a water reservoir.
    c. a disinfected delivery device.
    d. a dental unit with a water filter.

215. On the California RDA Written examination, only the clinical name, not the brand name, of a material will be used.
    a. True
    b. False

216. ZPC should always be mixed on a cool, glass slab incorporating the powder into the liquid in small, but steady, increments.
    a. True
    b. False

217. When mixing a material, make sure all the powder is incorporated into the liquid prior to adding more powder.
    a. True
    b. False

The California RDA General Written and Law Examination Prep Book © 2017, 2018 • KB Dental Arts – Publisher

218. It is acceptable and customary to trim a provisional intraorally.
    a. True
    b. False

219. When fabricating a provisional it is important to check the mesial and distal contacts.
    a. True
    b. False

220. A Registered Dental Assistant in Extended Functions may adjust and cement permanent indirect restorations.
    a. True
    b. False

221. A digital sensor used for digital x-rays requires the use of an impervious barrier prior to placement in the patient's mouth.
    a. True
    b. False

222. The _____ is the part of the orthodontic fixed appliance that initiates and establishes tooth movement in the arch.
    a. bracket
    b. arch wire
    c. separator

223. In accordance with Dental Board regulations, the dental unit water lines must be _____ between each patient.
    a. flushed with water for 20 seconds
    b. flushed for two minutes
    c. flushed with air and then with water for 30 seconds
    d. flushed with water for 30 seconds

224. Indirect vision is the process of using a mouth mirror for vision in the oral cavity.
    a. True
    b. False

225. DA's or RDA's can perform a mouth mirror inspection of the oral cavity.
    a. True
    b. False

226. When performing a mouth mirror inspection, the assistant will diagnose their findings.
    a. True
    b. False

227. A Registered Dental Assistant or Registered Dental Assistant in Extended Functions who holds a permit as an orthodontic assistant or a dental sedation assistant shall not be required to complete additional continuing education requirements beyond that which is required for licensure renewal in order to renew either permit.
    a. True
    b. False

The California RDA General Written and Law Examination Prep Book © 2017, 2018 • KB Dental Arts – Publisher

228. It is unprofessional conduct for a licensed person to perform or hold him or herself out as able to perform, professional services beyond the scope of his or her license and field or fields of competence as established by his or her education, experience, and training.
   a. True
   b. False

229. Only the dentist has a duty to respect each patient's individuality, humanity, and autonomy in decision making.
   a. True
   b. False

230. As a matter of ethics, the dental assistant should NOT follow the wishes of an adult patient who asks that a suspected case of abuse and/or neglect not be reported, even when such a report is not mandated by law.
   a. True
   b. False

231. The dental assistant has an obligation to enhance professional competency through continuous learning, incorporating new knowledge into daily performance of delegated services.
   a. True
   b. False

232. The dentist relies on the honesty of the patient to gather the facts necessary to form a proper diagnosis.
   a. True
   b. False

233. The dentist has a duty to communicate truthfully. This principle expresses the concept that professionals have a duty to be honest and trustworthy in their dealings with people.
   a. True
   b. False

234. The diagonal slots on the head of the Tofflemire retainer are always facing the buccal.
   a. True
   b. False

235. A matrix band creates a temporary proximal for Class I tooth preparations.
   a. True
   b. False

236. A mylar strip is used as a matrix for anterior composite restorations.
   a. True
   b. False

237. When seated properly, the matrix band will sit 2mm above the occlusal surface.
   a. True
   b. False

238. Wedges should always be placed from the buccal.
   a. True
   b. False

239. Wedges are supplied in plastic and/or wood and are triangular and/or round.
   a. True
   b. False

240. Another name for the Tofflemire Retainer is a sectional matrix retainer.
   a. True
   b. False

241. It is illegal for an unlicensed dental assistant to obtain intraoral images from computer-aided CAD design units like CEREC.
   a. True
   b. False

242. The RDA may not mill the final restoration on the CAD/CAM machine as this is considered fabrication of a permanent restoration – a procedure only allowed to be performed by an RDAEF (licensed after 1/1/2010) or a dentist.
   a. True
   b. False

243. The dentist should always perform a final check of the RDA-performed computer impression prior to the final milling of a permanent crown.
   a. True
   b. False

244. During in-office bleaching, there is no harm done if some bleaching material touches soft tissue.
   a. True
   b. False

245. A poorly placed wedge will create an overhang in the restoration.
   a. True
   b. False

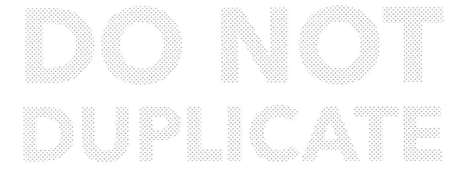

The California RDA General Written and Law Examination Prep Book © 2017, 2018 • KB Dental Arts – Publisher

Test Bank

Test Bank Answer Key

1.	C	41.	C	83.	D
2.	D	42.	C	84.	C
3.	C	43.	D	85.	B
4.	C	44.	B	86.	C
5.	D	45.	A	87.	B
6.	A	46.	C	88.	C
7.	B	47.	C	89.	C
8.	B	48.	C	90.	A
9.	C	49.	D	91.	C
10.	B	50.	A	92.	A
11.	C	51.	C	93.	A
12.	D	52.	C	94.	D
13.	B	53.	A	95.	B
14.	B	54.	C	96.	C
15.	C	55.	C	97.	D
16.	D	56.	B	98.	B
17.	B	57.	D	99.	D
18.	A	58.	D	100.	B
19.	B	59.	D	101.	B
20.	A	60.	C	102.	C
21.	B	61.	A	103.	A
22.	B	62.	C	104.	C
23.	E	63.	D	105.	B
24.	B	64.	A	106.	B
25.	B	65.	D	107.	D
26.	C	66.	A	108.	A
27.	D	67.	C	109.	D
28.	A	68.	C	110.	A
29.	D	69.	B	111.	C
30.	B	70.	D	112.	D
31.	D	71.	B	113.	A
32.	C	72.	D	114.	D
33.	B	73.	B	115.	D
34.	D	74.	B	116.	C
35.	D	75.	D	117.	A
36.	B	76.	D	118.	B
37.	D	77.	A	119.	C
38.	C	78.	A	120.	B
39.	D	79.	D	121.	C
40.	C	80.	B	122.	B
		81.	B	123.	A
		82.	B	124.	C

Test Bank

125.	D	167.	A	209.	D
126.	D	168.	D	210.	A
127.	C	169.	A	211.	C
128.	D	170.	D	212.	C
129.	A	171.	B	213.	A
130.	C	172.	B	214.	A
131.	C	173.	A	215.	A
132.	C	174.	C	216.	A
133.	C	175.	D	217.	A
134.	B	176.	A	218.	B
135.	C	177.	A	219.	A
136.	D	178.	B	220.	A
137.	D	179.	D	221.	A
138.	B	180.	D	222.	B
139.	A	181.	A	223.	A
140.	C	182.	B	224.	A
141.	D	183.	B	225.	B
142.	C	184.	B	226.	B
143.	A	185.	D	227.	A
144.	C	186.	D	228.	A
145.	B	187.	D	229.	B
146.	B	188.	B	230.	B
147.	C	189.	C	231.	A
148.	C	190.	A	232.	A
149.	A	191.	D	233.	A
150.	D	192.	A	234.	B
151.	A	193.	D	235.	B
152.	D	194.	A	236.	A
153.	A	195.	D	237.	A
154.	D	196.	C	238.	B
155.	A	197.	A	239.	A
156.	D	198.	D	240.	B
157.	B	199.	C	241.	A
158.	C	200.	D	242.	A
159.	D	201.	D	243.	A
160.	D	202.	B	244.	B
161.	A	203.	B	245.	A
162.	B	204.	A		
163.	C	205.	B		
164.	B	206.	C		
165.	C	207.	D		
166.	C	208.	C		

Notes

Notes

Notes

Notes

Notes

Notes

Notes

Notes